THESE

More praise for THESE LOWLY OBJECTS...

In *These Lowly Objects*, Cate McGowan has fashioned one of the great fictional characters of our time in Jules Lalande, Dadaist extraordinaire. From his Dickensian childhood alongside a second cousin (and later, wife), Isobel, McGowan tracks—in rich, rigorous prose—the Zelig-like Lalande's wanderings through fin de siècle Paris as he rubs elbows with Degas and Cézanne, fights in World War I, lands in New York with Breton, becomes a professional boxer, hangs out with Duchamp, and disappears in Cuba—or does he? Enter this remarkably imagined, enchanted world and discover the many delights of McGowan's marvelous creation.

—Robin Lippincott, author of *Blue Territory:
A Meditation on the Life and Art of Joan Mitchell*

Lyrical, stunning, and deeply strange, Cate McGowan's novel concerns a shape-shifting protagonist, Jules Lalande. Lalande disappeared years ago: various people—his estranged wife Isobel Wright, journalist Titus Pidgeon, and the people Pidgeon interviews, including historical figures like Andre Breton and Marcel Duchamp—chase his scent. McGowan's luminous novel tracks their efforts to conjure this enigmatic poet-painter-performance artist-thief-con man-duke-trauma victim-killer-healer. Twisty and original, *These Lowly Objects* is fundamentally about self-hood, its precariousness and perishability, and its surprising capacity for resurrection.

—Kim Magowan, author of *Undoing* and *The
Light Source*

LOWLY

OBJECTS

A GOLD WAKE NOVEL
BY CATE MCGOWAN

For all you chameleons—I see you.

And for Bill, who's always believed.

PROLOGUE

Never watch from the audience; dream your life as if you're always on stage.
—Jules Lalande, 1918, Zurich

Was it 1917 or 1918? Could it have been 1916? No matter the year. Dada. Boom boom. It was March, and in the Zurich dailies, Jules Lalande advertised his sincere intention to end his own life. Before a packed house, in the galleries of benefactress Berthe Weill, he stood backstage and waited and sipped on green absinthe "for benefit of his nerve."

To the baffled crowd, Lalande's plan appeared novel. What kind of man would invite strangers to watch his own suicide? What kind of man, indeed? They all gaped at the lonely table perched on the proscenium. It stood poised like a long-legged spider balancing a corked vodka bottle and a pistol on its back. Anyone could see the gun was clearly a lady's instrument. The ornate mother-of-pearl handle and silver barrel glinted in the dim spotlight.

In the back of the house, Lalande found a cloakroom where stagehands watched him wrap his chestnut-haired loins in long strips of circus-colored canvas, red, yellow, blue, and green, and then he slathered his sinews with a polish of lard.

"It's time for a show."

Lalande, gleaming in the half-darkness, hurdled down the center aisle and mounted the apron in a leap. A waft followed him redolent of wild beasts and grassy hollows.

As he warmed up on stage in a pre-suicide *recit*, which was a rant really, the near-naked performer pranced and paced. He covered it all. The important topics. Death, life, misery, happiness.

"No animal is fit to live in these times! No human animal, that is!" Many a member of the audience bobbed their heads in agreement.

He was close to winning them over, but what did he do next? He dug his testicles out from his bright jock, propped them on the table right there on the stage, and his cullions shimmered and jostled as if they were two pickled peaches in a jar. Three women fainted off their seats. One sobbed a little (from delight, perhaps). And, as he paused to relish the uproar, Lalande's balls shriveled on the cold slab.

The shocked crowd, still not sure what they were witnessing, held their breaths as Lalande lifted the weapon, poked his finger through the trigger guard, and aimed the barrel at his temple. He squinted, puckered, then pulled the trigger.

Click.

Nothing.

Silence.

Someone in the back row whispered, "The chamber was empty all along. Don't you see?" And then they understood.

Relieved applause rose to the rafters. Kindly gentlemen patted one another on shoulders and backs. Some ladies dabbed at their eyes with lace handkerchiefs.

"Shame on you all," he glowered and tossed the firearm to the floor. "Death is not a spectacle!" He bowed his head in a prayerful pose; contrition washed over the hushed room. The performer then looked up, smiled, winked at all the pale faces, and broke the pall with a hearty laugh.

Uproar.

"Oh, the nerve to trick *and* hector us!" someone hissed through his teeth.

"A charlatan, that's what he is!" a zaftig woman exclaimed as she swatted her fan at a friend's thigh.

"Don't you get it?" an old man asked and chortled as his monocle dropped, and he held his sides in abderian glee.

All the ladies and gentlemen stood and pushed, clambering toward the exits.

Outrage topped outrage, for then, in the growing mêlée, the nude Jules Lalande stood on the stage and urinated in a high arc onto the crowd until his penis gained a certain hardness, and he lost his stream.

After his scandalous performance, all organizers barred Jules Lalande from public events. At least that year, whichever year it was.

TITUS PIDGEON

No more painters, no more scribblers, no more musicians, no more sculptors, no more religions, no more royalists, no more radicals, no more imperialists, no more anarchists, no more socialists, no more communists, no more proletariat, no more democrats, no more republicans, no more bourgeois, no more aristocrats, no more arms, no more police, no more nations, an end at last to all this stupidity, nothing left, nothing at all, nothing, nothing.
—Louis Aragon

FOLLOW TITUS PIDGEON

If, on a particular March morning in the late-1930s, you stood on a corner on the selvedged sidewalks of Paris and paid attention to certain passersby, a man named Titus Pidgeon would have walked by as he made his way to police headquarters. If, in that boundless city, moments before a second great war, a time well after the first, you were into spying or snooping or even casual voyeurism, and if you, an observant person, were to look up after tying your spit-shined oxfords, you might easily have felt compelled to follow the interesting Titus Pidgeon, a stooped figure, a man who just happens to be a sartorial mess: all unpressed tweed and crumpled linen. Not exactly tall, not exactly short, certainly trim. And if you were to shadow that unkempt figure, crossing street after street on a dim morning, tailing at your own jeopardy and hazard, you might have shuffled only steps behind your quarry, finding yourself at the center of the great city designed anew by the amateur architect, Baron Haussmann. You would have crisscrossed through a jumble of perfectly formed city centers, *les quartiers,* not sullied by the stink of the Old City, where you also walked, where the smell flowed out from the bowels of decrepit sections of that megalopolis, where even the most romantic still held their noses. You would have traveled through over a dozen arrondissements with no seeming destination, until finally, the frowzy man crossed le pont Saint-Michel of that fetid river, the Seine, to the île de la Cité. If you stood at that intersection of old and new, you would have watched your mark duck into the chief law enforcement's immense structure, a building wrapping through the neighborhood, a splendorous edifice, its elegant frontage belying all the calamitous investigations transpiring within the stone walls.

La Sûreté nationale, 36, quai des Orfèvres.

And if you stood close enough to peer into that building's marble lobby, you would learn the slumping man you've followed was much more impressive than he first appeared.

Titus Pidgeon, reporter for *The London Times.*

❋

TITUS PIDGEON MEETS ISOBEL WRIGHT LALANDE, AND SHE INFORMS HIM JULES LALANDE IS DEAD

His visit to Paris's police headquarters provided Pidgeon with no information. After a long and tedious morning in the offices of le Préfecture de police, glad-handing, bowing, and generally smiling when Pidgeon's nature inclined him toward anything but cheeriness, he finally escaped the obsequious gendarmes. The men were beyond verbose! And they said nothing of consequence— not even an intriguing tidbit or nonessential anecdote. Jules Lalande was a phantom.

Now to the 5th arrondissement. This afternoon, Pidgeon would interview Madame Isobel Wright Lalande, the wife. *À bon chat, bon rat.* To a good cat, a good rat. Oh, these damn French and their inane idioms! He preferred straightforward English platitudes: "Set a thief to catch a thief." Tit for tat and all that.

As he made his way, Pidgeon sensed someone was shadowing him—he was sure of it. Discreetly, but most definitely. Yes, he had picked up a stealthy follower.

So, Pidgeon led his unseen pursuer on a slow chase, with the reporter doubling back two and three times where he had already traversed. He would get to where he needed, but not on time. Damn surveillance. He crossed streets, wound back around for repeat passes, revisited the same route four times, then stood in an alley for an hour and waited.

Shoe leather. The tale Pidgeon wanted to write demanded it. He was confident he could find the elusive Jules Lalande, the so-called master criminal, a bloody bastard who'd evaded everyone for decades. Assignments like this one got their hooks into a reporter. If he could deftly compose his findings, with just the right balance of facts and intrigue, his article would be the kind of exposé readers would devour. Perhaps his editors would even make it a serial. And the sensation would sell some papers, he was sure.

Yes, the publisher was practically panting with

anticipation for this piece. But research about missing men could not be rushed. This was a mystery with many threads. Many frauds. And a wealthy, dapper criminal at the center. But it was also the sort of edge-of-the-seat conspiracy dime novels and tabloids (like his employer's) exploited.

After he was confident he'd lost his tracker, Pidgeon recommenced, meandering through the streets and faubourgs; he took his time. It began to rain more than a slight drizzle, so he ducked into a dusty bookseller to examine stacks of cheap books and prints displayed at the front of the shop. It was a dark place, and with his suffering sight, he had difficulty reading the faded print in some of the older tomes. After much digging, he found an art volume for only twenty centimes. The book had a shot spine, but the color reproductions inside were superb—Matisse, Miró, Gauguin, Picasso.

By four o'clock, he found his way in the afternoon drizzle to rue Saint Jacques. He spotted the address and shook out his bumbershoot in the dark courtyard, then pulled the bell. The solid crimson doors swung open, and a well-pressed maid stood with her hands on her hips. She *harrumphed*—no greeting—and, with a critical gaze, she disapprovingly appraised his clothing. He looked down and smoothed the creases in his trousers, then handed over his card. Her eyebrows rose as she mouthed his name. She took his measure once more, then stepped back and pointed to the stairs. He shuffled through the foyer, and she called after him, her speech impeccably cadenced English with slow-rolling Rs.

"Knock before you enter, *monsieur*. Madame may be sleeping. Third floor." He double-stepped three flights of sweeping stairs, all iron and marble, and he huffed from the effort. As he reached the landing, he whiffed the thick scent of art: pungent turpentine and oil paints, sharp paraffin, sweet and soft pastels. He adjusted his sideways mustache, combed his fingers through his stiff hair, then followed his nose toward the half-closed door at the end of the hallway. He tapped the molding and identified himself with a half-lie.

"Writer and editor, *ici*, for *The London Times*, Madame. I have traveled here to speak with you about your work." He heard a long, feminine sigh. Clattering objects and racket. And then a voice from behind the door.

"Speed! Is there anything more stupid than speed? You came bounding up those stairs like a herd of animals." It was a gravelly woman's voice, an English accent tinged with snarkish French vowels. Pidgeon heard hobbling, as the woman's bullhorn voice carried closer. "People will tell you matter-of-factly you must know how to do anything in two days' time, to draw, to paint, to sing. But, *absolument*, nothing is accomplished without the patient collaboration of time."

He peeked inside, and a slit of dim illumination shone from the skylight. The woman, who was in her thirties (or forties or fifties?), wore a cerise cloche pulled low over her eyes—the hat glowed in the grey light. Indeed, she looked much older when the filtered sun shone down on her face. She pulled the door fully open, and he bowed low.

"Madame, how do you do? As I said, I'm a writer and editor for *The London Times*. Titus Pidgeon." He affected an accent: less Cockney, more noble and official, but, unfortunately, he was afraid it only came across as effete.

"Ah, a writer *and* an editor! How important! *Bienvenue*.

Well, come in, what are you waiting for?" He hesitantly stepped inside, and she slammed the door.

Madame Lalande frowned as she went back to her easel, settling in her seat like a feline, and she drew thick lines, her arm slashing in fragile swoops, her small-boned fluidity a wonder. Her eyes, a sapphire blue (or were they jet black?), danced over his face for a moment as she assessed his appearance much the same way as the maid had.

In the close studio, complex strata of discarded papers sprawled across the floor and sofas; murky jars and cups and palettes and half-finished clay sculptures jumbled atop the tables. There were stacks of boxes and paint tubes—so many colors—balancing precariously on the mantel and windowsill. Folded easels lined the back wall. And a fat cat lazed in the corner, licking its hocks.

Pidgeon moved to sit down on the nearest chair. Madame Lalande barked.

"Do watch out for that dressing gown. Don't mess with its folds, poor thing! No touching! I am painting that."

The posed prop, a negligée of salmon satin, lolled on the corner of the only empty chair in the room.

So, Pidgeon sat on a cluttered couch behind Madame and peered at the canvas board over her shoulder. She furiously dabbed and poked a vermilion pastel stick into the picture's foreground where she recreated the same satin fabric he'd left undisturbed. The composition revealed an intimate scene a peeper might appreciate; it was a young woman emerging from her bath with a maidservant in the background. He studied the artist's handiwork as the drapery took shape. The work suspiciously resembled the art of another master. Ah yes, he'd never seen such a beautiful copy! Madame's skillful hand moved onto rendering dainty fingers gripping the edge of a halfway-seen bathtub. Yes, yes, the artwork on the easel *was* a copy, but the lines, so luminous! Soft lines, real variegation! He gaped, couldn't help himself, though he knew the danger: an impartial reporter should never show interest in anything. But this drawing, this robust, full representation of such a private moment! So lovely. His eyes grew tired, though, and aspects of her creation turned fuzzy.

While Pidgeon remained transfixed, squinting to make out the strokes and details of the picture, Madame Lalande stood then and relieved him of his umbrella and book, which she yanked out from under his arm.

She leafed through the color plates, but because twilight had already darkened the room and lengthened the shadows, she held the book close to her face, eyes straining. Madame Lalande was more far-sighted than he.

After a moment of studying the book's contents, she shook her head and ranted with indignation.

"Modern painting! Bah! These young *artistes* don't work from nature. It's all surface, surface, surface. And lies, no proportions. Don't talk to me about those bushy-tailed young chaps. They ruin our peaceful cafés with their crazy talk, destroy our world with their shallow ideas!" Her face colored with anger, and she pointed at his book, which she smacked on the table. "I wish I were a dictator. I'd arm a police force and, without an ounce of mercy, order them to shoot those *moderne* imbeciles."

Pidgeon shrugged, watched Madame Lalande's hands as she reached toward her worktable where, amongst a jumble of pastels and papers, her fingers found a blue stoneware teacup. She grasped the vessel and swung her free arm through the air like a terrifying conductor. She continued.

"Like pathetic animals, those *moderne* wretches who hide behind their stupid white shields of canvas. Such nonsense." Pidgeon smiled, conceding.

She lifted the rim of the cup to her quivering lips, took shaky swallows, and eyed him at the same time. Her voice softened with a tone of secrecy.

"You know what this is?" she asked. "Tea, *n'est-ce pas*?

"Yes, that's what I would surmise."

He noted a woman of Madame Lalande's stature, a legendary hostess, had not offered him any refreshment when he'd arrived. Such a shame, he thought, Madame had declined in recent years to her current state of inhospitality.

"It's not regular tea if you're wondering. It's cherry stalk tea. For the bladder."

Pidgeon nodded; he knew people with bad constitutions drank this type of tea for its diuretic properties. And he'd read about Madame Lalande's poor health. All her significant losses over the past few decades had most certainly exacerbated her underlying conditions. At least she still had her art, poor woman. He'd ask his questions and leave as quickly as he had come.

"Madame Lalande?" At the utterance of her married name, the woman's eyes narrowed, and she exhaled with a sharp breath. She responded with venom.

"No one calls me by that name. It is forbidden in this house!" She slammed her cup on the table, and the tea sloshed to the floor, and the cat scooted to hide under the window drapes. The woman's face blanched as she stood and stomped her foot. She pointed to the door. "Sir, I trust you can find your way out!"

"But your husband's whereabouts?" Pidgeon persisted. Madame Lalande sniffed, and before he could think of another question, she grabbed his elbow and the book and hooked his umbrella over her slight forearm. She pushed him toward the door with a strength he had not expected.

"Jules is dead." She jabbed her finger at his chest. "I am not the person who will talk to you about my dead husband. There is no truth to any story. Though you probably wouldn't know veracity if it disrobed before you. Find Tommy Floyd if you're so curious. I hear he is in London, your own filthy town." She pushed Pidgeon by the shoulders as he backed out slowly until he passed through the entry, and she then tossed his umbrella and book past him, far across the hall, all the way to the stair landing. As she pressed the door, he slipped a toe in to catch it. One more question, he had one more question, if he could just ask it. She shoved the door with all her might, and Titus Pidgeon, his foot bruised, relented.

JULES LALANDE

*I have gone far back, further back than the horses of the
Parthenon . . . as far back as the Dada of my babyhood,
the good rocking-horse.*
  —Paul Gauguin

WHERE IS JULES LALANDE?

For more than three decades, Jules Lalande was at least
thirty men. A few women, too. A bulky man, a wiry woman,
a person short and tall. All were he. All were none.

Oh, Lalande! He was a cunning fellow, a sharp blade, a
magician with all manner of disguises; he could devise a
unique appearance for any name or job. With expertise, he
sculpted malleable faces in minutes. He saw possibilities in
every visage, even with his weak eye, the one he'd earned
through debauched violence, through throwing punches in
the ring. Some putty here, there, painted and flushed; some
places darkened with rouge, others lightened with zinc. He
knew all the chameleon tricks. Hairpieces cut to various
lengths and tinted subtle hues. Cotton muslin stuffed in
cheeks and up the nose. Strange round or square eyeglasses
pushing out ears at sharp angles or magnifying eyes to
saucers. Hats—small or large, round or peaked—worn to
define fake professions (balmorals, bearskins, porkpies,
berets, birettas, gats). Baggy or tight clothes fitted for a
birdlike or bovine frame.

As for the legend, Jules Lalande (or whatever he liked
to call himself on a fair day), he only hoped someone still
mentioned his name—or any of his monikers, really

(Dorian Rassup, Dorian Libellule, Jean-Paul DuBois, Jeb Calder, Blue Currin, William Wilde, Burlington Duke). He hoped for some remnant notoriety, some vestige of commemoration, or even a morsel of reverence a few continents away from where someone might still venerate him. Dada was nothing without its scandals, its stories relayed and spread as fast as wildfires in dry forests.

#

Most mornings, he awoke to ringing quiet in this strange place. The dead air of the Cuban coast—it was deafening. He squinted at the cheerful sunlight streaming in from a curtainless porthole and focused (with his better eye) on a hairpiece draped like a marmot upon his pile of clothes. Sitting beside the rodent-like toupee, his fake mustache curled into an apostrophe and flopped in the breeze. When he stood, his feet did not recognize the strange floorboards, and in the galley, he flexed his stiff hands.

He'd found the boat in Texas. Now, he docked somewhere along this bright coast. His Spanish wasn't passable—yet. It would take him another month or two to climb inside the language, to gain an accent and a native's fluency. Then he'd know exactly where he was. His location? He knew he had to be close to Havana. Or Santiago. Maybe. But who needed a map or compass anyway? Words were the way to find what he needed, but perhaps not today. It was too humid; perhaps it wasn't such a good morning to write. And Jules couldn't find a damn thing to write about anyway. No more memoirs, no more stories or letters about someone he wasn't.

With nothing else to do on the boat, no words to conjure, he'd walk away from the soundless water and head into town. A big breakfast at the good Señora's was in order. But first, he had to adhere his disguise. After he placed the blonde hairpiece on his head (he'd shorn his own brown pate down to centimeters short), he stuffed cotton batting into his cheeks for fake jowls, then jumped off the boat onto the sighing dock, and headed away from the water.

On the walk, the road was dusty. A pink glint of quartz dazzled in the dirt as Jules kicked it. Shiny dust distracted him, the fantastical designs moting mid-air. He strolled inattentively. Deep jungle edged the road, each side a bumper for his weaving saunter. And then, he absentmindedly ambled through a spider web spanning the width of the way. As he swiped silken strands from his face, he stopped and gazed with wonder as the arachnid commenced to spin repairs in the large tear. The mending of the hole, even at a furious pace, took the better part of an hour.

With the web finally rewoven, the spider returned to her previous work, lacing a filament around the chrysalis of a malachite butterfly. But Jules had stopped watching. He was far away, remembering, fancying his past, the parts he'd played.

※

JULES'S BEGINNINGS ARE A CURSE

Before Jules Lalande knew when he was dreaming,

before he realized he was awake, before he was even aware, years and continents ago, his story grew out of Lucerne's soil; his roots would nourish him, encouraging him to grow into a rare specimen, a strange wildflower, some new genus, some hybrid no one could classify. Especially after one eventful June nightfall in his childhood.

The air—so full of sweet scents and birds skittering about—tempted the boy outside. In his sleeping clothes, he climbed out his window, then shimmied a vine down a ledge. It was easy, though he had never attempted it before. His legs were wiry, strong. Off the drive, the coarse gravel tickled his bare feet. He walked along the lane, the mountain a shadow of darkness, the soft trace of dew or something else drifting along the path.

In the distance, a train whistle shrilled like a baby. Jules picked up the pace, found a stick, and batted at limbs as he cut through a thicket, then walked down to the meadow where he knew the day's flies were fast asleep in the tall grass. He came to the back of the village, where the streets were not easily navigable.

The roads were seasonal thoroughfares, slushed with mud or powdered with sun-bleached dirt or silent under layers of snow. Many of the roads (they barely qualified as such, and the word "streets" was too generous a term for what they were) were really paths trodden through the grass. Or they were two parallel trails where farmers' and herders' wagons lurched over stones on the steep grades. Or they were tracks of pebbles or mulch bordering squares of tended farms and overgrown properties along the way. And as travelers rambled through the countryside, the roads passed evergreen stands and tall chalets and meadows where old cows chewed cud during the longer summer days, and then the routes finally aimed far into the Alps, disappearing beyond the clouds like smoke.

He walked away, down the hill from his family's mountainside villa, where a maid chased away dusk with candles, plucking out darkness one candle at a time; Father and Mother were singing folk songs and playing parlor cards, too. But Jules was not interested in games, no; he wanted to find the railroad tracks and walk alongside. His curls slackened from sweat; he grew tired, sleepy, but he wanted to see the new train, wanted to feel it blast by.

A chorus of voices found him. Flashes of torches and a procession on a holy day. They snaked down the sloping trail behind him. When they came upon Jules, the parade of people gasped at the sight of him.

"Behold, such beauty! This must be a sign of the Beloved—an angel!" All the torches flashed at him. He smiled. What else could he do? The peasant women, all cabbage breath and heaving chests, pulled him close, held him in their suppleness. A priest made the sign of the cross. Two men in rough shirts hoisted him onto their shoulders.

"We will carry you home, little one."

#

Father was impressed by his son's new status with the commoners. Later, many times, Father told Jules he thought he'd seen a vision. Father glanced over his cards and through the study window and saw his son carried upon pious parishioners' shoulders, his boy paraded through the village like a living icon. Every evening after the procession, Mother allowed Jules soft caramels at bedtime, and Father did not scold the boy for lying awake to watch the night sky or for sneaking out of the house. No one said a word when Jules ventured on his midnight jaunts down to the tracks to wait for the thundering train.

Because Father interpreted his son's veneration by worshippers as a sign from God, he insisted on painting Jules as the Christ Child in the Temple. For months, the boy posed in the bright studio, holding a scroll of paper, wearing his linen dressing gown. Many days, he and his father waited for hours until sunlight appeared; however, a paltry luminescence seldom materialized. When the sun appeared, it was as if the clouds had dropped a drape over the mountains. Waiting for daylight's whims proved agonizing. He was always the model at the ready. So, to stave off boredom, he learned to watch the bees outside the window joists on the flowers as high as the sill, the insects flirting with dripping stamens.

He also counted the books on the shelves, all alphabetized by author and leather-bound, mostly unread, their spines untouched and striped with gilding. They were French books, Father's native language, a language Jules did not know as well as German. If asked, Father said books were one of his passions. He preferred as many as possible, just in case someone accused him of preferring base provincial pursuits.

"*De nouveaux livres et des idées nouvelles font une fois avec le sympathique, fils.*" ["New books and new ideas make one sympathetic with the times, son."] But Jules never once saw his father break the binding of a book.

The shelves in the vaulted room ranged from floor to ceiling, the volumes flushed tight to the edges. Posing for hours as Jesus, he studied the tomes' spines; they winked and glittered at him, begged to be pored over and read. And when Jules posed, when his father required him to stand still as a statue, the sun beaming brilliantly as a gemstone through the tall panes, Jules did not care one whit his legs had gone numb. The books called to him. From his place, he could discern the titles and authors printed sideways on the spines. Day in, day out, he memorized the words, and when he knew all the titles by heart, he whispered nonsensical poems composed from all the language he'd absorbed in his boredom. He started with the As, memorized a row of books through the Hs:

La Rabouilleuse, Illusions perdues, ETUDES ANALYTIQUES: PHYSIOLOGIE DU MARRIAGE, UNE DOUBLE FAMILLE, GOBSECK, ADIEU, L'ELIXIR DE LONGUE VIE, Balzac, LE PEAU DE CHAGRIN, La Lanterne magique, Banville, Les fleurs du mal, Baudelaire, Constant, Adolphe, Flaubert, Salammbo, Memoires d'un fou, JOCASTE ET LE CHAT MAIGRE, Hugo, Les Miserables.

He rearranged the list to his liking. The poem became:

DES ILLUSIONS PERDUES

Études analytiques: physiologie
Élixir de Gobseck
De famille de Rabouilleuse
À de mariage de double au revoir
De peau de Balzac de la vie
Des fleurs magiques de Banville
De lanterne de douleur des rapports constants
Mauvais de Baudelaire Adolphe Flaubert

THESE LOWLY OBJECTS

Salammbo d'un Jocasta aliéné et du chat mince
Hugo et les personnes malheureuses.

Every day, for months, the deafening lull, except the sound of Father's swishing brush, became his solace, for Jules had devised his own world in the studio. Waiting for the sun to open its eyelids and illuminate the room, waiting for his father to complete his large painting, waiting for such lovely words to fill his head, Jules's reverence for language grew, and it filled his world.

"Father, may I go out to play?"

"No, son, sit still."

"Father, I need to . . ."

"Not now."

"Father, I am hungry."

"Wait."

And his poems, begun as a silly way to kill time, saved him.

#

Strangely, as Jules grew older, spoken words were no longer part of his world. In fact, for a long while, he altogether eschewed words. He began thinking in pictures. And, yes, he didn't know why, but he stopped speaking for an entire year. It all started after the spring thaw when he barricaded himself in the school supply closet. His teachers were frantic.

"*Sohn, komm raus! Komm sofort raus!*" ["Son, come out! Come out right now!"] Jules shook his head. Herr Gruber, an old man in bifocals, attempted to yank Jules, but the boy fell limp, and the instructor could not lift the boy's dead weight.

"*Warum tust du das?*" ["Why are you doing this?"] Jules turned away and grasped a mop standing in the closet's dark corner. With no other alternative, the school sent a messenger for help—they fetched his mother. When she arrived, she opened the cupboard door and pleaded.

"*Komm raus, mein Sohn. Du blamierst mich.*" ["Come out, son. You're embarrassing me."] He sat on a box of lye soap and gazed at his feet. He did not acknowledge her or anyone else. Fearing gossip, his mother grabbed his wrist and tugged Jules out (he did not fight her), then she whisked him away. And he remained silent. On the road home in the big coach, his mother gazed out the window and *tisked* and sighed.

He would never return.

At home, he ran upstairs to the huge attic, and he remained in his odd confinement for months on end. The slanted walls pressed down on him with a comfortable closeness, and he tacked up all his sketches, drawings he'd made of the view out the dusty window, plastering them in patterns. The fading gold rose wallpaper was a burnished landscape of wispy petals repeating, repeating. Out past the windowsill inhabited with flowerpots, he admired the terrain, the one thing he could not control. The sightline pushed all the way up the high mountains.

One day, in the corner of his lair, he found a hand-stitched flannel shirt in a discarded trunk of clothes. He imagined the shirt had once belonged to some great English-speaking ancestor on his mother's side, a writer, maybe Byron or Wordsworth or Blake or Milton. Perhaps the piece of clothing possessed magical properties, and so, despite a rare heatwave, he wore it every minute of every day. It was long as a dress, finely sewn, with feminine stitches feathering the seams. The faded collar of Queen Anne's lace fastened snugly at his chin with a wine-colored ribbon he tied in a sad bow. The same torn lace hung in ivory trails from each wrist. Unfortunately, stiffened with dry rot, it soon fell apart. He slept with it then under his pillow.

This behavior had its effects on the family. Mother, always an uncomfortable, awkward woman, never exactly cruel, never exactly kind, professed she felt no pain when it came to his strangeness. Perhaps it was her English upbringing, but she refused to understand why her son refused to speak.

"*Und ich werde dich sehen, wenn du mit diesem Unsinn fertig bist.*" ["I will see you when you are done with this nonsense."] She then resigned her maternal duties and no longer climbed the steep stairway to his attic.

Jules continued to take meals in his lair's solitude. For eight months, he uttered not a single word. The days wore on like a dull ache. He never departed the house to play or visit his railroad tracks. No one ever knew why he gave up the world and talking for those months.

By the end of his cloister, the servants blamed the boy's strangeness for shoving his mother prematurely into heaven. At her funeral, Jules remained beyond language and did not cry out. Not even one sob. And his father noticed.

The resentful servants ceased to address Jules.

After weeks of mourning, Father took his withdrawn son to Paris. Jules slept as the trains and a carriage crossed uneventfully through Switzerland and France, but as soon as they arrived in the marvelous city and Jules spied the

Seine and saw the cobwebbed majesty of the new la tour Eiffel, he opened his mouth and croaked.

"Father, the tower! Look at how noontide falls on the tower!"

#

Perhaps Father loved collecting paintings more than anything—more than collecting books or even painting a portrait of his son. He certainly enjoyed acquiring art more than he cared for Jules, the boy was sure of it. Father had a growing reputation as an affluent collector. And so, the man bought and bought.

Jules and Father spent the winter in Paris, and father took him everywhere. They ferreted out expensive pictures so the man could build what he called a "significant collection." Maybe Jules's period of muteness had inspired a newfound affection in his distant, only-living parent. Maybe Father found himself concerned Jules would lose his will to speak again, or maybe his son would embarrass him in Parisian society. Perhaps he thought Jules was simple-minded. No matter the reason, Father continued to seek out the boy's company.

They spent their mornings and afternoons visiting other collectors and antique dealers off narrow side streets. They traversed lanes sliced with light and shade. Bundled up against the cold (the air hinted at a chill in other seasons, too), they would exit many establishments empty-handed, and the sad jingle of bells on door handles would announce defeat as the father and son stepped back into frozen Paris.

One December day, they found themselves in

Montmartre, searching for an elusive artist. They visited cafés, shops, charcuteries. No luck. Then they happened upon a corner bar.

"Degas? You just missed him. But you may be able to catch him if you exit through the back. He walks slow." The bartender polished a beer glass with a dirty grey cloth. Jules and Father ducked into the brasserie's alleyway. They came out far along the boulevard, found a stooped old man shuffling down the *chaussée*. His father recognized the decrepit artist somehow, tapped the wizened chap on the shoulder. At his father's touch, Degas skidded to a stop, turned, and started to speak, but sudden music burst out above. They looked up.

On her balcony, a prostitute sang as she hung wet laundry out to dry until a gust of cold wind from the river fluttered and freed one of her delicate petticoats. The lacy, pale thing soughed across the street, and when the wind died suddenly, the undergarment wafted down, whiffling like a slip of falling paper. It fell into the frosty mud under a naked tree. She stopped singing.

"*Mérde!*" she shouted down at the street and pointed at Jules from her perch.

"*Vous! Jeune garçon! Va chercher ça pour moi!*" ["You! Young boy! Fetch that for me!"] Jules did not hesitate. He scurried across the lanes, dodged traffic, and scooped up the woman's petticoat while Degas and Father watched with amusement. When he returned, the old whore, who was now on the sidewalk, snatched the damp thing from his hands. She scowled, then patted him on the head and disappeared back inside her run-down building. Degas chuckled and leaned down close to Jules, took in his face, studying it feature by feature before he spoke.

"Fils, tu as un chemin avec les femmes. J'ai été si." ["Son, you have a way with women. I used to be so."] The craggled man smiled, beard brushing his breastbone, eyes wild and unfocused. Jules stood on *le trottoir's* cold pavers and peered up at him, silent. And then Father took advantage of the moment.

"Monsieur, nous sommes désolés de déranger votre solitude, mais nous aimerions acheter un de vos tableaux. On nous a dit de vous demander directement." ["Monsieur, we are sorry to disturb your solitude, but we would like to purchase a painting of yours. We were told to ask you directly."] Father's voice grated, high-pitched and sycophantic. Degas looked down and smiled at Jules again.

"Suis moi." ["Follow me."] The boy's pride soared.

#

Jules and Father stopped at the Louvre after visiting Degas' studio, after procuring one of his magnificent paintings for a pretty penny. Rolled in a tube and off its stretchers, the Degas masterpiece nested between the two as they settled on a bench. Feeling triumphant, Father had tugged Jules into the museum, and now they gazed at some significant painting from early in the past century, stared at the historical mural as large as the side of a house; they both sighed at the monumental work of art before them.

"Avez-vous déjà vu quelque chose d'aussi beau, Père?" ["Have you ever seen anything so beautiful, Father?"] Oh, how Jules ached at the beauty! The figures thrashing, the dense colors, the emotional scene of women and men dying!

"Oui j'ai. Ce Degas." ["Yes, I have. That Degas."] He

pointed to the tube containing their purchase. *"Il rivalise avec n'importe quel autre, pourrait accrocher aux côtés de Delacroix et Géricault."* ["It rivals any other, could hang alongside Delacroix and Géricault."] With great feeling, Jules reached out to grasp his father's arm, but the man pushed his son's warm hand aside and hastily pulled on his gloves.

"Pas le temps de se moquer. Il faut avancer. Hilma nous attendra avec notre repas." ["No time to dally. We must move on. Hilma will be waiting with our meal for us."]

Jules followed behind, and, when Father turned the corner in the large, echoing museum, the boy propped Degas' rolled-up painting in a corner as if the tube had transformed into a leaning column, a fluted relic. Yes, Jules left the Degas where it belonged. His father did not deserve something so remarkable.

And so, Father hurried away, two steps ahead of Jules the whole walk home; he did not notice Jules's caprice until they were removing their boots in the mudroom. They pulled off their hats, untied their soggy boots, and then Father placed his hand on his son's shoulder.

"Le Degas. Regardons de plus près." ["The Degas. Let's take another look."]

"Nous ne pouvons pas." ["We can't."] Jules looked at his feet, wiggled his cold toes in his wet socks.

"Où est-ce." ["Where is it?"] Father's voice quavered, beyond angry. Jules shrugged.

"Le tableau est perdu." ["The painting is lost."]

The man howled.

"J'étais vraiment maudit avec une bête pour un fils!" ["I was truly cursed with a beast for a son!"] Father slapped him across the face, once, twice, then stormed into his

study and slammed the door.

✳

JULES'S DREAMS WEIGH HEAVY

The nightmares began before he could distinguish between dreaming and reality. He always harkened back to that same immutable feeling of his childhood—loneliness.

The servants packed and padlocked the boy's trunk and off he went to Lyon to live with Grand-Maman. At his grandmother's, the old woman feared he would wet his feather bed, so the boy slept on a cot in the hallway. And Grand-Maman knew the servants could best tend to his incessant crying if they didn't have to travel all the way to the bedrooms. Ah, he was such a pitiful child!

The old woman had a household to run; servants' chores and adult things were much more critical than some grandson who cried like a mewling infant. But Grand-Maman had a plan. Soft boys needed hard work. He required back-breaking labor, no luxury. Books and art were not a part of this kind of world; the sooner Jules knew this, the better.

\#

Winter wheat filled the lush spring fields. Sticks and branches crackled under his slight weight. He wore thin, cotton trousers, the cold air blasting his legs.

And then there was the hard hand of his grandmother collecting wood for the stove. Picking and handling became a continuous process in her household. And at day's end, the glaucous twigs, when set in the enormous parlor fireplace, would blaze with an angry flame, all fierce and snapping. He feared the burning more than the collecting.

"Grand-Maman, I am tired. Can I go home now?" The old woman's response frightened him.

"Now, little man, you've been bad. You will never go home. *Jamais plus*."

Then came his first real understanding of death. It went something like this: he ran with the boys through a barn, then into an abandoned graveyard. There, he concealed himself, huddled down, screening behind a tombstone sunk sideways in the moist earth; it tilted at the angle of a loose tooth. The dead man's name, long since eroded away by the elements, was unreadable, the lettering a shadow in the crumbling granite. The man rested with no words to mark him. The boy imagined a faceless, nameless man lying deep in the earth.

Nearby, a mortuary's stench fumed from its doors. No one in town ever acknowledged the smell, as if the marble walls could cordon off rot, prevent it from infecting the living world. For some reason, the reek comforted Jules; the idea of decaying flesh and acrid chemicals assured him of every human's equality. Everyone would come to a place like this someday. As he sat under the nameless grave marker, his skin tightened at the thought.

So, he shivered with the chill; it overcame him for a moment, but he shirked it off, then ran over the meadow to the Morisot's farm. He shuddered again as he kneeled in the tall reeds and pulled his slingshot from his back pocket. Groping on the ground, he found a smooth, round stone, yanked back the strap, and took aim. In the Morisot's pen, the chickens scattered, all but one. And on the hard soil, blood gathered in a pool viscous as syrup; it gurgled from the bird's neck wound. Jules wailed at the sight of the dying bird, and Madame Morisot came running.

"Oh, my dear! Is that you Jules Lalande?" Madame Morisot shambled into the yard and discovered blood and feathers. She pitched onto him, pinching his ear. "Lalande, I took one look at you when you arrived here. Trouble is what I thought. Back to hell, you little devil." She marched him across the length of four farms and through a close copse of alders. He lost a shoe somewhere, caught it on a root, then cut his heel to the bone.

Grand-Maman's anger! She whipped him mightily, then sent him to the larder room with no supper. No one noticed he wore only one shoe, and no one saw the trail of blood from his wound. He wept for hours, licking his heel to clean it, sat near a tub of butter and fell asleep wrapped in a tight ball to stay warm. Later, he heard the servants scrape his trunk from the attic. His dreams weighed heavy on him, for he knew he would depart to another place. Again.

#

The boat rocked, and Grand-Maman's maid, Solange, sang and shushed his crying. The spit bucket filled with his bile. Though the short journey only tossed him across the channel, it felt as if someone had cast him to the ends of the earth, away from everyone and everything. His bandaged foot throbbed, and he gazed through the porthole, where diving ivory birds somersaulted like demons in flight. The sky moved up and down, up and down as the boat creaked, and the bench swayed, and more bitter liquid rose from his stomach. What had he done to deserve this?

✳

JULES AT THE HOUSE OF WILDE

After arriving in England at the House of Wilde, seat of the Dukes of Burlington, in less than a week, Jules's foot had scabbed over, and he was fluent in English. He possessed no accent and banished his native German's rolling Rs, flattened his tonsils and lips, and he eschewed the French of his grandmother, those guttural and back-of-the-throat pronunciations. Yes, he compressed his tongue and stiffened his face to produce horizontal English sounds. He mimicked. And he understood.

He gleaned much more from his lovely new caretaker, Governess Hansen, and his uncle's valet and property manager, Alban Frost, than they suspected. The subterfuge was fun. No one assumed he comprehended anything. They supposed his speech was nothing more than mere imitation; they reasoned he mimicked like a myna bird, repeating every sound he heard. But he grasped it all. And how!

When he walked to the village, the shopkeepers offered him a piece of candy. He would smile and say, "Thank you kindly, sir," in his bronchial, upper-class accent. The servants took it for granted he no longer spoke in climbing tones or round vowels. Many townspeople forgot his Continental heritage. Now he was an Englishman. At least for a time.

His uncle, his mother's brother, Jonathan, the 8th Duke of Burlington, only called on the house once. During his uncle's visit, the man talked with Jules and treated him as an equal. The child found unexpected succor in this kindness. His uncle's hazel eyes, the color of a golden morning sky, mesmerized the boy, and the freckles dotting the handsome man's nose were like points on a map. He was tall, still vital, close to his older years. Two streaks of grey and a slight curve to his shoulders only somehow enhanced his bachelor swagger.

Uncle ran after Jules in a game of Blind Man's Bluff; he lashed at the boy's bare legs with a switch and peeked from beneath his mask, then made an expression like a grotesque mouse with two long fangs. That day, Jules laughed. He could not stop laughing, and he made a hiding place in the bower, the stinging scent of pine cloaking him in the prickly darkness of the afternoon. Uncle sought him out then and gave Jules a toy boat with the most exquisite rose-coral silk for a sail. Jules cried, of course, when Uncle left.

#

It was two years after arriving and some months after Alban Frost and Governess Hansen died in suspicious circumstances. Jules found himself alone. Though, not for long. That day there were no ominous signs. Morning dawned much like every other—roosters in the stables crowing fecund calls to awaken a sunrise before effulgence dowsed the lake's mists. The manor appeared as a monstrosity to the twelve-year-old. It also held much magic. His second cousin, Isobel, was gone for her term at school, and so Mrs. O'Kelly, the family's head housekeeper, was his only ally. Most recently, he slept on Mrs. O'Kelly's floor in her warm, dry room. He felt safer there.

When he sat down to breakfast, Jules could tell the servants were excited about something. No one would serve him until he had tied an apron around his neck to protect his best linen shirt, the one Mrs. O'Kelly insisted he wear.

"Why this one?" he asked as the plump woman smoothed out the sleeves.

"Never you mind. Just wear it, sir," Mrs. O'Kelly said, seemingly happy she had him as her charge (even though it meant so much more work!). She followed her gruffness with an assurance the cook would make his favorite morning meal of a poached egg and kippers.

"Eat, boy! It's good for your constitution. You'll see. We'll both live to see ninety."

The rest of the morning and afternoon, he couldn't believe his fortune—left alone to play! And no one was bothered he did not practice his numbers or write his paragraphs in the schoolroom; no one noticed when he did not visit the stables for his daily swordplay.

Who was coming to Wilde? Such commotion. It couldn't be Isobel. Oh, his beautiful cousin never stayed gone for too long, but she'd traveled great distances this last year and would not return soon. And they wouldn't make this kind of fuss for her. He also knew from experience the visitor could not be his uncle. No, the man preferred London; he would not visit Jules.

Mrs. O'Kelly, too busy to banter with Jules, had commandeered the home for the last-minute cleaning.

With her usual enthusiasm, she smacked carpets on the back landing and instructed the lower maids to double starch and press the already stiff sheets. Indeed, when he escaped outdoors, he sneezed all the way down the stairwell, while the women in the house kept to themselves, shining and plumping everything, polishing and pushing the grime away. All those preparations for a guest—and he was invisible to an army of servants.

Jules suspected no matter how diligently they cleaned, they would not wholly rid the haunted rooms of the fear crawling out from the cracks and waiting for the dark. He went to the woods, and from his vantage point in a low tree branch, he admired how the house's windows shone like new pence pieces, and he watched the kerchiefed maids bend to their buckets, slopping water across the wrinkled panes.

After his long day of lonesome play at the lake, of throwing rocks at butterflies and lying on the mossy boulders in the woods, Jules moseyed home. Mrs. O'Kelly sent him to the large washbasin. And then she brushed his hair. In the mirror, the gloaming's refractions cast rainbows onto the floor. He turned and gazed out the floor-to-ceiling casements at the closely mown back lawn and flowering gardens. They heard clattering at the front of the house; a forward coach had pulled up. He stayed behind in the room as Mrs. O'Kelly ran down the long stairway, into the foyer, and to the front door.

He ran across the corridor and stood in the second-floor gallery, watched a second coach arrive, its horses sauntering around the circular gravel drive. A coach lantern, already lit by the groom, swung in a soft rhythm. The carriage stopped with a great creak and a tinkling of horse bells, and out stepped a young woman, all rear bustle and lace bonnet and fringed cape. The greyness of her clothing overwhelmed her vulpine face.

The footmen lugged trunk after trunk from both coaches. Even after the stranger stepped down, her graceful gloved hand still held the door strap tightly. She took her measure of the property, grinned and shook her head in amazement, craning her neck to peer up at the four stories of Wilde; she then stared down the front lawn sloping toward the bright roses growing at the edge of the tree line. Out there, the pines grew big as explosions. And a covey of birds looped in a ballet above the lake in a great show for the young visitor. The woman's face took on a glow of something he had never seen before. Not joy, exactly. Greed?

Who could she be?

After finishing their task of unloading the groaning carriages, the servants carried the last trunk through the front door. Jules peeked at this whole production, first through the gallery's windows, then through the staircase landing's balustrades. Mrs. O'Kelly opened the heavy, two-story door, and three maids curtsied in turns to greet the woman as she entered. The young woman's voice quavered—it echoed through the marble vestibule.

"Whh-yy nice to make your acquaintance." She had the voice of a child, and it lilted most assuredly like Mrs. O'Kelly's. When the kind housekeeper curtsied deeply, the young woman stifled a giggle, ducked her head coyly into her cape collar. "Oh, what a beautiful home!" She stood high on her toes, then clapped her hands together, and twirled in a circle.

"I-I will show you to your room?" Mrs. O'Kelly

stammered, inevitably confused by an unseemly display of effusiveness. They came up the stairway. Jules scurried beneath a carved bench set far back against the wall, and he listened to Mrs. O'Kelly explain the house rules as they climbed—"We prefer to eat at seven, eleven, and six-thirty. But now the timing is for you to decide. Tea is served at three every day but Sunday."

The two women did not see him as they passed; he hid there, tiny and scared as a hedge bird. They made their way to one of the best rooms, a plum spot in the house at the right corner of the main wing, just two stories above Mrs. O'Kelly's strictly downstairs servant room.

And then Governess Hansen appeared.

At the edge of his sight, the specter rose up from the floor at the end of the corridor; she hovered a few feet from the ceiling and made her disapproving expression, nodding her head in anger and holding her long, silvery forefinger to her lips. *Shhhhhhhhhhhhh!*

Usually, Governess Hansen visited him and played jacks on the nursery floor or rolled marbles to impossible places under the best furniture in the grand parlor. Confident Governess Hansen would not like this new person, Jules gazed at the vision and attempted to draw her close to explain. However, Mrs. O'Kelly stepped back out into the hall, beckoned him.

"Jules! I see you under there. Come out. Come out this instant and meet your new governess, our new mistress, Governess Boyle." Mrs. O'Kelly's voice sharpened with embarrassment as she stood in the doorway of the mistress's room. He glanced down the hall again. Governess Hansen had evaporated, and there was only a dusty corner where she had floated.

He stood and sulked his way across the deep carpet into the airy room, blue and white like a porcelain teacup. Then he bowed grandly.

"Pleased to meet you, Miss." He whispered it almost inaudibly so as not to upset Governess Hansen's ghost (if she remained). His eyes, half-closed, aimed downward, fixed on the young lady's boots, their scuffed brown tips peeking out from beneath her tight barrel skirt. He looked up, forced a smile.

The governess's face brightened, her thin eyebrows rising. Nervously licking her plump lips, she sighed with satisfaction.

"My, you are ever, ever more marvelous than the house!" She grabbed at one of his curls, but he ducked behind Mrs. O'Kelly's full skirts, then ran back down the hallway to the nursery to look for Governess Hansen.

#

This new governess meant only one thing to him—he would part from dear Mrs. O'Kelly's close attention. He'd sleep one last time in the housekeeper's quarters, and then he'd move to his own room. Mrs. O'Kelly explained, "All men need their individual space."

That night, in the basement, he lay under the blanket on his pallet, and his sleep would not come. It grew late, so late, and above his head, the pace of feet bumped back and forth in Governess Boyle's room. Even though it was two stories above him, he perceived another unusual sound— the muffled hum of a woman singing. He imagined the governess as she brushed her chestnut hair in soft strokes, as she admired herself in the tall mirrors.

The droning upstairs continued, and he still could not doze with Governess Boyle's racket, and Mrs. O'Kelly had begun to bark orders to the maids in her dreams. He instead set himself imagining distinct figures in the murkiness, went to the window, and gazed out at the deep shadows on the lawn. Often in his long days alone, he found patterns of animals or faces in the swirls of clouds or of pasture. And he performed this seeking out of forms with nighttime nature, too.

As he had many times after dark, he stood at Mrs. O'Kelly's window and fashioned beasts from the muted outlines. Squinting, Jules visualized an elephant forming from a bush and tree, and he traced the leafless sapling, which grew at a sharp angle along the edge of the grass, then transformed the configuration into a waving pachyderm's trunk.

He searched for another shape to transmute so he could push away the old ache preventing sleep, the longing he felt for his parents, for Grand-Maman, for his cousin, Isobel, for something he could not explain. And then, way out near the forest, a tiny figure materialized close to Jules' imaginary elephant. But this apparition was no fantasy. It was plain as the ground below. It appeared slowly at first, suddenly shimmered, then solidified into the form of Alban Frost, the property manager for his uncle, the man who had immediately followed Governess Hansen to the grave.

The spirit jolted forward in spurts, and Jules cried out, yet Mrs. O'Kelly did not stir. The ghost skimmed the surface of the yard in a board-straight, singular mass, his arms stiff, clasped to his sides. And as the moon came out from behind the clouds, the ghoul formed into an opaque figure. No gleam passed through him, yet all of him shone incandescent: his hair, his jacket, his skin, even his shoes. A mystical monolith. Jules remembered how Frost had dressed during those last days, and there he was in the same shiny waistcoat now illuminated by a gash of lamplight. Frost progressed in the most unnatural, erratic movements. The dead man then stopped after a slow jerking promenade across the privet, and he cocked his head ever so slightly and peered up at Governess Boyle's fully-lit room.

Jules wondered if perhaps Governess Boyle was at that moment looking out at the far-reaching property. Could she see the apparition, too? And then it became apparent to Jules those thumping sounds above him were not Governess Boyle's; they were something different altogether; the thuds and melody were not Governess Boyle's feet stepping in time or her mellifluous voice.

And the steady knocking on the ceiling continued. Jules stood at the window frozen for such a long moment, watching the scene, fixed the phantom with a gaze crossing minutes, and overhead, the pacing accelerated. Jules's arms were cold; the hair on the backs of his fingers prickled.

Frost spied Jules half-hidden at the pane.

The specter's visage swiveled, and his attention shifted focus ever so slowly toward Jules; in seconds, then, his face zoomed terrifyingly close, and now the spirit's eyes cleaved onto the boy; Frost was only inches from Jules, so near, fogging the particular window glass of the transom from which Jules watched. The ghost's skin mottled in strange colors, peeled in places off his forehead. And Frost did not blink, just gaped with no eyelids at Jules, really, no pupils or irises, either, only pearlescent bulbs, bloodshot as if he had been crying.

Jules's fear subsided for some reason. Or maybe it increased. He had never experienced such ambivalence. But Frost grimaced, tried a smile, a crooked, slight grin, his pale eyes hooking into Jules's with recognition of pain or feeling or something indescribable for the young boy, and the barrier all but fell away. Jules went back to his makeshift bed and fell asleep in moments. He felt no terror now. He felt lonely no more.

#

With some of Mrs. O'Kelly's load lifted, the burden of caring for a child no longer her duty, her shoulders squared, and she performed her cleaning tasks with good-natured zeal. Her kindly feelings trickled down to everyone in the house. After breakfast with the new governess, dear Mrs. O'Kelly cheerfully suggested Jules show his keeper around—"Young sir, I am sure you would like to give our mistress a proper tour of the house and grounds." And off Jules and the governess went.

"Oh, show me the lake. Mrs. O'Kelly told me all about that." They made their way through the groomed woods, and Governess Boyle followed Jules down the path. The lake *was* rather significant. It was his favorite place, really, with its cattails and film of algae on the surface; its bend hooked around and away, so there was no way to see its edge beyond low-slung tree limbs. The sky above, a subterranean bruised blue, promised a perfect early summer day.

Governess Boyle sat in the grass with her legs folded beneath her while he collected bright bellflowers and tied them together to make azure ribbons. He waved dandelion seeds, and the fibers whorled through the air.

"Your uncle is a fine man. Has he ever married?"

"No, madam, never. I've never had an aunt." He shrugged. He knew nothing, really, of the duke, other than he had visited Wilde only once, and he had heard about his reputation as a famous artist.

Jules decided right then he did not like Governess Boyle, though he affectionately draped a long flower chain over her chignon, fashioned it into a crown, twining it round and round her head. Tight.

"Too much, my dear, too much!" Governess Boyle laughed, shooing the flowers off her head. She gave him a wild-eyed, affectionate look. And though he grinned an adorable expression, he did not mean it. Yet the moment must have touched her, for she jumped up, grabbed him, and swung him into a hug.

"Oh, you are too wonderful! This place is too wonderful! We shall make a life for ourselves! Your uncle will see!" Governess Boyle still held him close. He could feel the woman's heart hopscotching in her breast as she spoke, and he smelled a sour scent of something he did not understand. Callowness was not it. Ambition, maybe.

He peered over Governess Boyle's shoulder, and Governess Hansen emerged slowly from the center of the lake and stood in the shallows, her apparition's hair undone, black and shimmering with a bilious tint from the surface scum, loose and sinuous. The water reflected her aspect; her face had fallen in a bit with sadness, it radiated without color, but she was so much more beautiful than Governess Boyle could ever be. She frowned, her face drawn into an overwhelmingly sad expression, and he sensed her pitiful longing even from across the distance.

The odious new governess still clamped Jules in her hug.

"Please, miss, I can't breathe. Please, please, put me down," he said, and Governess Boyle complied. He glanced again to where Governess Hansen had been standing, but she was gone. This new woman could ruin everything. He did not like her familiarity, but disdain was easy enough to hide; he could pretend child-like diffidence until he devised a plan for her departure.

They trooped around the grounds a bit, made their way quietly, trekking through the astringent smelling acacia trees and pine forest. And when they disturbed some brush and startled a rook, the bird took flight with a dark blast of feathers and a loud *whoosh*. Startled, Governess Boyle tripped over a tree stump, then giggled and pulled herself up. "Oh, my!" She brushed pine needles off her sleeves and climbed up the hill.

She and Jules stood then and gazed at the looming house on the summit. Even in the noonday sun, it was vast and forlorn. A gargantuan place, Wilde had the bearing of a castle or fort, a structure covered in mist as if some fairy tale ogre resided there. Mrs. O'Kelly once told Jules his recent ancestors thought it romantic to fashion the structures out of the already substantial house (it had survived centuries without towers).

As he stood with Governess Boyle, Jules did not relay the home's renovation history, but instead, remained silent as he stood with her. Together, they gazed at the towers tagged onto the corners of the two outside wings, the large assemblies built with dark stone. Such a chaotic appearance.

"Look!" She pointed at the towers he hated. "How royal looking. And I am the headmistress of this castle. A fortress." The most absurd aspect of the home was those battlements, so ostentatious, deeply crenelated, awkwardly contributing to the hulking silhouette. It appeared less like a storybook palace and more like a hospital or prison.

She jiggled the house keys on the chain belt at her waist, and spoke with insufferable levity, "Yes, head of all of this. Of course, after your uncle, the duke. Of course."

They returned to the house and explored the far reaches of Wilde's interiors. It took them the better part of two hours. He pulled Governess Boyle into every chamber and every room, chattered about all the games his cousin, Isobel, and he had played before the adults sent away the young girl.

"We ran down this hall often, and one time, Isobel stubbed her toe on that corner." They both laughed. He cautioned Governess Boyle, "Careful, that step is loose," when she lingered on one of the back staircases. And then they climbed to the west tower.

As they mounted the last step, the sun ducked inside some clouds, and the wind combusted the air. When she stepped up and peered out, Governess Boyle turned a pale color from the height, but he distracted her, singing parts of a song he knew—*And shall I never see thee more, / The idol of my heart? / And wilt thou seek a foreign shore, / And from thy true love part?*

He whistled the entire tune again, high and sad.

"How lovely! You have such a vibrant voice." She rubbed his arm, and he pulled it away, pointing to the horizon.

"Look, you can see the village. And the lake is ever so small. And the birds like it here, too. It never feels lonely when I'm up here with the birds."

"You feel lonely?" she asked. He did not respond. Mourning doves perched on the ledge and cooed. The birds pricked warily away as Governess Boyle circumambulated the looming tower, as she stared out in every direction. East. West. South. North.

"Miss, on a fine day, I think you can sometimes see London. I imagine I see Cromwell Road, you know, where my uncle lives. I wave and believe he stands on his roof and waves back."

Governess Boyle tittered and enthusiastically waved her hand toward the city. He went downstairs.

#

A courier arrived with the post after tea, and Governess Boyle all but shut herself away in her room the rest of the day. She remained cloistered well into the evening. He took advantage of his freedom and searched for Governess Hansen, wanted her to see his loyalty was always with her. Well past dinner, he roosted in the stable loft and listened to the tintinnabulation of larks. *Ti-ti, ti-ti ti-ti.* The ghost of Governess Hansen finally came and sat with him, and, though she did not speak, Jules knew the spirit still cared for him—new governess be damned.

#

"I'm glad to see you've become such fast friends!" Mrs. O'Kelly studied Jules and Governess Boyle as she stood at the sideboard, stirring a pot, quietly directing the cook, who limped painfully in and out of the room. Everyone knew Mrs. O'Kelly, a housekeeper by trade, ran Wilde's kitchen. Poor Mrs. McDair, the cook, could barely walk anymore, but no one wanted his uncle to discover this.

Jules and Governess Boyle sat at the end of the long table and finished breakfast.

"We will meet Isobel's coach when she arrives tomorrow—perhaps you did not know, Jules?" His heart jumped. Governess Boyle smiled. He continued eating his bread, batted his eyelids, bashfulness a game. Of course, this news was superb, but he would not show happiness. Not yet.

After he finished, Governess Boyle hurried him away.

"Mrs. O'Kelly and I must conduct some business. Perhaps we shall start you on some writing exercises . . ."

Governess Boyle walked him down the hall to the dark, three-desk schoolroom. It had no windows because as Governess Hansen once remarked, "They serve as a distraction." Jules sat down at his desk, and he dipped his pen in the well, then commenced to draw loops on paperboard. He diligently worked on his letters, and after a few rows of Os, he amused himself by drawing some hares.

After this fun, he tiptoed down the back stairs and along the hallway to the kitchen. The corridor's shined-up floors, even downstairs, were difficult to traverse without his boots scuffling noise.

Outside the kitchen storeroom, he held his breath. And then, Governess Hansen materialized two feet away. They stood facing one another in the dim hall. Jules did not say a word. But the spirit smiled, a real smile, though it was hard to discern what a tall, thin apparition, all somberness, understood of the living world. She pushed up close to him, and she mimicked his stance as he positioned his ear to the door. He breathed in, and Governess Hansen smelled of cellar and moss. They were listening to a conversation about the deceased governess, with the new governess attempting to discover information about her predecessor.

". . . and what of the former?" Governess Boyle asked Mrs. O'Kelly.

"The last one? Oh, she was delicate—almost as handsome as you," the housekeeper answered.

Jules swallowed. What a lie. Governess Hansen looked down at him and scowled. He thought the following words in his mind, confident Governess Hansen would understand—*No one can ever be pretty like you, Governess Hansen. No one will EVER be as pretty!* Governess Hansen's image, vaporous and not entirely transparent, shifted and wavered a bit. He was sure he saw a hint of another smile on her dark lips. The new governess continued.

"I do hope her loveliness was a pleasure to him!" Governess Boyle's voice faked flippancy.

"Yes, it was," Mrs. O'Kelly agreed, "but that's the way *he* likes everyone . . ." And then her voice caught. "I mean, of course, that's what the *duke* prefers. Yes, indeed."

"Isn't that who we were just speaking about?"

"Yes, the duke, of course."

Quiet. Uncomfortable seriousness in the kitchen. Governess Hansen's piercing eyes stared up at the ceiling, looked to something far away. Jules thought of Alban Frost, and the apparition touched his arm. He felt a deep cold surge through him, all the way to his feet, settling there in the warm hallway. The women's conversation continued.

"I received this forwarded envelope in the post yesterday from Duke Burlington himself," Governess Boyle said. "Look at the seal, embossed and so grand. The first note from the duke enclosed a second letter. He instructed me to deal with the matter and not bother him. I am not to disturb him in any way with particulars. Would you read this letter and tell me what you think?"

"Oh." Mrs. O'Kelly sounded as if someone had squeezed the air out of her. He imagined the old housekeeper's face; he knew Mrs. O'Kelly could not read a word—it was her great embarrassment. Governess Boyle had now alienated her only ally, but even as Jules and Governess Hansen lingered outside the door, they heard the impatience in Governess Boyle's voice.

"Should I read it to you then?" The governess had a condescending tone, and there was the crinkling of paper.

"No, Miss, please, please, just tell me what it says."

And then Governess Boyle blurted out the news— "Young Miss Isobel is returning to Wilde. She will remain here for good."

Jules rejoiced! Could it be? Isobel. Here? For good? But he froze his face, made sure he did not look too pleased. He looked at the ghost of Governess Hansen, and she nodded. Then, Governess Boyle recommenced her interrogation of Mrs. O'Kelly.

"What does it mean, Mrs. O'Kelly, do you think? That the child's parents have released her?"

"But she is usually here anyway." Mrs. O'Kelly sounded baffled.

"Yes, sent here for summers—but this letter states that Isobel may never go back to the school." Governess Boyle's tone was haughty. Jules could hear Mrs. O'Kelly shuffle her feet, clanking the pots, placing cutlery and utensils in the safe. He looked back to Governess Hansen's ghost for some reaction, but all he saw was the doorway and beyond. The hallway felt larger. And darker, too. It was also warmer.

"The school won't keep her?" Mrs. O'Kelly's tone turned weepy.

"They will not."

Mrs. O'Kelly sobbed, "What has she done?"

He heard the rustle of papers—no doubt, Governess Boyle handing Mrs. O'Kelly the letter. And then another sigh from Mrs. O'Kelly.

"This is not for me to say," Mrs. O'Kelly spoke with quiet tension. There was a mortified pause. Jules's knees ached from locked stillness, but he remained transfixed.

"She has done something terrible," Governess Boyle stated. A leaden monotone replaced her usual voice, its lightly dismissive timbres.

"Does the school say so? Oh, this is horrible!" Mrs. O'Kelly wailed now.

"They go into no particulars. They merely express their regrets that it would be impossible to keep the young miss. I wonder—it can only have one meaning. She is harmful to others!"

"Miss Isobel? Her? Never!"

He heard Governess Boyle sit, her skirts whispering about her. Mrs. O'Kelly's resolute faith in Isobel reassured him.

"No doubt, they thought the girl was somehow ill-behaved. But a *child*? Harmful? An abomination? That is not possible unless she is terrible." Meanness trickled into Governess Boyle's voice; it was not difficult to miss. But it did sound, too, as if she wanted to believe Mrs. O'Kelly.

"It's too, too shocking," Mrs. O'Kelly sobbed, "to say such spiteful things! Why she's scarce ten years old."

"You're right, it should be impossible for someone so young."

Brave, now, Mrs. O'Kelly continued her protestations.

"Meet her, miss. You might as well believe it of our sweet, innocent boy." There was not a sound, but it seemed the new governess agreed to reserve judgment until she could observe Isobel firsthand. Jules sensed tacit assent.

Jules turned the doorknob and swung open the closed door without knocking. He stood in the doorway, where he held his paperboard drawing of hares. He displayed it in front of him, fingers black with ink, and he mustered the most innocent of expressions. Mrs. O'Kelly pointed to him tenderly.

"Bless him! We have ourselves an artist!"

#

He diligently worked the rest of the day on his schooling, ignored Governess Boyle's inquiries about his cousin.

"Jules, have you ever known your cousin to misbehave?" He pretended he did not understand.

"Well, Isobel is well-behaved. Everyone says it, miss." He moved his pen around his page, dipped in the well and pulled too much ink.

"Has she ever done anything, well, that was mean?" Governess Boyle grabbed him by the shoulders. He worried she might even start shaking him if he didn't give her the answer she wanted.

"Nothing naughty. Never." He lied.

Later at tea, Governess Boyle continued her queries. This time she directed them at Mrs. O'Kelly, who poured milk from a jug.

"Has Isobel ever been difficult?" Mrs. O'Kelly paused and smiled at Jules. A drop of milk splashed onto the carpet.

"Why all children are mischievous, miss!" She reached over to Jules and tugged a curl, which sprang back to its rightful place.

"I just worry, with a wicked spirit, she might . . . damage . . . or be harmed!" The young woman's voice dawdled off.

"You worry she'll harm him," Mrs. O'Kelly pointed at Jules, "or do you worry about yourself?" They were all quiet, and then all three of them laughed at such silliness. Children corrupting adults! Hah!

Jules pretended he did not understand any of it, and he laughed with the adults. They nibbled the rest of their scones and sipped tea, and Jules faked drifting in his chair. Still, behind closed lids, he listened to them discuss his cousin.

"Did *SHE* see anything in the girl?" Governess Boyle asked.

"You mean the previous governess? See something that wasn't right? She never told me."

"But would she have told you? Was she careful?"

"About some things."

"But not about everything?" Governess Boyle was prying again; Jules heard Mrs. O'Kelly shift her weight. The floor creaked angrily. He tried not to laugh, stilled his flickering eyes. A hush ensued; Mrs. O'Kelly finally broke it with a careful assessment.

"Well, Governess Hansen is gone, so I won't tell tales."

"Did she die here?"

"Not exactly, she went off."

"Off to die? How strange!" The heat rode up Jules's neck. Mrs. O'Kelly stood by the window, where he could hear her wringing her apron, tossing the words over her shoulder.

"Please, Miss, not in front of the child. She never came back from holiday, is all. We expected her, but instead, the duke sent word she wasn't returning on the day she was to arrive. Please, now, I have to prepare for Miss Isobel's arrival." And then she left Jules alone with Governess Boyle. From the window, the sun carved a wedge of afternoon sun onto the table and across his pale arm. He fell asleep.

※

JULES AND ISOBEL PLAY CHEAT THE DEVIL

Over time, the two children became accustomed to playing their games in Governess Boyle's midst. Isobel and Jules amused themselves at all hours, in the nursery, outdoors. Their favorite game was Cheat the Devil, but they often played dead, too. Though she was younger, Isobel was better at the game than he was. Isobel pronounced, "When you Cheat the Devil, you never die, and you don't have to wash the cabbages that grow behind your ears." He giggled, and Governess Boyle sat on the floor, her skirts puffed, inflating around her like a striped air balloon.

"When you Cheat the Devil, you live in darkness, and you never breathe. You can walk without legs, but that's no matter because the Devil can't catch you."

Governess Boyle yawned, stifling it with a long splinter of hand.

"Come now, you two, I must tuck you in."

During the early evenings, Governess Boyle tried to teach them how to play cards—bridge and other confusing games. Jules liked hearts best. But the deck was missing The Queen of Spades, and Isobel always won—she did not play fair. Governess Boyle allowed Isobel's minor dishonesty, but it was frustrating how his cousin always had her way.

Isobel sat up, walked over to the cold fireplace, and stood inside it. The mantel and surround gaped wide as a giant's mouth. But then again, all the chimneys in Wilde were massive. Isobel climbed up on the bricks inside so Jules and Governess Boyle could only see her boots dangling, shiny buttons winking in candlelight. She called out, her girlish voice high-pitched, echoing from inside the massive cavern. Her words were incisive.

"When you Cheat the Devil, you never go back!" Governess Boyle flushed.

"Come, come, we'll have none of that."

And Jules made a case for himself.

"When you Cheat the Devil, you never go to bed," he shouted, defiant as he tossed his cards in the air. A draft from the chimney flailed the cards across the nursery as if they were leaves in the autumn wind, which was appropriate, as he often imagined the shafts were brick tree trunks pushing all the way through the slate roof above. Beside each fireplace was a black firedog, the andirons sooty beasts baring their ferocious teeth. He patted one on the head.

Governess Boyle snapped, "When you Cheat the Devil, you have to be good, or the angels won't protect you. Ghouls come. They haunt you."

"But this house is already haunted," Jules said.
"To bed." And that was the last of it for a while.

✳

JULES, THIS VERY NIGHT, YOUR LIFE WILL BE DEMANDED OF YOU

Anyone who stayed indoors for long periods at Wilde grew ashen and tired. Jules and Isobel did not encounter any shut-in maladies; they preferred to play outdoors. Wilde was a fortress, after all, even as Jules sadly noted there was no moat. The place was dusky even in the sunlight with overstuffed sofas and the scary paintings of long-dead forebears and dark libraries and crimson carpets and high-ceilinged rooms nonetheless felt cramped. But the one place Jules detested more than any other? The rickety stairs to the towers frightened him.

When it was too hot outdoors, they lounged all day on his bed, which resembled a ship with four masts. And Wilde boasted more than three hundred windows, their undulating panes often distorting the natural light inside. With the house's bounty of windows, it should have been a bright place, but instead, the majestic oaks pressed up close, so the interior spaces were as porraceous and dim as if the tenants lived under the sea.

#

One summer night, the wind sighed in the nursery flue, and Isobel came to fetch Jules. Governess Boyle was fast asleep. They tiptoed past Isobel's room with her dolls and pillows tossed about the floor and crept into the nursery. Outside, the moon shone through the trees, and, again, he saw Frost's ghost gazing at them from the lawn.

"I dare you," she said, and he did.

He cocked his head inside the chimney. The cold, wet air licked his face, and he did not recognize the voices speaking, the low mumbling snarls from above (or below?). He did not understand what he heard, but he knew whatever the language, the speakers meant him harm.

#

Governess Boyle was jumpy as a cat. Her rosary beads were never far from her side.

One afternoon during tea, a sound ruptured the quiet in the house. A loud cry rang out, followed by the shrillness of a breaking dish or glass. Every person within earshot rushed to the source, which was the big library, and found Governess Boyle as white as the cream she had just spilled. She stood frozen over the broken pitcher, and the liquid bled across a reading table. Governess Boyle was pointing at the window.

"I'm sorry, but I was startled. I thought I saw someone at the window looking in at me," Governess Boyle said. "I must have been dreaming."

Mrs. O'Kelly smiled and set to swiping up the cream with her apron, her fingers like pincers as she picked at the delicate debris of broken china from the dinged table and shiny floor.

"You've been working so hard, my dear."

Isobel and Jules pointed out, "But the library is on the

second floor. How can anyone look in from that height?"

#

It was the time of summer when the Perseids burst through the galaxy. If no clouds were obscuring the view, a person could spy dozens of meteors sketching luminous lines across the dark heavens with the Milky Way as a backdrop. The sky's debris hurled toward earth late at night into the early morning. Governess Boyle called them the "Burning Tears of St. Lawrence"—she said they appeared around the anniversary of Saint Lawrence's martyrdom in Rome.

As often as Isobel and Jules could secret out of the house, they stole away from their rooms to the lawn outside. And a couple of times, they thought they saw Governess Hansen's specter lurking at the rim of the pines. She watched the miracle of the Perseids with them.

#

The last summer was eventful. Frost and Governess Hansen visited so often Jules knew something was not right, something was about to happen. Jules was confident their appearances were an augur. The air around Wilde was still as if it, too, was anticipating something momentous. In August, vultures roosted in the low hedges well into each afternoon.

But Jules nonetheless relished the time he and Isobel spent together. They played games, stargazed, searched for their former caretakers in the places where they had all once played together—in the loft in the stables and in the yawning, quiet woods.

Many times, as they were walking, when they avoided Governess Boyle and lost her somewhere in the house or on the grounds, Isobel would murmur their personal lore. She'd reminisce about the skin on Frost's shoulders. She'd whisper about how it was smooth like a swan's back, so alabaster, and how the dark fullness of Governess Hansen's hair had rustled against his skin. They remembered it was all like a fairy tale, as Frost and Governess Hansen had joined each other into one body and writhed in each other's limbs right where the children could watch.

On those walks with Isobel, alone, he recollected. Those were the times when he thought about his parents the most; his memories went back home, how he'd often heard sighs from Mother's and Father's bed. Though, he would not have Wilde's reminders much longer.

#

By the last season, Isobel had won over Governess Boyle; the woman was wholly convinced the girl was an innocent, adorable. They often heard her exclaim to Mrs. O'Kelly, "How absurd that her parents disposed of such a wonder!" Such folly.

And at every turn, the household soon felt the effects of Governess Boyle's growing aspirations. During casual conversations, she manipulated them into telling her how she was beautiful or smart. She asked Jules every day if he thought the duke would find her an attentive keeper. Her neediness for approval knew no bounds.

Stalwart Mrs. O'Kelly kept a close eye on the young woman, who had become imprudent about discussing her sightings of ghosts. Governess Boyle was convinced the spirits of both Governess Hansen and Alban Frost often appeared in the house, and she talked to herself often, too, hiding in her room for long periods. Mrs. O'Kelly grew weary. And wary.

After a while, Jules and Isobel only saw Governess Boyle when she took them to church on Sundays and in the afternoons out by the lake. He and Isobel slyly pretended they had no idea what the poor woman was seeing. It was a good game. As good as Cheat the Devil.

#

The church, St. Bartholomew's, was a wonder. On Sundays, they walked the distance from Wilde. To mark the end of the season one late-summer Lord's Day, they wore their best summer clothes; village celebrations would continue well into Monday. The day was already giving way to the slanted, longer shadows of early fall, to the gilded radiance before winter slammed everything shut. Governess Boyle and Mrs. O'Kelly waited outside for Isobel and Jules. As Catholics, the women could not blaspheme by entering the sanctuary of a Protestant church (though before the Tudors, it had belonged to the Vatican). Jules did not care one bit about injuring God; he had long ago given up believing. He was only there for the sights.

Above the south door of the church, he read two inscriptions. Both messages were in Latin. The first celebrated the rebuilding of the chancel in 1646, and the text was what one would expect; Psalm 116:12—*Quid retribuam Domino pro omnibus quae retribuit mihi?* ["How can I repay the Lord for His goodness to me?"]

But the following text was confusing; it was Luke 12:20—*Et stulte, hac nocte animam tuam repetunt a te.* ["You fool, this very night, your life will be demanded of you."]

Inside with Isobel, Jules gazed up at the vaulted ceiling. It was an azure blue sprinkled with silver stars, so real he felt he was out on Wilde's lawn at night. Elaborate murals depicted biblical figures, saints, and landscapes. The stained-glass irradiated; it draped jeweled capes on the shoulders of all the village children.

And the choir stalls voluted with carvings, and there were misericords, preserved even after the churchgoers no longer stood for hours in prayer. Jules sat in the pew, observed those holy images in the twilight, and he had the odd sensation all the static figures were moving. Those writhing creatures were not meek beasts. They were the terrifying hoofed demons of the Middle Ages, their legs shaggy with long hair. They snarled with agape mouths and their eyes bulging, breasts puffed for a fight. At the top of the reliefs, the ugly fiends burst into leaf and transformed into full, beautiful elms.

Outside, after the service, the villagers milled about gossiping. A farmer's boy came up from behind Jules and pinned him against the fence, growling into his ear.

"The man who built this church, when he died, the bearers brought him to be buried, the people heard the dead man's voice speak from his coffin. He screamed, 'I am not ready!' And you know what, little flower boy?" The boy pushed Jules against a post, and Jules glanced over the kid's shoulder to search for anyone who might come to his rescue. No luck. Jules had no choice but to speak up for himself.

"I don't want to hear this."

"Oh, yes, you do. What, going to piss yourself or something?" The boy snickered, then continued. "You know what? The man's attendants opened the coffin after they heard him scream, worried that they'd buried their master alive, but there was no life in the dead man's face, though his beard had grown two feet." The boy pointed his gaze to a relief stone figure. It was a spade-bearded knight chiseled into the marble of the portal's architrave. "And when those people buried him beside the altar, the dead man's voice hollered again. 'I am not ready yet!' To this day, they say he likes boys who look like girls. Like you."

The boy chuckled at Jules's expression, mistaking amusement for fear.

Puzzling words, teasing, meanness. Jules could care less. He waited for the real horrors to come, comfortable as he was now with terror. He relished the evil of his predicaments, anticipated the fright pressing on him, quietly as always, as if the fear was a slow tide breaking among the stone flags and soaking the warm earth.

The big boy pushed him down and continued, "The man *was* buried alive, you know. And he comes back to find boys like you to exact his revenge."

From the ground, Jules looked up and over the worshippers where some horrible, misshapen man laughed as he loudly regaled parishioners with another ghost story. Two ghosts! *How ironic*, Jules mused.

The man talked about his vision.

"It was a human shape, all right. And the spirit wore a large hat with a feather like a flag. He told me that he wasn't dead. That he was still alive. Can you imagine?" The man cackled again, and so did the mean boy, and so did the crowd who'd been listening.

Jules could not spot Isobel, Governess Boyle, or Mrs. O'Kelly anywhere in the courtyard.

No more ghosts. Jules wasn't afraid. Just angry. No more things he could not invent or control. This was all madness. No more.

And so, Jules ran. He ran away on the remote road, over the water meadows, and breathless, finally slowing on a high hill where he stood above a row of willows and saw the roofs of the village, all the homes' peaks stacked in a disorderly manner like hats on a bed. Bad luck. Yes, hats on a bed were bad luck.

He looked for landmarks he would recognize. There was the village's tithe barn. There were Wilde and the church. He felt as if he could keep going higher, float above it all. But it was only a late summer evening gloomy with stretched shadows, with laughter following him everywhere he turned.

＊

JULES TRIES TO UNDERSTAND GOVERNESS BOYLE

The governess, poor thing. Governess Boyle. She was easily thrilled by the children's antics. They could get her laughing if they made ridiculous faces or if they played a simple game of hide-and-seek. He was sure she was almost as young as they were.

Her muted clothes, prim, were much the style of ten years before. Now they were dowdy and out of fashion.

Perhaps her dourness was on account of her Catholic upbringing or maybe it was because she hailed from the Irish countryside where her father had been a poor school teacher. In any case, he was confident someone had her as a child; she had a naïve confidence in her bearing. He also noticed she read too many romances. Those books, he was sure, contributed to the cloying, enthusiastic way she described almost everything as "lovely" or "magnificent"—especially when it came to descriptions of Wilde. He did not understand how anyone could consider Wilde "lovely." Coarse-hewn stone surfaces, both inside and out. Cold. Monstrous. To him, lovely was something different. It was the warm sun on his face, starlings wheeling around the tower, white roses in the garden so full of bloom and life, so fragile, dropping their petals like veils in the breeze.

He did not know the governess's history until close to the end of her stay when she told them a bedtime story.

"Come now. I have a tale to tell you about my home." Governess Boyle patted the large bed. She'd spread his uncle's silk coverlet neatly across it. Jules and Isobel climbed up and made themselves comfortable. Isobel wound her tiny braids through her fingers, and Jules drew designs on his cousin's back. They listened to Governess Boyle's story.

"In the country in Ireland where I grew up—oh yes, much more desolate than this place!—is a secret garden. You can pass on the road and never know the patch of quiet exists; the wall around it is so high, and one would assume that the ornate iron gate is locked, too, but it isn't. A person might think the place belongs to someone, but it doesn't."

Now the children were listening, and Isobel pushed Jules's scratching hand aside.

"Yes, the strangeness of this place only begins with an open gate. There is a carved stone seat next to the gate, set back from the wall. Yes, it is inviting, too, if you can imagine! Almost comfortable! On that seat, someone carved a verse with a clumsy hand: 'Friend or stranger, rest here, there is virtue in the rest.'" Governess Boyle slipped her plaits from her comb, and Jules fetched her ivory brush and pulled it through her tresses much as he did when he groomed the horses' tails in the stables.

"Oh, what does it look like, this garden? Tell us, governess, tell us!" Excitement filled Isobel's voice; her breathing grew raspy.

"A passageway of tall box hedges leads to a lawn, and beyond that lawn, there is, on one side, a beautiful ironstone building with columns. No doors or walls. This place is open in all weather, like a shrine. On the other end of the lawn, there are more columns in the same sort of stone, forming a walkway around a courtyard. That courtyard is open to the sky, which is a dark blue there, so magical. It's quiet, enchanted." Governess Boyle was animated now; she tipped forward like a conspirator. "As a girl, I often read there. No one could ever find me." Governess Boyle's face took on a softness; the deep worry lines on her forehead smoothed. She was so young looking when she did not fret.

"What was this place?" Jules asked, suspicious Governess Boyle was lying.

"In a word, a graveyard. An old family built it for their dead children; one was lost as an infant to some sort of pernicious disease, I suspect, another was lost in some war, others to Lord knows what. Funny, that such a sad place made me happy."

"How quaint," Jules stated flatly as he stopped his brushing to smile at Isobel.

"No, not quaint, it was a sad place, where grief rolled around at every turn, and there was this perfect misery."

"Then, why did you like it?" Isobel asked.

❋

JULES RUNS AWAY FOR THE DAY

Cannons were his idea of heaven. If Jules could have one in real life, he would. What a jolly way to awaken! Someday he planned, perhaps when he was away from Wilde and an adult, to turn out of bed in the morning and slide into a half-sized cannon parked in his room. Jules, pajama-clad, would scuttle into the muzzle, and a servant would then tug the iron beast by a rope, creaking it forward on its wheels; his manservant would then swing open a large window, clanking the big gun to a stop at the opening, then ignite a fuse, and Jules would explode out the tube and blast skyward. He would start each day flying!

Or he could join the circus.

\#

A fair was in town; he'd seen the posters in the shop windows when he'd walked past them on a spring Sunday before church. And so, he told no one when he filled his pockets with coins, stole away one weekday morning through the woods and escaped Wilde to spend time at the traveling fair on the outskirts of the village.

CATE MCGOWAN

Fairs, carnivals, amusements. Those were places people visited in family packs, all intent on having fun. He was alone, of course, but it didn't dampen his spirits. First, he stepped his way through an arcade, a real treat. Candy, crackers, rock crystal twined in colorful wrappers. The tents smelled fusty, and the carnival barkers hawked their wares in Cockney and some language he couldn't understand. The games gallery was bustling, but the tents' colors faded at their corners, and in broad daylight, instead of red, the canvas stripes were a tomato pink.

With a tuppenny, he bought a toy, a paper canary affixed with a string to a dowel, and he sprinted in circles, flinging his toy through the blinding sunshine. It fluttered and whipped and darted, made whistling sounds like a real bird.

And when he stopped spinning, he found himself in the off-limits performers' area—he'd somehow slipped under the chains barring the public. He hid behind a hay bale to watch a circus family go about their day. Fascinating. He knelt in the muck, dirtying his blue breeches, but he remained hidden, stifling a sneeze. The people he observed were a strange lot! He couldn't make out their conversation, but the painting on the side of their caravan featured reasonable likenesses of each person in the act. Below their group portrait, blue-lettered words announced them: "The Flying Walseckis." In flanking images, there were also depictions of a firing cannon and a flying lady in her undergarments. The colors were as festive as a bakery at Easter.

The tall man who stood closest to Jules was wearing an open robe, his muscles bursting from a leotard underneath. He paced around, twirling a chunky mustache, his bald head waxed and lustrous. A petite woman lounged in one of the wooden chairs planted at a lopsided angle in the mud yard; she sipped a cup of tea and giggled. A couple of other men, stumpy, entered and exited the shiny carriage; the wheels wobbled each time they went in or out. The squat men fetched bowls of food: steaming dumplings, slick finger-shaped potatoes. The smell of butter and garlic reached Jules, and his stomach growled. The family spread their feast on crates lined up in a row in the yard, with the circled caravans of all the other acts muting the carnival's sounds. He stood to get a better view of the food.

The woman saw him then, motioned for him to join. Jules hopped over the wet patches of ground, gripping the stick of his bird toy. And as he reached her, the lady smiled, jerked his arm. Her sharp nails dug into his forearm, but Jules could tell she was eager to have him join them.

"Eat, boy? Yes?" So, he nodded assent. He could not demur. It would be rude. She offered him her fork, and he watched as the others fetched their own forks from their robes' pockets and ate straight from the bowls. He marveled at their flamboyant garb—embroidered kimonos and coats and long underwear underneath. He'd never seen anyone like them before.

"Good? No?"

"Thank you, yes." He nodded. As he chewed a soft potato, the butter slid down his throat, and he shifted his weight.

"Good!" The woman's braided blonde hair wobbled in a pile on her head as she furiously shook her head with delight. She went inside the caravan and came out with another chair and pointed for him to sit. He chewed and smiled a lot, said nothing more. He was sure they wouldn't have understood him anyway.

But he watched the family chat as they sprawled in their wooden chairs. Their talk, animated and loud (Polish?), staccatoed over the wagons and tents, muted the horses whinnying in an enclosure at one end of the carnival. They even drowned out the jangling calliope music. And they laughed and relaxed and chomped, food spraying from their mouths as they delighted in each other's company. He had never seen such joy! He thanked them after he finished the last crumb, heartily shook hands with each person, and departed with a full belly. The big man, the small blonde lady, and the two fireplug men waved.

Later, outside the big tent, the emcee in his top hat and scarlet coat called the carnival attendees to a show. From the back row in the audience, Jules found himself bored watching a high-wire act. He waited for his new friends and was excited when he spotted the Walsecki woman, now with plum-colored lips and rouged cheeks, sashaying into the middle ring as the master of ceremonies announced her. She raised her arms above her head, waved at the people. She wore a lemon-colored headdress with roseate feathers scattering in all directions like a fountain. She resembled his bird toy.

"Ladies and Gentleman, you are about to witness the most amazing feat known to humankind. I give you The Flying Walseckis, the human cannonballs!" The female Flying Walsecki threw off her ruby robe, arms high in the air; she wore a golden satin costume bodice revealing a heaving bosom. Her legs were bare. The audience clapped with enthusiasm as she climbed a ladder and slid feet first into the giant cannon at the outside of the ring. The two small Walsecki men pulled on a large chain to precisely position its aim. And then the drummer in the band began a snare roll, and a trumpet hailed, and the mustached man pulled out a bucket and packed gunpowder into the gun's chamber. He lit the wire fuse with a metallic torch. The drum rolled and rolled. The long string sizzled down as it sparkled, and then *BANG!* The lady, arms at her sides, legs straight, toes pointed in her pink slippers, was sunshine flying through the tent, a buttercup bullet, a sparkly missile gliding high. Effortlessly, she plopped into a net at the other end of the arena, her headdress still firmly atop her head. She flipped onto the ring and waved. *Ta-dah!*

The first of the two men followed, his sequined costume glittering in the spotlight. He soared like an exotic bird. The other stubby man came next, but his blast wasn't loud like the other two. The poor man's trajectory was short, and he barely hit his mark; he tucked up tight so as not to miss the net. The crowd gasped in horror as he flung off the receptacle, flipped onto the sawdust, and lay still. There was a breathless moment, but then he hopped up, and the band's drums and trumpets played. *Ta-daaaah!* The errant flyer pumped his arms in the air and beamed, and the audience hollered approval and stomped in the bleachers, and Jules went home with his bird on a stick, happy with a full stomach, the echo of wild, approving claps following him.

#

Late, it was late, but all of Wilde's lamps were blazing. The torches' flames made the drive as bright as an early sunset. Good, someone had stayed up and waited for him;

someone had noticed he had run away. It was midnight, at the earliest. He was hungry again.

As he neared the door, there was moaning, crying inside. Isobel, Mrs. O'Kelly. Jules pounded on the front door with his cold hands, and a maid opened it.

Mrs. O'Kelly was there on the bottom step of the grand staircase, her face and eyes red from crying; Isobel was standing behind her.

"Governess Boyle has fallen!" Isobel sobbed and flounced onto the step; her skirt gusted around her like a wind. She pushed her face into her arms and wept.

"Boy, you worried us. We could not find you." Mrs. O'Kelly held his shoulders.

"Now brace yourself, young master. Be a man. There's been an accident." She patted at her face with a handkerchief. "When we searched the house for you, Governess Boyle slipped on the loose step, the one in the back staircase. Isobel saw it happen. The poor, poor, poor woman broke her neck. Instant death. There was nothing we could do."

Jules's vision darkened; his world took on grim shadows. Mrs. O'Kelly grabbed him into a tight hug and swayed. He peered around the woman's girth to spy Isobel. His cousin smiled and winked, drew her fingers across her throat, a cutting motion. His legs went numb, and he fell to the cold marble of the large foyer, and it was the last he saw or felt anything for a long while.

✳

JULES SITS WITH DEATH

Outside, the rain slapped the landscape like a spanking hand; the waves cursed the shores of the lake, and inside, he and Isobel sat on the edge of a worn bench and gazed at their dead governess's countenance. What a thing! A face so still, opalescent as a bone china plate held to a window, no blood pumping through, no shifts of expression to mar it. And in the room, there was gloom. Burning candles and votives wavered in a draft, but they could not chase away the dark. Mrs. O'Kelly had lit the display. He sat there for so long the smell of death, wax, flowers—lilies, hundreds of them—weighed down on him like a lid. The mildew of the house in the rain, the closeness of the air, the putrid seal of decay made him want to run out into the cold downpour. But he stayed.

So many mirrors in the room, all reflecting his cousin, their former caretaker, and himself. More white lilies than he had ever seen in his short life, more than at any stall in the French markets he had once visited with Grand-Maman, more flowers than on any church day. The room was full of mirrors repeating the same pose: Isobel and Governess Boyle and Jules. Isobel and Governess Boyle and Jules. Angle after angle. His family. All artifice.

The lilies fumed. And the wet stones outside glittered in the torchlight as if gems were set deep in the pavers. If he could somehow ignore the mold, his senses would fill with the lushness of the scene. But the rankness seeped through; it crept in through the window cracks. No, their manor was not safe from the strange desolation of life.

Mrs. O'Kelly had insisted to everyone Governess Boyle deserved a Catholic wake and burial. This was a strange ritual, the way attendants "laid someone out" with a shroud, votives, crosses, and silver coins over the closed eyelids. The old woman had ceased addressing Isobel; she would not smile at Jules anymore either. She did her work, but she averted her eyes when the two children entered a room. Mrs. O'Kelly knew what Isobel had done.

Oh, the lamenting lilies with their heavy pollen—the powder colored his fingers as if he'd dipped his hands in turmeric! The tainted ecru, the wilt of fawn at the edges of flower petals—this fading he associated with himself. The stain of the pollen, the color of blood, the break of bones— those were horrors for Isobel to own.

Governess Hansen and Alban Frost had vanished as soon as the rain came. He knew they would not return, even if he and Isobel searched.

He tried to stifle his repugnance at the wan, dense flesh of the dead woman. Governess Boyle lay so still, had so much in common with the waxy armfuls of lilies in their great glass jars. The ebony furniture lurked like monsters in the candlelight. Isobel had done this, he knew it. One push was all it had taken. It did not matter he had not liked Governess Boyle. She did not deserve such a fate.

Life. Those somnolent lilies. They would wither. Life. Death. Today, the flowers drooped their lolling trumpet heads, distributed their incense. He reminisced on the powdered scent of Governess Boyle's skin. But those lilies would wilt come Wednesday; someone would throw them in a heap after he left for school, after Isobel shipped off somewhere. The servants would close the house and find employment elsewhere. He could only imagine what his new life would have in store—Mrs. O'Kelly and the maids had already packed his trunk.

And then he heard a voice. It was as real as the scent of lilies and the sharp odor of rot and the melting candle wax. The murmur was not Isobel's, no; she had drifted off to sleep in her serge pinafore, slouching on the side table, drool collecting in a puddle on her sleeve.

The whisper, he heard it, yes, plainly! And then it grew to an urgent call; it lifted up in an ululation—*"Go! Go! Go! Go, child!"* The voice raised as loud as trumpets or a pipe organ. *"Go! All is well!"* He looked to Isobel, but she did not awaken. He held his breath and opened his eyes again to spot Governess Boyle's shroud puff like a sail.

And the echoes left him, ricocheted down the hall, out past the landing windows, and then disappeared.

He gazed at his cousin's peaceful countenance. Oh, beautiful Isobel. Oh, evil, disturbed Isobel. Even her breath now was a strangeness to him. Wicked Isobel, almost as pacific as Governess Boyle. Could she have done it? Could she have? Could she kill someone? Could he love her if she had?

✳

JULES, CHAMPION OF THE SCHOOLS (AND THE WORLD?)

Jules was the youngest of the students. A mere twelve. The duke was duplicitous and told the boy to lie about his age. "Tell anyone who asks that you are thirteen. They won't know the difference." It was the last time Jules ever saw his uncle, who moved to America or to Africa. No one knew where he finally settled.

6th-form boy. New bug. Even the sound of it was disdainful. The school was not a pleasant place. Days were all the same.

Wake to a cold room. Drowsy dress. Waistcoat. Cutaway jacket. Scarf. Scramble to the dining room. Walk past the prefects in their bespoke attire, the dandies! Look to the ground when passing. Be invisible, or there will be a licking.

Lower chapel service: an ugly old church. No beauty. Not like St. Bartholomew's. A service for a meager ten minutes? Shameful.

The notice board: no duties.

First school: Science class, bottles, tubes, Petri dishes, scalpels. Unpleasantness. Cut something, anything. Slice open. Even the bugs—sad how they end up here.

Second school: Music, drama, art. Pleasant offerings. Scare professors with wit and weird acting. Fake a limp, off to infirmary. Artificial tears, off to infirmary. Clipe rage, off to infirmary.

Third school: Poetry, literature. So ghastly. Prudes with crumpled up faces and weird proclivities. No real poetry, only old English *blah*.

Elevenses: back to the house.

Fourth school: Latin, Greek. The beauty of the old times. Fluency by the end of term. Repeat in notebooks over and over—*Ligamina volveant cordis mei*—May my heart bands be loosened.

Fifth school: Mathematics. Equal signs, equations, theorems, lines, curves, tangents. Each side the same. No guessing, no creativity here. Clean fun. Easy, too.

Dinner at noon. More slop.

Gymnasium. Only a few hours of the ring. Cut and

lunge, punch and badger.

Prep: nurse bruises, no friends.

Supper at the corner table. The foreign boys, the outcasts, anyone not correctly English. Unwelcome as an unwanted erection.

Prayers, more prayers! The House Master worries. Checks watch, dangles fob absentmindedly.

Bath: Float in tub, wrinkled skin.

Bed: Masturbate to French erotic poetry. Sleep.

#

It was his goal to escape the school someday, though they locked the doors at 9:30. When he slept, he often dreamed of Isobel, of Governesses Boyle and Hansen, but most times, he dreamed of running in the fields around Wilde, and somehow, they metamorphosed into the pitches of Lyon and then he awoke so many times screaming, convinced there was blood in his bed, on his hands. His room was always a pip, so there was no finding a clean handkerchief to muffle his cries. His pillow soaked through with tears.

He took to sports where his performance was superb. And he mastered most activities within weeks. At the outset of his school career, the only exciting activities were marksmanship, boxing, gymnastics, swimming, and fives.

Soon, he was a member of the house shooting team, regarded as the best. They won seven trophies over this period with his perfect aim. And on the river, the house's boat (with him rowing stroke) won the top prize. He was just beginning to impress people with his potential as a rower when he abandoned it and all other sport for tizzy pooles, cricket bats, and padded gloves. His disregard for authority strained the patience of his tolerant and long-suffering House Master, but his personal popularity got him elected to Pop. He won a place in the cricket second eleven, his fives colors, and a silver cup many times over in boxing.

#

When it came to the ring, his fortunes never lagged. Early on, he had learned *la boxe Francaise* or *savate*, a dancing sort of mess, from the French groomsmen at Wilde. The various skills of fighting included low-line kicking, English bare-knuckle, grappling maneuvers from *la lutte*, and the dirty tricks of the Apaches. His weapons training at Wilde had included, among other things, the revolver, knife, *épée*, and *la canne*, as well as an improvised kind of combat with whatever was at hand—a jacket, belt, scarf, umbrella, or even a hat. He supplemented *savate* with essential skills from Japanese jujitsu. But he hated it all—it was too much a stew of methods making no sense.

Now, old-fashioned English pugilism was more his style. He found upright, manly fighting more natural, comparatively speaking. There were rules! And he often went to the ring for the school. In two months, he chalked up victories with his first encounters. And with his new prestige, no one expected him to lose in his weight class.

He handled the pain; some would even say he relished it. It was naff, really. For his win against Wellington, he received the referee's congratulations—a rarity. His Captain of Boxing, who was time-keeping, saw judging slips (it was not a decisive win, after all) and complained the match was relatively close on points. Sour grapes. After many events like that one, he experienced some disfigurement, and his eye did go blind within the ninth year. He did not notice the malady until much later. Of course, his injuries and inurement to the resulting pain only added to Jules's legend.

During the Quadrangular Tournament, he had the misfortune of breaking his nose early on, so he entered the finals with a tender face and anger to burn. In that event, his ire was his opponent's undoing, for the decision went in his favor. He won that tournament and henceforth became captain of the school's boxing team. No one ever defeated him.

At the school, he learned to fit in by not fitting in. It became his greatest lesson. He was a success.

#

A ROUT!
April 10, 1903, from the *Sunday Standard*
Ralph P. Conover and Simpson Speake

London. Jules Lalande, a new sensation, boxed against Wellington on Saturday, and their best chap, William St. James, was out of luck. The defender, a large eighteen-year-old, could not hold a candle to scrappy fifteen-year-old Lalande. Now we wonder how did St. James keep his cap for three years running? The fight was a rout! In the first round, Lalande came out hard and fast. Before long, the young bloke had beaten St. James soundly—he closed one of St. James's eyes, gave the other a nasty knock, split his bottom lip and made him bite through his tongue. It was a hasty decision for Lalande, now the champion of the colleges. We applaud his vigour.

✳

JULES'S ART SCHOOL JOURNAL

13 AVRIL 1905, LES VACANCES DE PÂQUES

"See that ripe apple, Jules? It's round as an Odalisque's full *derriere*! Paint it like that, cup it in your hand, draught it out, Lalande!" Today, Master Emmanuel Laroche wrapped his tongue around the word *derriere* as if he'd licked it, but then again, he pronounces every word with *la verve*. I reason the man is too big to speak with the usual hushed tones other masters use. No, this atelier is a loud one, where everyone knows everyone's business.

Still-life paintings. I am painting still-lifes. *Mérde*. But once I am an expert in fruit, Master Laroche promises I might move on to 15th or 16th-century Italian masters. One day even a real woman. This afternoon, all the other students labored away, depicting the face of a live model, a beautiful one at that. How I wish I were allowed!

Yes, dear journal, still-lifes are the lowest of the low. I feel the shame right down to my splattered boots. You ask, where are all the Chardins hanging in the Louvre? Why, they are skyed, strung up close to the ceilings, of course. No one ever copies those, no one, never. Museum patrons never congregate in front of the smaller paintings. And no one ever applies for a permit to reproduce them. Pity all those lonely pots and pans and vegetables.

In my world, faces and bodies are what matter, and that is it. Did Delacroix and David and Titian waste time on such things as fruit or dishes, domestic scenes, female stupidity? No, they were artists who worried over history and events that mattered. Great scenes, busy scenes, figures reticulated, interdependent, woven in death and love. And the colors! The red and right, the subterranean and majestic blue, the cerulean, all tempera and oily shininess on canvases large as rooms.

Often, I stand in the dark galleries and the halls of the Louvre, and I close my eyes after staring at those paintings. There's too much to take in at once or even many times! In the lamplight, my imagination runs away with what I see in the art. I think I spy motion in the epic scenes—Sabine women raped by soldiers, Romans feasting half-naked on piles of food, Orientalist harems waiting. The scenes come alive! Yes, they are so real that I think I catch sight of an arm twitching, an eyelid blinking, a horse quivering. And I like to copy what I remember and admire:

     –Nubian purple-black princes
     –Red-haired men with freckles
     –Long, silken-haired Madonnas
     –Shiny armored conquerors
     –Alabaster breasts
     –Thick legs
     –Flowing togas and capes

The figures, there on the gallery walls, are so perfect for gazing upon, yes, but once I return to my studio and I try to reproduce them onto my own canvases, under my direction, they transform into distorted and ugly things. Gangly, disproportioned, off-scale. And now Master Laroche has relegated me to painting fruits in a bowl under his watchful command.

For hours today, I worked on the scene before me, sketching, shading, laying a foundation, palette knife blending and smoothing, brush hairs shedding whiskers in wet paint. Just a dab of ochre for gleaming fruit, a bit more cadmium red for the apple, some umber in the shadows. As I worked, the scene darkened in the late afternoon, and the window greyed in the retreating sun, and I could no longer see.

I painted anyway. Finally, in half-darkness, I had to stop, so I folded my easel into useless angles, hung my canvas on the wall to dry, and swished turpentine over my expensive brushes (only the best will do, Father always said).

Chattering students scattered outside in the alley, leaving for the evening, leaving me alone; I could make out each individual classmate's voice—some were whooping at the streetwalkers who'd come out to work after hours, their gaslight silhouettes against a flaming sky. I cleaned and dried the last of my brushes, rolled the hair in linen.

Finally, I stood back and peered at the tableau Laroche had assembled on the table before me. Today was the last day before the rush of the holiday, but I did not clear away the offensive fruit models I had painted. I left them as they were, draped in deliberate folds of velvet. My own vision of those fruits ended when I had finished my canvas. But visions are alterable, I know this—and so are all living things.

While we are away, a new assemblage will emerge.

The apple now leans against the flat pewter bowl. But the metal vessel will soon feel a gradual withdrawal of the apple's touch, as the incarnadine skin will wither. Yes, the flesh will shrink away into its consoling core. I pity them all—the pomegranates, the apple, the pewter bowl—sitting alone through days of quiet. Days will pass; the room will fill and then empty of brilliance. The slowest pouring, in and out. Afternoons, the long shadows will consume the fruit with lavender fingers, will sink glaucous caresses across the rotting flesh. The darkness will move by hours as accruing mold will fall into creases of decay.

I think now of all living things and their demise to time. And today, I imagined this slow transformation of the still-life props like the change was unfolding in front of me, a deliberate dream, a sluggish nightmare. I know the future of these lowly objects. Perhaps still-lifes are majestic after all.

Life's gifts are simple: the way the illumination keeps coming back with offerings; the sweet smell of perfection in decaying fruit, in all living things; the way the oil paint will be tacky to the touch years after I've spread it on canvas. Always there is the promise of fruit forming, of pewter reflecting sky, and there is beauty everywhere, *grande ou petite*.

At this thought, I smile. I now will join my friends at the café. There, everyone will congregate at the tables outside under the bright awning, happy, lusty.

I am sure my fate is like these lowly objects I leave behind.

28 MAI 1905

Today, I dispensed early with my painting exercises at the École and found myself wandering familiar side streets, places where Father and I had once explored. Perhaps my roving was nostalgia. On a whim, I ventured into the gallery of Eudoxe Badeau, who often sports a hooded cape and a worn-out hat (men like Badeau always don worn-out hats). Long ago, I'd visited the gallery with Father, who purchased many works there. And I know through rumors at the École this Badeau still represents the great artist, Monsieur Paul Cézanne. On many occasions throughout the years, Badeau and I have also met briefly, often in the street passing one another.

As I entered his shop and closed the door behind me, not as quiet as I would have liked, I made out Badeau and another man in the back. The proprietor sat folded into a corner, his long, skinny limbs tucked at right angles, almost too much for his chair. His lankiness and tallness were exotic in such a staid place. When I slammed the door, his mustache whiffled, but he did not even glance toward the entrance where I had come in. He was arguing with the other man who stood leaning against the wall, and Badeau looked troubled—he wrung his hands furiously. After I stood watching this with amusement for a good five minutes, Badeau finally looked up and smiled, happy to see me.

"Lalande! Good friend! Meet my close competitor, Mizelle." I nodded, started to speak, but Badeau interrupted before I could say anything. "You've met Cézanne, the great artist, haven't you? Your father bought some of his work from me, no? Well, the great artist is in town for a short visit. And he just left here looking offended!" Badeau's voice was a whisper, his mustache working up and down. "You see, I refused to lend him one of his own pictures for an upcoming show. I was afraid of the damage that might come to it. That exhibition space is likely to collapse—so much glass!" I nodded, though I really had no idea what he was talking about. The Grand Palais was sturdy as a midwife. I responded with a lie.

"Yes, the Grand Palais does look rather flimsy. But it *is*

the man's work! You must yield." I could not believe Badeau would not return the great master's work.

"Yes, yes, but what if Cézanne's painting is ruined?"

"Well, then he will paint another."

"Oh, you are so even-tempered, Lalande. How will I sort this out? Monsieur Cézanne never comes to town, prefers Aix and its scenery. But he is here in Paris only for a few days. Perhaps you can go with me to speak to him? I will bring the painting along as a goodwill gesture." I smiled, not sure how this man knew me well enough for such a daunting task. Yes, I am still uncertain how I was appointed to this mission, dear journal.

Mizelle, the other dealer, a short, stout dandy, put on his hat.

"Badeau, I hope you know what you're doing." Mizelle bowed and left.

29 MAI 1905

Last night, I could not sleep; I was too excited. I have never looked forward to something such as this. This morning I dressed with care, and I walked with a jaunty step, my new waistcoat tight and fitted. I presented as fashionable and smart. Badeau and I met at his shop and went off to Monsieur Cézanne's sister's home. I toted the painting in question, wrapped in brown paper, tied with twine, and walked beside Badeau.

Mademoiselle Marie Cézanne, the master painter's sister, answered the guest house bell, and Badeau bowed and proffered the painting forward, a peace offering. She took it inside, and then we heard his voice.

"Come in, come in." Monsieur Cézanne sat with his back to the sitting room door, and the smell of cigar smoke greeted us.

"Ah, so you brought my child." The master turned, a high turban upon his head, smiled from the divan, and beckoned us inside. Badeau nervously glanced at me, snatched the painting out of Mademoiselle Cézanne's hands, then handed it over to the master himself with a flourish. The artist grabbed the wrapped canvas, held it close to his chest, and caressed it absentmindedly as one might pet a dog. We had tea and made small talk. I could not string together full sentences. I was too nervous and in awe. Cézanne! I was sipping tea with Cézanne!

And then, when we were about to leave, something strange happened.

"Thank you for your hospitality," I said as Badeau and I bowed, and the master stood and bowed in response. But he looked unsteady, did not right himself. Instead, he placed one foot in front of the other, staggered, and then fell flat on his face. He lay prone for a moment, then lifted his head, the turban still tight upon it.

He pushed up quickly to his hands and knees.

"*Mon Dieu*. Dizzy spell! I get them all the time!" He was embarrassed. He stood, and when he did, blood gushed from his nose, soiled his smock. He fell back this time into the wall and slid to the floor and sat there, pale and sweating. Badeau wrung his hands, and Cézanne's nose continued pouring. I acted. I hurried to the pump for a bucket of water and dabbed the blood away with my own handkerchief. (Hah! I unpainted Monsieur Cézanne!).

"Here, hold this under your nose, tight there. Tilt back more," I said. And Badeau was useless, wringing his hands, whining.

"Oh, dear, Oh, dear. Oh, dear."

Cézanne spoke. He grabbed my hand, trusting: "The doctor, I need one. A doctor is what I need." I knew what I had to do.

I ran with all speed, my constricting waistcoat a hindrance. I pulled at the buttons to loosen the fit, and they ripped off and left a trail behind me in the street—Cézanne had ruined it anyway when he splattered fat drops of blood onto the delicate silk. I sprinted the whole way to the rue de l'Isle to retrieve my old family physician, Doctor Albert.

The maid answered the door.

"Please, fetch the doctor. The great painter, Paul Cézanne, has taken a fall." There was desperation in my voice. I gasped for air, as the doctor came to the door. I wiped my face with my sleeve. In my haste, I had not worn a hat or jacket.

"Oh, and we were just starting the last hand," Doctor Albert said. A tall man, he peered down at me, saw my desperation, and his demeanor shifted. "Right. Let's go!" He waved goodbye to his bridge game in the front study, found a jacket and his bag, tapped on his top hat, and pointed me to his carriage. We made quick time back to No. 10 quai Voltaire. There we found rotund Cézanne sitting on the stairs still quite shaken, his upper lip quivering, the turban discarded next to him, his grey hair thin and standing at attention. He held the banister with one heavy hand, the other dabbed his nose with a bloody cloth. Badeau sat above him, quiet.

Mademoiselle Cézanne knelt on the foyer rug. She was praying.

The doctor opened his bag, and I soon slipped out the back entrance, forgotten by everyone as they tended to the great artist in a flurry of ministrations and fussing. What a day! I, Jules Lalande, helped Cézanne! Monsieur Cézanne! I cannot believe it! Perhaps I'll call on him tomorrow. I'm tired now. I've calculated I ran a good seven miles. My clothes are a mess. But I'm walking on air.

30 MAI 1905

Today, as I promised I would, I took it upon myself to call on Cézanne to inquire after his progress.

"Oh, dear, dear, Lalande, how can I ever thank you?" Mademoiselle was gracious with her tea and cakes and even unveiled a new painting her brother had just finished. It was marvelous. But Monsieur Cézanne was nowhere to be found.

14 DECEMBRE 1905

The Exposition—1,725 works! And 397 artists! And Cézanne's painting is the one the crowds are talking about! Today, I devised another plan to see the master. The newspapers hailed the old man's return for only a few days. He will be in Paris tomorrow.

15 DECEMBRE 1905

Today, the chill finally came to stay. I stepped into Badeau's; dead leaves swirled onto the floor from the wind outside. The door closed with a draught.

"Badeau, I can retrieve that picture Master Cézanne borrowed. Remember? But only if you would like me to do that for you." He was too busy to notice my nervousness; I needed a chance to speak with Cézanne.

"Yes, yes, good, good. Come back as soon as you have it. I have an interested buyer. You might make something if you can recover it for me. Your first commission!" I went straightaway to Cézanne's sister's home—I've walked the route numerous times over the past few months. I softly rapped on the guest house door, no need to announce myself with a bell. And the master answered!

"Good day, Monsieur Cézanne—I've come for Badeau's painting."

"Ah, you mean my painting? But I've sent it this day to the old miser! Weren't you the young man who helped me back in the spring?"

"Yes, I am Jules Lalande." I bowed deeply.

"Do come in! Out of that cold." Cézanne's voice was all levity, his fingernails dark with fresh paint. I followed him to the back of the house, to a large, dazzling room.

There, in the middle of his studio, from tall windows, dulled winter noonday swept across an easel and canvas; a roaring fire crackled, and the scent of success permeated everything. The master was already back at his work, smudging at a distorted myrtle tree, filling in a strange landscape composition.

"May I help you with something? I must thank you again for your help that day, but I should get back to work now." Oh, I wondered, how to start with my questions? I felt no sense of fear. This was my moment. He would not discourage me.

"Sir, I do some painting. I am just starting out, and my father, who is a man of taste and an art lover, a dabbler with the paints himself, believes I am not a hopeless cause."

"Well, young Lalande, if you must choose this life . . . Draw lines." The artist's brush kept stroking the trunk of the large tree in the painting; in the fireplace across the artist's room, the dancing flames snapped; the logs gave into themselves. A spaniel exhaled from the hearth. "Draw lots of lines. Not always from nature, young man. Do you see a tree in this room?" I looked around and only saw furniture and books.

"Paint from memory; paint from your imagination. Don't rely on real-life or photographs or real paintings by the masters."

"Thank you, sir."

I walked home, my steps springing.

Just tonight, dear journal, I've begun a self-portrait, my first masterpiece. I am copying the pose Monsieur Cézanne struck for his own self-portrait I saw hanging in his studio today. I will not use my mirror. Perhaps someday this work of mine will hang in a museum.

ISOBEL WRIGHT

One was thrown in a cold English pond.
One holds the sweetest song.
One holds a letter buried in a garden.
One holds a teaspoon of his grandmother's ashes.
    —Jules Lalande

ISOBEL RESCUES JULES, SOMEWHAT

Her second cousin, Jules, hobbled from a line of tall shrubbery all thinned out along the path. There was a limp in his step.

Come to me, cousin, I see you crying.

She sat in the lower meadow and waited for him. All afternoon, she'd whiled away the hours pulling purple weeds, splitting the stalks with grass-stained fingers, swirling the vinegary taste of the vegetation with her tongue, imagining a pretend family.

Here came Jules, his walk sideways with a kind of hurt. It was delicious to watch. When he neared, he whimpered loudly, but it was a grateful whine, relieved. He sat beside her in the crushed-down plants, held up his right foot, then scuffed off his thin-soled boot. He wore those shoes every day, just as their governess demanded, but the boy kept the footwear untied, the heels scrunched down, tongues and laces looping over his exposed, smooth skin.

"I was bitten out there, Isobel," he pointed toward the dark woods, no sunlight inside. "A big dog. I got a dog bite." Jules smelled like play, his hair full of summer sweat and dark things, too. The back of his ankle was red, and the four dots of blood trickled bright crimson. She knelt and held his foot in her hand.

Isobel commanded, "Sit still!" She didn't like how the bite was puffing. Jays argued, wrestled in the willows along the lake. The birds debated the wound, all the threats in the world. Behind Wilde now, the sun hid its face, but the top of Jules's head still glinted with heat.

Isobel was hot, too.

She latched her mouth to his heel, sucked at the punctures just as she'd read cowboys did with snakes—perhaps she could treat a canine injury the same way? There was the taste of tin in the wound. She drew more blood and spat it into the grass. It was also delicious. Jules was quiet, concentrating.

"Will it kill me, Bel?"

"I don't know; it might."

※

ISOBEL FEELS SOMETHING

Isobel stood on the lake's shore. She was dizzy as she followed the path of the choppy waves.

"It's brimming with fish!" Alban Frost stated with enthusiasm. He grabbed Isobel's hand and tugged her and Jules to the water. Isobel then wormed a hook for Frost, used one of those lures the breezy caretaker preferred. They stood shoulder-to-shoulder on the green shore, the depthless ink of water, murky and mysterious like the world beyond the estate.

The buzz of some strange bird off in the distance broke

the quiet every so often. And above, the sun glared down and blinked, as if the gathering rain clouds were eyelids. The water was a pulse, like a heartbeat, and underneath Isobel knew there were flashing shoals of fish, forests of waving weeds. Frost, Jules, and Isobel stood silent, rods in hand. The lines sizzled out over the water, breaking the surface occasionally. They waited for a twitch, for something.

She watched Frost tug his line with force, an injured thumb wrapped in cloth like a mummy. Injuries were typical for Frost. Since her parents had sent her away, since Isobel had left her last school, she'd watched Frost hurt himself so many times. She quit counting. Mrs. O'Kelly stocked an inventory of dressings in the house's kitchen pantry. Every day it was something else. He'd come out of the horse barn or the tack room or the storage rooms where all the winter furnishings were packed away, and he would bleed and curse: "Damned screw! . . . Bloody shovel! You'd think . . . Blimey."

Just yesterday, he'd hurt himself. While repairing the fences with the gardener out beyond the stables, far into the meadows, he'd slammed his thumb with a spike. Now he couldn't handle anything with much of a grip. Isobel watched him struggle all last night, his clumsy efforts with tools, candles, forks, fruit.

She wondered why he'd attempt to fish with an injury?

"Miss Isobel, I need your help today with fishing. Jules can come, too. My blessed thumb . . ."

The post had arrived early in the day, and they received a letter from the duke, her first cousin once removed. She smiled when she heard the bell tower.

"Mr. Frost, shall we go up to the house? Governess

Hansen just rang the bell," Isobel asked

Without waiting for Frost to reply, Jules spoke, "No, Governess Hansen can wait."

So, they fished. Jules inhaled, tossed his line out, the lure sailing a distance with a hiss, then it landed, marring the mirrored surface of the water with a ripple. He exhaled smoothly just as the bait hit with a splat. Isobel's line followed, falling far short and plunking down, announcing her failed attempt.

"Now don't scare off my fish," Jules said. She pulled in her line, recast. It skimmed the surface. Jules smiled.

There was a lack of noise again. At least for a few minutes. They stood on the bank for a while, everyone together in peace. The quiet between them was an understanding, a conversation without speaking. There was only the sound of the poles creaking and some oaks rustling.

Frost finally spoke and spat out the words.

"Isobel, they've found you another school," he said as he kept his eye trained on the body of water and tossed his line out again, this time farther, where the bigger fish lurked in the shadow deep.

She gulped, said nothing. No, it couldn't be right. Sure, she'd worried them all with her penchant for killing small animals. Especially Governess Hansen. Just as she had scared her parents with her strange proclivities. She handled her pole and gazed at Frost again. He stood close, expression innocent, unblinking, avoiding direct eye contact. His skin was translucent, baby thin with blue veins visible through the wispy auburn hair on the nape of his neck. He was so beautiful.

With a flick of the wrist, Isobel sent her line back. She

could feel the warm sun on her shoulders now, and she envisioned the worm in the water, irresistible to the fish; she waited for the line to quicken with a strike.

#

Like an alarm, a shrill voice came from up on the hill through the screen of trees.

"Where is everyone? I rang the bell!" Governess Hansen was there. In moments, she'd maneuvered down the slope in her profuse skirts and was standing there, hands on her hips. "Well, gentlemen," she said to Jules and Frost, not even glancing at Isobel. Frost stood straighter, ran his fingers over his shirt to check if he had tucked it in and buttoned it down the front. He hadn't. Governess Hansen eyed the poles. Her intricate braid wound high around her head, and anger clouded her lovely face.

"Mrs. O'Kelly's queried about those fish for our meal," Governess Hansen said, pointing to the creels.

"I'm certain we'll catch more soon enough," Frost mumbled. And then, the governess hoisted her silk skirts past her ankles and returned up the slick grass hillock.

For a moment, Frost, with heavy eyelids, squinted and watched the woman's precarious march. Stiff from standing still, he stretched one leg, then the other, and tottered a moment, then jogged up the hillside to offer her an elbow. Isobel watched the two of them mount the berm, the wind catching Frost's hair, swirling it on end into a bird's feather crest.

And she pulled in her line, her back to the bank and the house, and wondered if Frost was tired of pretending, the way she was.

"We should head to the house, too," Jules said. "And be prepared for unpleasantness."

He carried the poles behind her. She listened as his breeches swished with his gait as he strode closer.

They trekked back the long way on the crooked forest path, switchbacking over the rise. It was all gravel and tree roots, with better footing than the hill. Up nearer to the house, they could hear Governess Hansen and Frost, even Mrs. O'Kelly, in a lively conversation inside the house, and the murmur of their discussion carried through soughing branches and bird screeches. The voices were high-pitched.

Jules and Isobel hid behind an overgrown holly bush; it pricked Isobel's arms.

"She can't go away so soon, especially with all her problems," Mrs. O'Kelly said. Her tone was imploring.

"She has ideas of her own," Governess Hansen stated matter-of-factly. Frost was silent. "You know, we can't change everything every time she comes into trouble. That's why she's come here. It's the last resort. That's what the master said, after all." In addition to the loud voices, there was the clattering of pots, then the thud of a door closing.

"Maybe you should . . . You must be patient, Governess. She's just a child. And with all the changes—" Governess Hansen interrupted Mrs. O'Kelly mid-sentence.

"I understand, really. I want to help the girl, but the master was explicit, she is only here for breaks in schooling. She must go back."

"It's too difficult for her," Frost finally piped in. "You know." Isobel sensed tension as she heard Frost choosing his words carefully. She could feel Jules eyeing her, but she pretended not to care, glanced down, and began scribbling ghost designs in the dirt with the toe of her boot.

Then, as if suddenly inspired, Jules laid down their poles, strode across the kitchen garden, and burst through the scullery door. Isobel followed.

At the sight of the two, Frost and Governess Hansen silenced. Jules was the first to speak.

"Would you like me to brush the horses?" he asked Frost.

"No, not now. However, perhaps you might dress presentably for dinner," said Governess Hansen, glancing at Frost, turning her back to them all. Frost let out a huge sigh. He smiled at Isobel, patted her on the shoulder, then stepped outside toward the stables, his boots worn down at the heel from his daily walks around the property's acreage. At the window counter, Mrs. O'Kelly shaped miniature cakes with her hands, her back to them all. Isobel watched Governess Hansen and leaned against the large center work table, gazing out the back windows, watching a spider the size of a saucer zigzag across a new web. Jules, his chin down, crossed his arms and piled crumbs from the counter into mounds. His smooth forearms flexed with each gesture.

#

Her family was gone. *So what*, Isobel thought?

At home, after her parents had disappeared, she packed up all her things at her cousin duke's behest and went away to Badminton. When she was expelled, she was shipped to Godolphin. Then Harrogate. But this house was where she always came for holidays and between stints at schools. The burden of Isobel's care ultimately fell to those who lived and worked at Wilde.

Jules was already here when she arrived. The first night she met him, he leaned in her doorway and watched. He watched her all the time. She didn't mind. Ever since Governess Hansen and Alban Frost came here to manage the estate, ever since she had moved here, they had become a strange sort of family.

In recent months, she felt a new sensation when Jules watched her or walked by. Maybe it was his smile as he burst out of the nursery or his put-on Irish accent when he greeted her with "top 'o the morning" as they passed in the corridors. And when she finally settled into the house this holiday, Jules became her staunchest ally.

In their lessons, he laughed at all her silly jokes, while Governess Hansen sat and screwed up her puzzled face, and Mrs. O'Kelly, always in the kitchen or shuffling through the long hallways carrying a tray of something, would hear the laughter and step into the room, wiping her hands on her apron.

"What'd I miss?" she'd ask. Isobel would glance at Jules, and he'd wink.

"Nothing," he'd say and smile at Isobel.

Staying at Wilde was preferable to her family's other estates. And though it was only twenty miles north of her last domicile, more rooted in the country, it felt like a continent away.

At night, the governess allowed her to open the nursery windows. And so, in Isobel's new world, she saw and heard things she would never see and hear at home. She listened to crickets and marveled at the bats' silhouettes skittering across the lake, and then before she knew it, she'd fall into a deep, comfortable sleep. The lullaby of hooting owls and churring bugs drew her deep and away. When she'd have conversations in her dreams, Governess Hansen would mention the next morning she'd heard Isobel crying out in her sleep, but the girl could not remember what she had talked about or to whom she had spoken. She knew, though, her dead parents were there in the bottomless dark.

#

After breakfast, Mrs. O'Kelly came in, waving her big wooden spoon at them like a baton, and then she swept up the corners, tried to look busy. Jules stood and grabbed Isobel's elbow.

"You two, go find something else to do. Don't you have your studies this morning?" They both laughed and ran outdoors and down the hill, giggling all the way down the slippery slope.

Isobel and Jules stood on the shore, breathless. Their shoulders touched. Jules fixed on a point in the middle of the water, and he bit his lip.

"Swim?" he asked.

She nodded. Jules laughed, stripped down to his undergarments, his clothes a heap of warm color on the bank, and waded in. She followed, only wearing her linen petticoat and bodice. The water was bracing as she ducked under, and, as she surfaced, she crossed her arms over her chest and kicked her feet to stay afloat. Minnows licked at her toes.

Jules swam under, too, brushed up between her shoulder blades as he surfaced like a sea monster. He sliced out far then. With a sidestroke, she caught up, found him bobbing and waiting. She, too, dipped for a while, facing the shore, facing away from the center of the lake, then floated on her back, circling with arms and legs splayed. She gazed up at the grey sheets of cloud marbled with moisture. Jules kicked plumes of water over her.

"If you ever tire, I will hold you," Jules said.

"I'm almost there."

From the house, they heard Governess Hansen call, then Frost beckoned with the steeple bell, the loud peals ringing in ripples. They pretended not to hear, paddled around each other, spat sharp-tasting water through their pursed lips.

They settled somewhere in the middle where a warm spot bubbled up. A breeze puffed above them through the pines and the birds whispered in twilight song. Black lace reflections of tree foliage bounced across the lake's surface. And then, not tired, just exhilarated, she floated over to Jules, draped her arms over his shoulders, wrapped her legs around his waist. She watched the drops sparkle on the tips of his eyelashes, and he held her with no effort.

ISOBEL SETS A FIRE

With Jules gone, there was no stopping her. The fire gladdened, happy in its dance as it gnawed its way through the beams of the house. It traveled all the way to the roof, licking the dark carpets, rough and ugly, charring all those beautiful books to black, and Isobel absorbed the scene from the lawn even as the flames singed the ends of her scribbled locks. The conflagration was mesmerizing with its happy orange color. Like the sun, but better.

When the lamps exploded in the large foyer, the smell of something sharp like fuel pushed her farther away from harm; she walked to the woods and smiled, satisfied with herself, satisfied she'd succeeded in destroying the awful place.

The third governess, her name unimportant, was still inside.

So much better than pushing.

✳

ISOBEL, CAREFREE

In her memories, she focuses on his ropy muscles, the ligaments of an athletic boxer. His smooth chest, the lock of hair over his brow, the boxer's nose and puffed lips. He shadowboxes, while everyone around him lounges on blankets, the food baskets are brimming, and the women laugh and drink from a passed bottle of wine.

Emerald grass. Smoke the same color as the water. Grey industrial filth whiffling out from the stacks farther up the river.

There is much gaiety this day. And Jules's trunks, striped red, white, and blue, are the subject of laughter and a patriotic song or two.

✳

ISOBEL DREAMS OF STEAMSHIPS

When it was inevitable Jules would stay with Isobel, he stole away often in the morning, then woke her by whispering bits of the day into her ear, quotes and dreamy things he'd studied in some book. He breathed newfound knowledge. She'd wake to him murmuring, kissing her throat, and pulling the hair off her face.

"Oh, Isobel, the men dance together in the remote villages of China, waiting for the crops. But how is the dance perceived by the village women? Braids through the hair and stripes of colored ribbon indicate marital status to visitors." He had a memory that pulled things to it like a magnet, and his sweet way of sharing rolled her closer to him. Jules professed facts and questions in a sing-song until sighs and underthings floated up toward the ceiling.

Isobel's laughter, when it came, pleased him. She encouraged him with her smiles. And he attempted to earn more, a giggle, maybe, or even an explosion of amusement; he acted silly to make her happy.

Often, they would lie atop the bedcovers, gazing out the window, watching the wind handle the junipers with gentle strokes, and they'd share their dreams of steamships. Jules would say wistfully, "A boat could drift in this wind," pointing to the jostling limbs.

#

They understood each other without speaking. And then there were times when nothing remained to be said anyway. Especially in bed.

"How do you like this strange new haircut?" he once

asked. He had shaved it to the scalp. She did not like it, not at all, and she threw a bottle of perfume at him as a response. He ducked, and the penthouse smelled of gardenias for weeks. The reek made her sick. Or maybe she could attribute her nausea to pregnancy. Six months.

However, there were so many moments of friendship and kindness between them. Jules gave her trinkets. He left gifts out in the open where she discovered them, and, whenever she found the objects in his absence, she longed for him, already out of the apartment and going about his day exploring the city. He was passing through, and she knew, too, there would be a day when the presents would look back at her with nothing to say. One morning, after the door clicked behind him, there was the tapping of a wind-up metal bird hopping about the bathtub. When she set it on the windowsill, it slowed down to a gentle pecking. It took a long time for it to wind down to a full stop, a half-hour at least. But she watched it lose momentum, sat on the floor, waited.

She kept a list of all his presents: a wooden brush for scrubbing fingernails, two gold foil-wrapped spheres of chocolate, three balls of silk thread—lime green, hyacinth, and azure, a milkweed pod, a bar of lemongrass soap, and the hopping, wind-up bird.

The uncertainty between Isobel and Jules, though, was brutal. During their time together, what Jules called their "nesting time," they mostly entertained themselves. But he often went out, left her alone. And then she'd read about his antics in the morning papers. Debauchery, crazy performances. He once made love to a mannequin on a stage to the chinking of a piano tune, and a crowd went wild, an almost-riot. Another time, he passed off a basket as the very one in which Moses was found. He called the object "Flotilla."

With Marcel Duchamp as his inspiration, he also often painted canvases with simplistic shapes (or assembled nonsense) and showed the work under an assumed name. She remembered one painting, interlocking squares in shades of russet and maroon, which he called "Nude with a Barbell." The title was more impressive than the work of art. If she could call it art. This was about the time when his forgeries evolved into such fabulous creations no one could tell a fake from the original.

#

On their last night together, they danced. Jules and Isobel turned and swiveled; he tried some fancy steps, and she leaned into him as he grinned, though she wasn't sure if the expression was really one of distance or sadness. They circled in slow shuffles to a tune she hummed. The shiny floors creaked in the bistro. They were the last people in the place, and it felt right to be there inside the moment with him, moving to their own song for a long time. And then the baby cried, and they stopped dancing. The next morning Jules was gone.

#

During those dwindling days, she looked out and thought about how she used to like the streets when winter was undecided—the rain came and went, like the sun. And when strange weather appeared, the sun and rain occupied the same space, so the streets were wet, but the sun crossed over through drizzle. It would rain all morning, and then a cheerful city sun appeared like a miracle.

She was fond of poppies because they were miraculous, too. The flowers were so fragile. Their fluttering silhouettes and thread-thin stems were too weak to support flamboyant scarlet petals and those contrasting black hearts. Like herself. Like Jules. She could so easily spot such a flower from afar as it poked up its head in the middle of a field, on the banks of a country road, or in the most unexpected places like cracks in sidewalks—and she found that it was a flower best left unplucked. As tempting as it was to tuck a poppy behind the ear, it would wither away so fast that a person felt quite sorry for picking it.

Jules was like this. He was just fine when he was a wild thing, but to pluck him up meant he'd wilt away. She knew one day he'd keep going. It was what people do. The wind carried away his words from her, like everything else.

TITUS PIDGEON

Tell me whom you haunt—"whom you befriend"—and I'll
tell you who you are.
   —André Breton

TOMMY FLOYD REVEALS NOTHING TO TITUS PIDGEON

Intrigued by Madame Isobel Lalande's hostility and lack of cooperation—why would she be so unwilling to provide him with information unless she had something to hide?— Titus Pidgeon took her up on the tip to visit Tommy Floyd. It was better to find eager witnesses. He made his way to South End to the gymnasium owned by the former heavyweight champion of the world, the toast-of-the-town American boxer. Yes, Tommy Floyd had quite the reputation in fashionable circles. He was a novelty, a circus act, a scandalous athlete. Pidgeon had heard curious aristocrats and bored monied sorts treated Floyd like an exotic pet, inviting him to their wild soirées.

Midday, the reporter arrived at the gym. It was a shady sort of establishment. At the entrance, roustabouts milled around, smoking cigars. Pidgeon climbed two flights of the warehouse building and found himself in an open space stinking of unwashed men. Acrid sweat, stale semen, it was overpowering. Pidgeon breathed through his nose as a tall, muscular man sidled up. The boxer had a flat face.

"What're you here for? Not for the fists?" The man assessed Pidgeon and his suit, and the journalist felt overdressed in the steamy close gym as all manner of half-naked men grunted, punched bags, threw jabs at each other, performed stretching and bending exercises.

A bulky man appeared from a back room.

"May I help you?" he looked suspicious.

"My name's Titus Pidgeon, sir. I'm inquiring about Jules Lalande—I believe you knew him? I'm a reporter for *The London Times*."

"I am Tommy Floyd. Sure, yes. That's an old story, though. I knew Jules, but he went missing in Cuba. Remember? It was in all the papers." Pidgeon noted the muscular American's flat accent was soft. He was not the gruff person one would expect at first glance. And the athlete had impeccable diction, even if it wasn't British.

Pidgeon responded, "Well, Mr. Floyd, I don't necessarily think that's all of it. Do you?"

Pidgeon did not interject as the famous boxer replied by relaying his story.

✻

TOMMY FLOYD TELLS TITUS PIDGEON HIS STORY

Not sure I can help you, but I'll tell you what I can.

Yes, you know, Pidgeon, it's crazy, your name's like the bird, right? How did you find me? Oh well, most folks find me, I guess.

So, yes, everybody knows that Jules was last spotted here in London. I can understand why you want to find him. Everyone does. Me, too. It's a mystery where he went off to.

Of course, you know I'm from America. I'm from Georgia, in the South. You probably know that.

My first win, not in the ring, mind you, was a colored boy—he was probably fifteen. I was older, a college freshman. I know you must think it's strange that I went to college.

That fight. It was a late fall afternoon, and I had stayed after my literature class. I wanted to talk to my instructor about Dickens and Marx, about the mistreatment of workers. I sat in the hallway for a couple of hours and spoke to fellow students.

Yes, you see, I'm a kind man. And I was a gentle boy, too. I could scarcely watch my mother cut a chicken's throat, let alone go after another human.

So, I was walking through town after class, it was dark already, and I encountered a boy on a deserted street at the border of the city in a pocket of a rough section. I was on the colored side of town. And you know what that means?

So, as I turned on the avenue behind that boy, I thought there was some safe distance between us. But he shot back a worried glance. To the boy, a looming white man—over six-feet-two with a cap on, both arms crossed, a cumbersome wool jacket—might have seemed threatening. I guess he'd thought himself the target of a bigot or something.

After a few quick glimpses, he turned around and ran at me, and I reacted—I punched forward. It wasn't really a fight, but I defended myself. As my fist grazed his cheek, I felt the boy's slick skin give with force; his jaw clicked. He was down on the clay street lickety-split.

And, well, after that, after I knocked him out, I knew it was no good, that if I didn't get out of there, the mob would be at me, so I disappeared into an alley.

But what started it all is that a colored boy thought I was after him, so I had to defend myself. And because of the rush of that angry boy who barged at me, I first understood what kind of inheritance I'd come into—I could hurt people before I even punched. But that's politics, and you don't want to chat about politics.

Soon, I learned I could calculate how to inflict the most pain in less than a second.

I just looked, knew, punched. I wasn't like others.

My fists are a tool, something I can use to get out of a scrap. Or even more, I make money with these hands.

We all use our hands and muscles. I just use mine and then use some winning strategies in the ring.

So, you're here about Jules Lalande. Let me tell you, Jules was different. He saw me as a gentleman, treated me that way.

We met in the ring. That fight was a killer. The mob cheered me on, sure, and I could tell Jules wanted me to win, too. I think it's because, in his mind, I was an intellectual inferior. That was before he knew me. He wanted me to take home the prize out of pity—even though I could beat him jolly. And I felt terrible at all the shit the crowd threw at him. Real shit. Animal stuff. Not just words.

After that match between us, we spent a lot of time together. Especially before his soon-to-be wife came along. I remember when I first saw her. Jules and I were at a party of some donor or sponsor or something. We were in New York. I had walked all the way through Greenwich Village, and I distinctly remember, as I walked to that party, I was whistling Mozart's *Requiem*.

Anyway, Jules stood with his arm around my shoulder,

but when Isobel walked in, I heard the entire Mass, all of Mozart's choral parts playing at once in my head. I had never seen a woman move like her. Jules's arm dropped from my shoulder then, and it never returned.

Over the years, I've learned to hide my anger. And I have the best outlet here in boxing. As you can see. But I take precautions to make myself less intimidating when I walk around London. As a big man with cauliflower ears, people assume I'm a ruffian or a mick revolutionary. I move about with care in this town. And I give a wide berth to nervous people on the streets, especially at night, particularly when I'm not in a fancy suit. If I'm about to enter a building behind somebody who's jumpy, I walk on by, then wait for the lobby to empty before I come back. I look like a lout, sure, and maybe people sense my ire about the world, I suppose.

I read. A lot. More than when I was in college.

But it didn't matter when the war came. I didn't want to kill anybody. I only liked punching. But I did slay others. I learned to aim, I learned to hide, and I found out no one looks out for folks like me. People with no connections.

That's when I started fighting in my free time. I was good. But you know all that. I won all the prize fights, moved up the ranks during the war. And that was the real battle.

But I shouldn't be talking about me. This is supposed to be about Jules. Mind you, my story's his story. Everyone knows this. Jules wasn't like anyone else in the world. And Isobel isn't worth the paper you write her name on.

She bothered me for months after Jules went missing. Right after, not too long ago, her letters would splat on my hallway floor every morning, slipping through the mail slot like a flying bug. She was desperate, begging me to tell her where he was. I didn't know! I still don't!

I tried to tell her no one had heard from him after Cuba. I kept my replies short, to the point, responding every few weeks with just a few words—"My name's Titus Pidgeon, sir. I'm inquiring about Jules Lalande—I believe you knew him? I'm a reporter for *The London Times*."

No news yet." I even started underlining that one sentence! But her letters just kept sliding through my mail slot.

Toward the end in New York, when we went on our weekly picnics—Isobel, Jules, and the baby—that woman wouldn't wear a mushy-pea variety hat. That wasn't good enough for Isobel. No, only the most alluring, expensive, umbrella-sized bonnets for her. She was just as theatrical as her husband. But with no heart.

Finally, Isobel quit bothering me. It was only a few years ago. I threw away all those letters. Sorry. I bet you could have used those.

What kind of man was Jules? Well, he couldn't fit all he was or could be into one skin. I won't say another word on this subject.

Let's talk boxing, alright?

❀

TITUS PIDGEON, SOME MEMORIES ARE SO RARE THEY NEVER EXISTED IN THE FIRST PLACE

Like most stories with no clear timeline, this Lalande

business was confusing; the din of the newsroom and its urgent deadlines and journalists and editors shouting at each other weren't conducive to puzzle-solving either.

"Pidgeon, get in here!" The reporter scrambled into his editor's glass office, and Mr. Talbot pulled a piece of paper from his drawer. "I want you to go visit one Lord Havelock Hereford. The poor chap was a dupe in some fraud. Maybe Lalande was involved. Find out if Hereford's really a mug or if something strange was afoot. And look the part." The chief editor's voice wavered slightly as he scanned Pidgeon's frowsy suit.

When Pidgeon arrived at Lord Hereford's, the gentleman was somber-faced as he shook hands with Pidgeon in the entry of his *pied-à-terre*. The reporter was aware he would need to be gentle—no one ever likes to be made a fool, especially those aristocratic sorts.

They sat in the book-lined room, and Lord Hereford smoked his pipe.

"Put your feet up there. Up, up. Yes." Hereford pointed to the opposite chair, motioned for Pidgeon to take advantage of the ottoman, then pushed back into his own seat, legs in front of him. Pidgeon parked on the edge of the cushion, primly upright, as Hereford spoke.

"Do you mind?" Pidgeon leaned back, pulled out and pointed to his own pipe wad.

"Why no, of course, of course," Lord Hereford replied. For Pidgeon, tobacco was most undoubtedly necessary—he predicted the nobleman would be verbose.

"Shall I tell you the whole story?" Hereford asked. Pidgeon nodded.

The journalist smiled and propped his notepad on the briefcase propped on his knee. He squinted. Hereford whiffed smoke slowly through his lips and then began.

"I met a lovely chap—who was *not* a card sharp, mind you—in a high-stakes game. I'd never seen the man before, but good friends vouchsafed for him.

"Well, I came to trust the card player, and I dare say, after a few encounters, this gentleman (and I was certain he was a gentleman!) convinced me to attend an auction. Indeed, I bid on something. That's really something quite frivolous for an old man to do—mind you, I never endeavor after that kind of thing. I only gamble with cards, you see." When Hereford spoke, he did not move his lips, such an English talent. Pidgeon tapped his pipe and gazed at the gory tapestry hanging above. A hart pursued by a pack of wolves. Garnet warp threads pricked through a silk weft background. Like blood droplets.

"Sir, why is this important? Why are you telling me this?" Pidgeon was kind in tone, and he continued taking notes, doodling the name of the stout he would sip on later: *Guinness. Guinness. Guinness.*

"Yes, yes. I'm telling you because I had a terrible fright with this man. I want you to roast the bugger."

"Can you describe this bloke? His physical attributes? Name?"

"Not sure on the name, I'm having a difficult time remembering. Landis was his name . . . No, crikey, no, I'm not really sure, or was it Lakely? I think he was about five-feet-eight, no, he was more likely six-feet. And, well, maybe he was forty years old? No, maybe thirty? He was definitely blonde or redheaded and had grey—light brown hair, yes, with one blue eye, one brown, I think. Kind of like your eyes."

Pidgeon cleared his throat, sat up. How could Lord

Hereford have trouble describing a man with whom he'd played cards during many evenings? Now Pidgeon was paying attention. The suspect sounded like he could be more than a petty criminal: the sly conniver had confused Hereford, a man of stature who possessed some wits (not a lot, though). Not an easy mark, but not a difficult one, either. Intriguing. The shady character was so crafty he could disguise himself in bright lamplight.

"His voice—how would you describe it?" Pidgeon asked.

"The man had no accent, except maybe one from the South. I mean the American South, of course. Quite a well-mannered chap, too. Indeed. Could play poker the best I've ever seen. And I don't even think he counted the cards. Not one trifle." Pidgeon nodded his head, tried not to look too excited, and now he was taking copious notes.

"Lord Hereford, tell me about the auction?"

"Well, as we played cards into that last night, this Lakeland chap—or was it Lawler?—mentioned some sale in passing. He made a comment off the cuff. Said he wished he could invest his own money in an object that was coming up on the block. He intimated that his liquid funds were being held up in probate. Well, the man's passion piqued my interest, you see. I was convinced. Blasted if I didn't trust him. He could play cards like the Dickens, you see? Did I say that? And he played honestly. Or so I thought.

"So, I bid on a bloody letter. Damnably expensive, too. Apparently, appraisers said it was historical, that it was important to times gone by, to the world of poetry. Didn't really mean anything to me, though. And old boy, I hate poems anyway. Never understood rhymes. I never liked Shakespeare, either."

Pidgeon casually peered up at the bookcases filling the

oval-shaped room. They were all leather-bound; many were first editions; many were indeed poetry and Shakespeare.

"Old boy, the piece of paper that I bid on? It fell apart on the way home. Smelled funny, too. Christie's had already paid the private seller when I called. The vendor went by the name of Rassup, but when they tried to contact him, his address was a fake."

Pidgeon could not help but smile. Of course, the item had fallen apart. It *was* a fake. Of course, they could not find the seller. This was a classic confidence game. Somehow, though, the Christie's experts had touted the item as an original parchment letter in the hand of Marlowe. It had been so rare it never existed in the first place.

#

Pidgeon awoke early the next day, bent at an angle inside his armchair, the fire spat down to ashes, and he skipped his usual cuppa. Instead, he made his way in haste to Scotland Yard where his archives contact had pulled information about the auction scandal.

#

BULLETIN—BULLETIN—BULLETIN

WANTED CRIMINAL
17 JUNE 1936

FROM: Chief Constable Mitchell Foote

Scotland Yard
Victoria Embankment
London, England SW1

TO: International Criminal Police Commission
French Division
General Secretariat
Paris, France

REGARDING: The open case of Jules Lalande, Duke of Burlington (suspected alias: Dorian Rassup).

From what Scotland Yard investigators can ascertain, Jules Lalande (Duke of Burlington) is the culprit in a recent string of fraudulent auctions. He may well be in Paris, where his English wife resides. We believe he is perpetrating crimes from France, where we suspect he runs his operation. We are asking the International Criminal Police Commission to open an investigation.

It is this office's general impression, though many believe the man to be dead, that Jules Lalande is still alive and working at the highest levels of criminal intrigue. The latest string of frauds perpetrated at Christie's definitely bears his mark. We are hoping our Parisian counterparts will help us in our search for Lalande.

Do not be fooled: this man is a criminal of the highest order. His Majesty's government is determined to find Lalande and bring him to justice.

The lead investigator on the case is Detective Chief Inspector Ralph Winderwheedle from the London home office.

#

FOR OFFICIAL EYES ONLY

INTERNAL MEMORANDUM—SCOTLAND YARD

TO: Detective Chief Inspector Rolf Winderwheedle

FROM: Chief Constable Mitchell Foote

CC: Chief Superintendent Ralph Sheridan; Lord Haverford Hereford, House of Lords, Parliament

DATE: 23 JUNE 1936

RE: Jules Lalande, Duke of Burlington

Winderwheedle *et al.*,
I am providing you with more background information on Jules Lalande, Duke of Burlington, though I am confident you are familiar with the complexities of the case by now. We shall refer to him sans title for the remainder of our correspondence.

The last confirmed sighting of Lalande was in the early Twenties when he disappeared off the coast of Cuba. All evidence indicates Lalande did not vanish or perish at all. About that time, he was seen in London, Paris, and perhaps Amsterdam. And, in his role as his alias,

Rassup, we believe Lalande continued to hone his skills as a counterfeiter.

To wit, though never proven, Rassup and Lalande are the same man. Their behavior is strikingly similar. And beyond their matching preoccupations with poetry and forgery, Rassup and Lalande have used many of the same disguises and passport tricks.

Perhaps Lalande's handwriting was not involved in the recent hoaxes, yet the scheme has all his flourishes. Guillot de Saix, the celebrated poet and *missioner* in France, when interviewed just last year, said he had met the *faussaire* Jules Lalande in Paris in the late 1920's and Lalande had continued to make a living forging documents for Charles Covington, the shady publisher and purveyor of erotica in the rue de Châteaudun. According to de Saix, Lalande admitted many times he was living under the assumed alias of Dorian Rassup.

Magazines and two-penny newspapers have fanned the flames of the Lalande legend. In the spring of this year, a retired American banker and bibliophile named Henry Boyce Baker read and recognized Lalande's name in a news account.

In any case, this American, Henry B. Baker, whilst on holiday in London, came to our offices to give a statement [see interview notes below, if interested]. Baker is confident he had dealings with Lalande, whom he met in New York in 1924.

Baker also produced eight letters he received from Rassup/Lalande during their brief acquaintance; all were dispatched on genuine European hotel stationery, dated 1924-1925, and are difficult to assess for relevance. [We are in possession of these letters. Please see the Yard's archives, if interested. Transcript of the final postcard included below.]

One note is signed "Eva, Dowager Princess of Iceland," another is signed, "Queen Mary." The last missive, dated 6 July 1925, bears a picture of a Cunard liner. It was mailed from Southampton, England, eight months before a long string of petty burglaries and forgeries in London.

Our experts have analysed these letters. And by forensic accounts, graphological analyses verify the penmanship used in the recent auction frauds may be our suspect's handiwork. The handwriting is unmistakable—clearly, it is a hoax, but may or may not be Lalande's. Our graphologists' report also discusses the curves of some upper-case letters mirror both the fraud items and Rassup's notes from 1924-1925. Baker never heard from Dorian Rassup after his last postcard, but said, "The correspondence certainly reveals him as an obvious deviant interested in buggery."

I hope this sheds some light on the slippery nature of this character, Lalande. Please be on alert for further crimes that may have gone unreported.
Yours,
Mitchell Foote

#

HENRY BOYCE BAKER INTERVIEW NOTES (COMPLETE TRANSCRIPT AVAILABLE IN SCOTLAND YARD EVIDENCE ARCHIVES)

Scotland Yard interviewed Henry Baker on 4 April 1936, when he visited London on an annual holiday: "Over a decade ago, Lalande and I met in New York City at a poetry reading. I remember it all like it was yesterday. The name he used initially was Dorian Rassup. I found him to be a strange sort of vagrant. His appearance, as I remember it, was rather derelict. He wore a velour hat down close to his eyes—as if he were hiding something."

According to Baker, Rassup produced and read his own refined verses in public settings. His poetry was "completely at variance with his character, especially when he presented his original work in erudite performances."

In his interview, Baker also stated, "Once, I walked Rassup to the train. Before he entered the station, he slipped a visiting card into my hand on which appeared the name 'Mr. Jules Lalande.' It was elegantly engraved. I questioned him about it. He said I should use the name in any further communication with him. As you can imagine, I was somewhat surprised to find my friend Rassup going by another name."

Baker also recalled in further meetings that Rassup/Lalande conversationally was the highest form of genius, but was nonetheless duplicitous, "a criminal to be sure." To read his poetry, though, "was like reading Poe or Maupassant or Verlaine or Musset or Whitman or

Swinburne. But associating with him was like encountering a treacherous fellow akin to Jack the Ripper. And you know? He never once signed any correspondence with his real name. I found the whole business suspicious. He also was most certainly a depraved sodomite."

Text from Jules Lalande's postcard correspondence sent to Henry Boyce Baker from a known Jules Lalande alias. Held in Scotland Yard evidence archives. Please return to records.

6 July 1925

Dear Poet,
It is cold here on the great pond, but the men are keeping me company. Perhaps we might meet upon my return to the Great Democracy. My jewels are safe, my language and my tongue never better.
Love, love,
The Queen

[Investigator's note. *Text analysed by technical graphologists: the ink is smudged and water-damaged.*]

※

TITUS PIDGEON SHOULD NEVER TRUST ARCHIVISTS

Early the next morning, after his fruitful research at

Scotland Yard, Pidgeon found himself in the centuries-old Burlington Archives at King's College in London. Lalande was the rightful heir of the Burlington dynasty, after all. The 9th Duke of Burlington after his uncle passed away. There was not a 10th. Not yet, not until an inquest could decide Lalande was dead *in absentia*. No one had provided enough proof either way.

At the college, Pidgeon first perused the stacks in the faculty library for a half hour. Such great literature! And those classics bolstered him as he mustered the courage to deal with the college's famously cranky librarians. After double-checking the directory, he descended two stories to the titularly named "Burlington Archives." Pidgeon gave his card to the man behind the counter.

"May I speak with the director? I am a journalist for *The London Times*. Titus Pidgeon."

"No, no, I'm afraid the director's on sabbatical. May I help you with something? My name's Walkner." The short, fat man huffed as he spoke.

"I'm interested in finding all the information I can about Jules Lalande, the last Duke of Burlington."

"Well, yes. This *is* the Burlington family's archive, after all." Walkner's tone was condescending.

"Would you mind if I browse a little?" Pidgeon asked.

"Sir, this is a reference room, but you have permissions with the newspaper. Only make sure to stay in the back row there." Walkner pointed to the wall behind shelves stacked with crumbling manuscripts. Pidgeon skipped the books and found cabinets, lots of low storage with many drawers where no sunlight ventured. He thumbed through the J files. Nothing on Jules. Only letters, all in neat grey envelopes, all from relatives and friends with J names—

Johnson, Josephs, Jilly—and there were many bills, too, from art dealers and suppliers going back to the 1850s. The reporter even found jam recipes. But no, there were no clues about Jules here, only daily items from Jules's mother.

Pidgeon moved on. He browsed the first edition books nearby. Some beauties, rare tomes, especially the ones about art and jewelry, 1800s décor. Propped against a volume entitled *Counterfeits: Great Crimes in Art*, he found an unmarked, inexplicable binder. It was sealed with wax in multiple places, on the corners and flap, and there was no number or label affixed to its leather cover and binding. No identification, no title. Pidgeon carried the file to the front counter, where Walkner sat peering over his half-round spectacles, checking his pocket watch.

"No sir, I've never seen that before. There's no number? Are you sure it has no catalog number? Well, then, I have no idea when or how it got here." The librarian trundled his stout body over to the sign-in and sign-out books. He leaned over and scanned, turning pages furiously. His tweed waistcoat stretched over his massive middle, the buttons pulling to reveal his dickey and some skin underneath. "Surely, surely someone had to have signed it in!" Walkner skimmed through multiple books, his finger tracing signature after signature. He propped his glasses up on his forehead and wheezed. "No, nothing's here. Nothing at all."

"Well, if I want to review this *non-existent* book, should I sign it out?" Pidgeon tapped the binding. He intuited the item was essential. Why else would it be there for him to discover?

"No, no, you're supposed to sign it out, but if no one signed it in, how can anyone sign it out? Just take it, take it. Less work for me." Walkner turned away, began sorting cards and filing them in a drawer. And then the man spoke over his shoulder as Pidgeon reached the stairwell.

"You know, at Wilde House, the college still maintains many of the Burlington estate's valuable documents. Perhaps I can write you a letter of introduction to Miss Thacker who manages those? Or shall I contact them and let them know to expect you? I could ring them up."

If Pidgeon hurried, he could make the 9:30 train.

#

Pidgeon traveled by rail the rest of the morning to arrive in the countryside. It was a long walk from the train station on a deserted lane. As he rounded a bend, the Wilde estate appeared over the vast park. The hulking, half-burned manor held court over a large lake (or pond?). He mounted the slate stoop to the grand double doors and pulled the chain. He heard footsteps, and the door creaked open. A thin woman stood in the entrance without a greeting or a smile, wearing her black hair pulled back in a tight braid. She did not say a word, but waved for Pidgeon to follow.

He stepped in. The dusty entrance hall reeked of mold, even though the structure was constructed of cold marble. It was dank like a mausoleum where darkness dug into the corners. They walked down a few corridors before she stopped, opened a door, and announced rather dryly, "The safe parlor." She raised an eyebrow as if he should be impressed.

"And I am Miss Eveline Thacker." She pointed. "Here, you will be safe from unfortunate draughts and the noise for which this property seems to be famous. Please note the structure of the home is sound and most of the rooms on this wing are locked." There was a glint in her eye, something frightening. She pointed at a long table.

"You will sit there." She then gestured at a hard, elaborately designed chair. It was a ladder-backed throne, carved deep with dragons and trees. He thought of Jacob's Ladder as he came around to his designated seat. She continued, "I will ring for the houseman. He will fetch what you require. What years did you say you wanted to read?" She crossed her arms as if to block his exit from the room. There would be no nosing his way around the dreary mansion.

"Miss Thacker, I did not say."

"Mr. Walkner from London informed me you were interested in the last of the Burlington generations. Well, then, we will bring you the most recent diaries and journals. Why Lady Elizabeth married a Swiss man, even for money, is beyond all of us . . . But I am indelicate and speaking out of turn. In any case, if you are interested in further study, you may ruminate on which course you will take after that." She stomped out, her feet hammering the checkerboard floor—white, black, white, black. Her footsteps' reverberation stayed with him long after she departed. It was a scary place; he did not like it.

Pidgeon sat still, heard other steps coming back toward him, the echoes ricocheting like balls off the high, dark walls. A tall man in crisp butler attire—cutaway, wing collar—arrived with a measured gait; he carried multiple slim volumes stacked in his outstretched, gloved hands. And with a bow, he announced the pile as if it, too, was a guest of the estate.

"Lady Elizabeth Lalande's diaries. I will wait here, sir, while you study." And then the man stood like a sentinel by the open door. Or perhaps he was more like a Cerberus. Behind the houseman, a hundred or so cats slowly filed in, in twos and threes. They came in one long, steady stream. By the time Pidgeon began reading, many had jumped onto the table and were walking the high window sills, or perching and cleaning, or scratching and clawing. He sneezed.

And as Pidgeon delved into the slim tomes, he covered his nose and mouth with a handkerchief. In just a few minutes of study, Pidgeon concluded Lady Elizabeth's reminiscences would not reveal useful information about her progeny or Jules's nature or where he might be today. No, the child, Jules, was not mentioned, not once. The diaries were merely long, scratching narratives of expenses and parties, society teas and balls in Switzerland, France, England. European gentry and their silliness. There was only one slightly lurid item: a kiss on a terrace somewhere in Italy. The entries were merely the petty doings of a shallow woman's life. No intrigue. This was not the jackpot Pidgeon had hoped. The cats were not the least bit perturbed he was there; they weaved between his feet, and he reached out and scratched under an orange feline's chin.

As he finished reading the last of Lady Elizabeth's drivel, Pidgeon looked up, and the attendant smiled with a wry half-grin. The houseman reached into the back of his waistband and pulled out a folder. He then motioned to his lips with his gloved forefinger, *shhhh*, and leaned in as he handed over a small accordion file wrapped with yellow string. "You might make better use of these papers than Miss Thacker."

Pidgeon pushed the stolen dossier deep into his suitcase, covered it with some inconsequential papers, and departed, made his way with his "guard" close behind him. Miss Thacker stood on the landing above and watched as he turned around one last time to take in the spooky place. The door creaked as it sealed shut like a closing sarcophagus. Pidgeon could hear someone latch four different locks.

#

The reporter waited until he was home to read both the binder he'd "borrowed" from the Burlington library and the contraband folder from Wilde. Even though he yearned to dig into them on the trip home to London, he held his fire until he was safe in his own environs. After pricking the needle of the Victrola onto a record (something German and thunderous), Pidgeon placed the two absconded folders side-by-side on the table.

How strange the process by which he had come to possess them. What would any of their information *really* reveal? He hoped for delicious revelations.

He stood on his carpet in the middle of the room, head spinning, found himself carefully gripping a paring knife to cut the wax seals on the Burlington Library materials. He had not noticed it before, but one of the red seals bore a monogram. <JL>. Pidgeon bent down and smelled the leather attaché. He sniffed a combined fragrance of cherries and cigars. On the record player, Wagner was reaching a crescendo, and Pidgeon's hands shook with excitement. The music was too much, too much for this moment. He paused, lifted the needle. He also decided it best to don some gloves before commencing with this careful operation.

And so, with great caution, he slit the closures on the library documents. He sliced in spastic, short motions, stopping three times to make sure he had not damaged the portfolio or its contents. It was as if he were performing surgery.

The last cut. Documents spilled onto the shiny table. No, the contents were unfortunately not a single manuscript or diary, just many scraps of dirty paper, written in a shaky, lovely hand. A familiar hand. It was almost Lalande's, but perhaps less slanted. An adolescent's handwriting? Upon inspection, there was really nothing of value. Such a disappointment! Just transcribed copies of specific passages from Shakespeare's tragedies. Such an unusual thing for a person to do. Why would someone endeavor this? There were already excellent Shakespearean editions, meticulously printed volumes anyone could purchase in a bookshop.

Someone had also annotated the scraps in an indecipherable language; Pidgeon suspected a kind of code system, a cipher. But without a key, any secret message was useless. What a waste.

The timepiece on his mantel dinged 10 o'clock. So late. Some Scotch first. Yes, he was thirsty for the stuff. Now, he turned to the absconded folder from Wilde. Ah, perhaps this information could provide more answers. Though he really wasn't sure what questions to ask. It was all such a grand puzzle.

He pored over every piece of paper, beginning with an old letter written in the previous decade:

Miss Lucretia Summerville
Head Librarian
Burlington Archives and Library
Strand
King's College
London WC2R 2LS

13 February 1925

Madame Isobel Wright Lalande
79, rue Saint Jacques
5e PARIS
FRANCE

Dear Madame Isobel Wright Lalande:

In this package, you will find a sheath of documents I discovered whilst organizing the estate of the heiress, Lady Elizabeth Lalande, sister to the 8th Duke of Burlington, mother to Jules Lalande, the 9th Duke of Burlington (your husband).

Because you have not provided copies of your New York marriage registry, unfortunately, I cannot address you as "Duchess." However, because the 8th Duke was your first cousin once removed, and the 9th Duke is your second cousin, our mandates allow you to view these documents.

For now, we will not use these papers for our current genealogy work, which is our primary task. Nevertheless, we ask you to return these labeled records to storage here once you have dispensed with your family business.

I am uncertain how anyone misplaced these

items, Madame, but I surmise Lady Elizabeth's servants continued to collect records even after her death right up to the confusing times of our Great War.

Many of these papers might hold emotional significance for you or your husband, or maybe contain something precious only to the family— perhaps the Duke wrote some of these letters in his own hand. Among other things, you will find artwork (drawings, watercolors) and original newspaper clippings. I also discovered rather personal journal entries and did not read them once I realized the sensitivity of their nature.

You may return everything at your convenience; they are still the property of the Burlington Archives at King's College.

Sincerely yours,
Lucretia Summerville
Lucretia Summerville
Archivist and Librarian

Enclosures

JULES LALANDE

> *what's become of (if you please)*
> *all the glory that or which was Greece*
> *all the grandja*
> *that was dada*
> —E. E. Cummings

JULES LALANDE MEETS DELPHINE FOLIN

Indigence brought invisible rewards: resolve and strength. With no income except a measly allowance, Jules immersed himself in painting. He ate beans from tins, wrapped himself in worn-out wool when it was cold. Many days, Jules didn't have money for bread. But he was happy.

He had not directly spoken to his father in five years.

Jules's state of contentment would change, though, when a rangy messenger, a boy of eight or nine, arrived.

The missive was urgent news from his father. The old man was ill; a spell with his lungs.

Jules ignored the message, continued his painting, dabbing ultramarine into a landscape. After an hour, he dropped his brushes into a jar of mineral spirits, abandoned the loaded paint palette on his cot. He slipped on three shirts for warmth under his wool coat, doubled two pair of socks, his only socks, and then tied on his worn boots.

His father lived in a new house now.

As Jules turned down the lane, late afternoon sunlight beamed over the row of elegant townhouses and manors crowding the sky, each structure the color of a dark bruise, brown or burgundy or blue.

He found the correct number, knocked on the red doors, and after a long minute, a butler peered at him through the peephole. As Jules entered the foyer, he caught a whiff of sickness and infection. The butler, with no words, pointed to the staircase, a spooling trail to the upper floors.

Jules found his father with his head propped on pillows in his canopied, four-poster bed. His father focused for a moment and squinted at Jules, who stood frozen close to the door. Jules scanned the room. There were murky, half-drunk glasses of amber tisanes crowding a table alongside the bed, the bureau by the roaring fireplace, even on a tray on the sitting area's ottoman.

"Son, have you come to see me suffer? I'm sure you're quite pleased by this sight." Jules did not offer a retort—his father had summoned him, after all. He moved close to the bed. The fire licked at the tops of the stone fireplace. His sick father, wrapped in a shawl and slathered with liniment, sweated profusely; he sat up to cough blood into a handkerchief, then pointed at the two priests standing in the corner next to the shuttered windows. In his delirious state, he cursed.

"Fucking God has nothing to do with this." They murmured their Stations of the Cross louder then, swaying with the rhythm of the rosaries' clicking beads.

Jules talked; he didn't know what else he was supposed to do, so he chatted about the most natural subject: his painting. And though he was there only an hour, he was exhausted and had difficulty walking home.

After Jules's initial visit, he called daily, hoping to offer comfort, hoping for a kind word from his father. Each day, Jules stayed for hours. But his father's affection never came. The man tossed meanness, and his bitterness was not the least bit attenuated by sickness. He often mentioned Jules's mother.

"You were a frustration, and your mother did not love you." The words were cruel, but Jules remained bedside, nonetheless, and read to the old man, mostly poetry and old newspapers. His father never smiled. At least Jules knew the nurses appreciated his efforts—his distraction provided respite for the over-burdened caretakers, who could shift their focus to fussing over medicines, cleaning the room.

#

Not long after Jules's first visit, he met Delphine Folin, the youngest nurse. She was about his age and hailed from a well-known family. He watched her angelic care for his father, her snowy linen uniform gliding over her slight figure, apron tied perfunctorily around her tiny waist, golden hair in a low plaited chignon. Healing was her calling. Her deep-set hazel eyes never wavered, never turned away as Father faded and fought. She smiled when the man's screaming epithets mingled with his coughs.

After spring came and went, the old man's lungs permanently filled with liquid, and he gurgled with each labored breath, but Delphine remained devoted; she sat with his father, often wiped his brow as he drowned in his own spittle.

One day, when the doctor arrived, and Jules and Delphine stepped into the corridor. They whispered.

"Remember, everything ends. And any end's not such pleasant business," Delphine said. She touched Jules's cheek with the back of her hand, and he felt ice—not an unpleasant sensation.

#

They escaped to the locked-up wing. On the floor of one of the many forgotten bedrooms ("Don't muss the sheets!"), Delphine smoked a cigarette as she sprawled flat on her back, legs splayed. The afternoon light sliced across the room. He sat above her, admiring her rosy skin, the aureate hair between her petite hipbones. She sucked in smoke and slowly charmed it back through her tiny nostrils.

Delphine, fair hair on her head—and everywhere else.

"Your father doesn't have long now. I've seen it before. And dying is something to behold. Beatific smiles lighten faces afflicted with the most awful maladies. I've seen it recently with your father. It's wondrous."

"And why do you care about this sort of thing?" Jules asked.

She hesitated, then sighed. "There is beauty in death."

Delphine was like Jules. She understood an ineffable pulse drummed below life's surfaces.

✳

JULES, LOST, THEN FOUND, THEN LOST AGAIN

Jules quit his painting. He had to admit it; his art bored him. It wasn't a painful realization, especially after he sold a series of self-portraits, peddled the last part of himself he'd been willing to commodify. A select few—gallery agents, discerning collectors—appreciated his work, he supposed. Favorable reviews even ran in the papers after his small contribution to the exhibition. He was satisfied with this modicum of success.

Delphine, however, was not impressed. It was his utmost concern—piquing and keeping her interest. He so desperately wanted to please her, and the more he tried, the less accepting she was.

One evening after a rough day of sitting with his cranky father, Jules asked Delphine where she lived.

"Upstairs in the servant's quarters. It's easier for me."

"Well, we could pool our meager funds, lease a place nearby. Of course, I would expect nothing of you in return." Jules was lying. Sort of. He did expect something in return. He wanted to amuse her, maybe make her smile. And he wanted her somewhere close. He searched for an apartment within walking distance of his father's.

He found a walk-up on the Ile St.-Louis, the island spreading the Seine's thighs. Delphine brought her valise; he left his paints in the garbage. They now lived at the cartographic center of Paris, where, just across the water, the ruins of St. Julie-le-Pauvre crumbled, and beyond, the sooty quartiers of Montparnasse sloped to the clouds. Downriver, Notre Dame winked at their sinful (yet necessary) cohabitation.

Jules was not miserable, even as his father's health declined, and he started writing down his thoughts during his meager hours of freedom. He began with criticism about his favorite poets, then moved onto breezy essays and nonsense narratives (he wouldn't dare let anyone read those notebooks!). He also wrote poems about Delphine. It was better than painting on canvas; Jules now mixed colors with his words, describing his visions with ease; he no longer needed a paintbrush and pigments as he recorded his troubled and hopeful thoughts.

Every day, the couple journeyed to Father's home. They were a team as they began their days, climbing into the pirogue they moored to an iron ring at the bottom of the quai, paddling the jaunty yellow craft downstream to the quai de Tuileries. Delphine was stern; he was bow. After tending to Father, they returned home each night to their "fortress," rowing with more difficulty against the flow of the river.

One warm morning, Delphine wore her bathing costume, packed her clothes in a basket. A galaxy of freckles formed on her shoulders in the sunlight. The couple coasted downstream, Jules ruddering his paddle, and every time they passed under a bridge, Delphine stood and kissed the pilings, hoping as she said, "For good luck." When they sculled under each overpass, he watched in amazement as she'd stand, kiss her fingers, then caress the mossy bricks.

Le pont Royal, le pont du Carrousel, le pont des Arts.

Transfixed bystanders stood on the bridges and applauded the beautiful spectacle—a pair of young sweethearts drifting down the Seine in a yellow boat, fornicating in broad daylight.

#

In those last days, when he sat in his father's room, there was no indication the sickly man was aware of anything. Jules leaned in and lay his head on the bed covers, breathing in sync with his father's shallow, water-gurgled breaths. In those last hours, the man's fingers groped, sought out something. Maybe, finally, Father wanted comfort. Jules grabbed his father's scrawny hand, but he jerked away and huffed. Taciturn Father.

In the end, in his delirium, Father was somewhere else, someone else. He outstretched his arms, humming and gesturing, sawing a bow across his chest as if he were playing an invisible violin. His father's glazed eyes took cues from a phantom conductor as he nodded and swayed. And Jules imagined he heard a Bach concerto, a murmur of a full orchestra. But he wasn't sure, and he fell asleep, exhausted after two days with no rest.

When he awoke, the candles had burned down, and Father was cold.

#

Burial arrangements for a famous patriarch and magnate called for pomp and circumstance.

On the day of his father's internment, after a funeral Mass, a cortège carted the man's remains across the faubourg to the cemetery. The procession wound its way through Paris, the slow-walking Belgian Blacks' heads dipping, their feather-plumed headdresses swaying to a four-beat gait, the hearse's driver steering the black reins. The only sound? The horses' somber clopping. Jules followed the carriage on foot behind the praying priests. Curious crowds fell in and out of the parade.

Outside their palatial home, along the route on the sidewalk, Delphine stood with her parents; they had dressed for the occasion in their fine clothes. Delphine wore her usual white. And, as Jules passed, he smiled, but she did not see him. Instead, she gazed dreamily at the coffin inside the carriage; Delphine's upturned, golden eyes radiated pleasure. Oh, morbid Delphine with her death fascination!

At the family mausoleum, the gates opened, and the pallbearers carried his father's coffin inside, placing him on a catafalque. Jules turned away. There was no way to say a proper goodbye to a man who had hated him. And Jules did not want to reciprocate those feelings; he did not wish to abhor his father.

#

After the funeral, Jules returned to Father's empty home, and a courier knocked on the door. A blue-uniformed man produced a telegram out of a pouch. It was from Isobel:

```
=SYMPATHIES
REMEMBER HE NEVER CARED
SOON
ISOBEL=
```

Jules went upstairs to look around his father's now-empty room. He curled up—fully clothed, shoes tied—on the deathbed. And he thought he once again heard Bach, and even if the nurses had stripped the bed and there was just the bare mattress, Jules made himself comfortable and fell asleep, forgetting he had agreed to meet Delphine.

#

The attorney's office was plush. Lots of burgundy velvet, deeply tufted chairs. The drapes were open, but the room was dark anyway. It felt evil.

"If you'd be so kind as to sit here at the desk. We will read through everything. You will initial the pages as we go." The fawning lawyer motioned to the maple desk. So many rumors had already spread through Paris about the great Lalande's last will and testament. No one had ever seen an estate with so many codicils and addenda. As the only progeny and son of the great man Lalande, Jules received the remains of the vast railroad fortune: 47 bank accounts, investments in over 345 profitable businesses, five family homes in Switzerland and Paris and England, art treasures—crates and crates of them.

There was a more recent codicil of the will, added just weeks before his father's demise, something of which the lawyers were adamant. If Delphine remained in Jules's life, he would receive nothing:

> *Moi, Vicomte Jean-Louis Lalande de la Marche, citoyen français et suisse à double nationalité, déclarons que c'est le codicille de mon testament, qui date du 16 mai 1913. J'ajoute ou modifie mon dernier testament comme suit: si Jules Lalande, mon fils, est en quelque sorte affilié à Delphine Folin, il ne sera plus bénéficiaire de ma succession.*
>
> *Sinon, je confirme et republie mon testament, daté du 4 janvier 1902, à tous égards autres que ceux mentionnés jusqu'ici. Je souscris mon nom à ce codicille ce 16 mai 1913, au 27 Avenue Rapp, Paris, en présence de Me André Clément, Avocat, et de Léo Adolphe Amette, cardinal et archevêque*

de Paris, attestant des témoins, qui attribuent leurs noms ici en ma présence.

[I, Vicomte Jean-Louis Lalande de la Marche, a dual citizen of France and Switzerland, declare that this is the codicil of my will, which dates from May 16, 1913. I add or change my last will as follows: if Jules Lalande, my son, is somehow affiliated with Delphine Folin, he will no longer be a beneficiary of my estate.

Otherwise, I confirm and republish my will, first dated January 4, 1902, in all respects other than those mentioned heretofore. I subscribe my name to this codicil this 16th day of May 1913, at 27 Avenue Rapp, Paris, in the presence of Mr. André Clément, Lawyer, and Leo Adolphe Amette, cardinal and archbishop of Paris, attesting witnesses, who ascribe their names here in my presence.]

His father had seen more than Jules had suspected, even at the end. And those vampiric lawyers would soon visit Jules and Delphine's "love nest" on the island. They informed Jules if she did not vacate their apartment by the end of the week, then he would forfeit all monies and assets.

"Monsieur, we shall bring the gendarmes for verification that you are no longer cohabitating."

Jules made his way home in the heat; the boulevard was broad and sweltering, then the river stream was choppy. He paddled with all his might against the current. How would he tell her? He walked in and gazed upon her naked skin. She was on the carpet, reading a book. He explained vast wealth awaited, but only if she were no longer there.

"I cannot have any of it—I cannot have it if I am with you," Jules winced as he spoke. It sounded so mercenary. But it *was* true.

"So, you've chosen money over love?" She flung her book at his head. It grazed his temple. Now he knew what he wanted. He had not known until the instant Delphine confronted him—he would go ahead with his plan. He'd pretend to pitch her away.

"No. I've devised a strategy."

#

Delphine was too precious to toss away as if she were the contents of a full ashcan. Yes, he wasn't sure he could live without her just as he couldn't live without air.

And so, Jules heeded the mandate, but only for appearances. The next morning, they made a public show of their separation in public on the street.

"I'll miss you, *mon chou*." Delphine carried her tattered suitcase, a blue cap plopped on her head. They embraced in exaggerated gestures. She tripped down the row, and the neighbors who watched from their windows confirmed the parting later to investigators. Yes, they witnessed the two lovers' goodbye kiss, a sad farewell for all time. She stayed with her parents.

Probate was straightforward, and Jules received his wealth. Who would check on whether he'd obeyed his father's express wishes after-the-fact? The attorneys were as happy to rid themselves of any trace of his father as Jules was. And the estate paid them a hefty sum, after all.

#

Three months later, Jules took a long-term lease on a grand home, it spanned a half-block and rose four stories over the boulevard. It was lavish. Delphine's room alone was an auditorium with its blue silk walls, pale chartreuse brocade drapes, and an entire wall of mirrors. The opulence suited a golden creature like her.

Jules wrote for three hours every morning and two hours in the afternoon.

And Delphine left healing behind, found a new passion. Sculpting overtook her—she studied with an aging instructor at the l'Académie de la Grande Chaumière. Monsieur Fyot admired her beauty, but, well, he was not as enthusiastic about her work.

One evening, she arrived home apoplectic. The old sculptor had told her she was more likely a painter, "*Très fine et très fraîche, il faut chercher la vérité.*" She finished a bust of Jules in the evening and never touched the sculptor's clay again.

Nonetheless, their lives settled into a routine of art. Every night, Jules performed Baudelaire for her, read each poem with care. They recited to one another in bed. And Jules soon took to the idea of receiving company in his pajamas.

"There exist but three respectable beings, the priest, the warrior, and the poet. Delphine, what do you want me to be?"

"A poet, of course." Jules completed a new batch of poems soon after. Inspired by the *les poètes maudits*, he wrote of death and love.

They made new acquaintances, too. The faubourg St. Germain opened itself to them, but they were suspicious of the *ancien regime.*

One such lady invited Delphine to her home.

The comtesse sat propped in a colossal bed against a mountain of lace pillows. The bed-ridden noblewoman jangled a small silver bell nestled on the nightstand; she rang it for the entirety of Delphine's morning visit. The servants never responded, yet there was a stream of dark-coated suitors pacing outside the woman's boudoir. The comtesse chose to ignore the men and bragged on her own poetry to Delphine, who balanced on the edge of a silk chaise.

"My poetry is divine; anyone will tell you this." The woman handed a slim volume of her work to Delphine. After ringing her bell one last time and receiving no answer, she *harrumphed* and dismissed the young woman, then rolled over to doze. Delphine tiptoed out the side entrance, avoiding the gigolos in the corridor.

#

The publication offers for Jules did not rush in. But he soon rectified the problem. The simplest way to publish a book was to print it oneself. After all, his father had left him a print shop (one of many enterprises still functioning after the old man's passing), so it wouldn't be challenging to commence. Of course, this endeavor would not suit the whims of temporary backers. It would not produce flyer manifestos to be handed out on street corners; no, Jules wanted his words read by the public at large, by poor workers willing to devour something scandalous.

On the Left Bank, off the place de Furstenberg, he found the print shop his father had passed onto him.

Through the dusty window, Jules spied a bored man sitting at a long empty table, a man with the face of a plump fowl and the waddle of an old turkey. And so, Jules went in and introduced himself to the birdlike Guillaume Morget, who bowed and laughed, squinting through his ink-smeared spectacles. He was a congenial man, agreeable to allowing Jules to take on the task of printing books.

"*Oui, oui!*" They shook hands to seal the deal.

Though he had never attempted to print an entire tome on his ancient hand press, Morget was enthusiastic, interested in publishing something more challenging than sales notices and funeral announcements. The two were a perfect partnership. Jules penned a press declaration:

LA CHORALE D OISEAUX PRESSE |A CHORUS OF BIRDS PRESS|

We will bring you utter nonsense. You will
discover the sun hiding on staircases when it is
raining in courtyards. Contact other merchants on
other corners if you have complaints. We are too
busy and perspicacious to worry about pettiness.
Birds will not sing alone here. We are in their
choir. Join us. Indecency is good. So is your
childhood bedroom and pinafore.

For Jules's book, the first for the press, Delphine took charge. She was sure she could interpret Jules's vision into a pleasing design. Morget followed Delphine's plans scrupulously, not only the typography, but her request for dark mahogany ink on deckled paper.

"*Magnifique, magnifique*! But it will be *très cher* just for the paper alone, and for italics, we must buy special typeset, you know."

"Monsieur Morget, you know money is no object."

Every night, Delphine and Jules composed poems for each other in their separate beds and for their press. They met in the kitchen for dinner, sent the cook away. And they'd read their work to each other, then make love on the tile.

Soon, they forgot about the press, though, and moved onto more exciting endeavors.

#

Jules wanted to try anything. Why not? Schopenhauer's words inspired him: "Social rules are made by normal people for normal people, and the man of genius is fundamentally abnormal."

No one had finalized the rules of human relationships; no one had defined them. Not yet. Nothing was "normal."

At cafés, Delphine and he had a game. Jules would stare fixedly at an attractive woman at another table. Then, he would leave Delphine's side to go sit with the woman. He'd engage in casual conversation with the female, speaking low, while locking his gaze on her. After only a few moments, she'd rise and leave—forgetting either her purse or gloves, often abandoning a companion or a party or even a husband. And Jules would follow her to an alley or a hotel. Somewhere secluded for copulation.

Yes, Jules seduced them as casually as he would pluck a

flower for his buttonhole.

When he talked to someone, anyone, his charm turned on like a bright beam. It was hypnotic, magical. There was no fakery, no con. No one had a choice other than to fall in love with him—if he wanted them to fall in love with him.

#

Next door to Jules and Delphine's home, at the end of the street, a prestigious art school concealed behind tall shrubbery. Students would spill out the gates every afternoon after their life-study classes and gather in groups for cigarettes, chatting close enough to Jules's writing window so he could eavesdrop on all the juicy gossip. One day, when the conversation below was dull, and words would not come to Jules, when he found himself not able to rhyme or compose any lyrical language, when his pages remained obstinately blank, he called down to a few students, invited them up for a drink.

"*Tous*?" one called back to him

"*Bien sûr*."

A class of 27 boys stomped up the stairway. Delphine chuckled, sent a couple of the lads for a cask of wine from the bistro around the way. For glasses, they drank from cachepots, old inkwells, even a thimble. They were polite and full of mirth. Delphine invited them back for the masquerade ball.

"Bring anyone you want. Especially women."

#

No other party of the decade could compare to the

ribaldry of Lalande's masque. The evening of the ball, a nude, gilded Delphine appeared in the courtyard riding bareback on a donkey. And Jules, her attendant, walked alongside wearing a brace of unplucked squab as a neckpiece. Resplendent in his dead jewelry, he hauled a canvas sack of live snakes. Jules proceeded through the crowded rooms, swishing a paintbrush dipped in red ochre across all the student maidens' naked bosoms. He even grabbed one of the orchestra's violins and played a jolly jig. Jules was unsure where he learned to play a fiddle.

Reckless, raucous.

Absinthe, gin.

An orgy of bodies.

Drunken students freed the snakes from the bag and wore the serpents like living bracelets around their wrists, the reptiles writhing through the fête, slithering across body armor costumes. Soon, everyone was naked, and the guests coiled around one another in the large foyer in another reptilian spectacle; they doused each other with champagne pouring from the fountain, copulating with whatever body was close.

Jules awoke the next morning to the stench of sex and dead animals and peered out the window to see a young woman, shining in the sunlight, tenderly offering her breast to a snake.

#

The rains came. And they did not halt. No respite of sunny days. Their neighbors worried; they griped. The torrents doused the city for weeks—the Seine rose and transformed the tranquil banks through the heart of town.

The lashing overflow from the northern feeder streams—the Marne, the Essonne, and the Yvonne—poured into the Seine. The river raged past the boot tops of the stone soldier sculptures of the le pont d'Alma. Of the four figures in the stone relief, the uppermost Zouave was the marker for flood-crisis stage. At first, the waters rose as high as the Zouave's ballooned pantaloons, then to his chest, and then the torrents drowned the figure's beard, swallowing the Zouave and submerging the bridge. Most of the city swam underwater. The archbishop, Jules's father's dear friend, marched to the river's edge toting a nail from the true Cross, dangled the spike over the currents, and intoned the waters to recede. And they did.

Jules and Delphine were lucky—the flood spared their home; the surge stopped two feet from their door. Only le pont Neuf and le pont Royal remained passable during the water's tenure. Rowboat transport was the only means of travel along many streets of the faubourgs adjoining the Seine. The next road over was underwater, and the beloved Ste. Clothilde flooded, too. Many of the fancy locals had no heat or electrical lighting, but a surprising number of citizens hunkered down in their damaged homes during the deluge. There was no epidemic of waterborne illness, which was a miracle.

From their dry perch on the third floor, Jules and Delphine observed the footmen and maids rowing their wealthy employers back and forth; soaked yet regal, they floated to each other's front doors for visitations and social engagements. It was as if Paris transmogrified into Venice. If parties were planned, then, by God, parties would be given and attended.

\#

Soon after the flood, Jules began to suffer attacks of vertigo; when objects fell from his hand, he felt he, too, was about to fall. He feared his midnight walks in the cemetery. At the corner of the street one night, he witnessed a neighbor drop a book to the ground, and his eye compulsively followed the falling object. He felt dizzy the whole walk home and had to lean against the side of the building to arrive indoors safely.

\#

They had smoked many times, but never in an establishment. Delphine wrapped herself in a maroon cloak. The cab moved out of the faubourg, their stylish arrondissement, then through a rundown neighborhood, where a factory on the river spewed vapor into the night.

They drew up to the curb and rapped on the glass of a house with no number, its ominous façade contusion-colored. A Chinese servant answered the door. The interior was barely visible behind the man; a street lamp across the road illuminated shadowy surfaces inside, which were all dusty. Another servant shuffled up in silk slippers and bowed deeply. There was incense—an acrid odor, mysterious, somewhat sweet.

Through a dark passageway. Down steep stairs to a basement. Delphine and Jules found themselves in a barely-lit room with divans, silk partitions and screens, black cushions, pipe stands on carved stools and side-tables.

Profuse smoke.

An acquaintance glanced up from his couch. His

unfocused eyes, softened by the drug, shifted, and he went back to nuzzling an Asian woman who lay next to him on his pillowed pedestal. The whore limply turned.

A rail-thin French man, the proprietor, sidled up and nodded slavishly. Jules handed him a wad of currency. The man's voice was dry like the flapping wings of an insect.

"Please, please, recline. We will prepare everything for you," the man said.

He scraped over one of the carved tables, brought in a gold-lacquered tray. On an ornately painted plate, accouterments lay assembled in rows. Long, lady-dagger length steel needles and patterned ivory handles; tall, urn-shaped pipes; porcelain candy boxes filled with glossy rocks of the lovely narcotic; a statuette adorned with a necklace of jasmine flowers.

Over a scented brass lamp, they melted the rocks, then Delphine and Jules dipped in the needles, shaped the drops, which shone with iridescence. They let the molten tablets fall into a pipe, set them aflame, and Jules, then Isobel smoked. They went through nine pipes before the evening ended.

"This unravels me," Delphine slurred.

"It's time to go," he said, wrapped her cloak around her shoulders.

"No, one more." But he refused to stay any longer, left her behind, left her swaying in her cloak to the distorted music crackling from the *tourne-disque*. The tune bellowed from behind the embroidered drapes as if it was playing from a long distance.

#

On a June afternoon in 1914, he sat alone in a park, and darkness descended on the day. All the potted flowers, freshly green trees, and ladies' beribboned hats could not brighten the news. Everyone gossiped.

"Haven't you heard? Archduke Ferdinand was shot in Sarajevo."

"Where is Sarajevo?"

"His wife was with him."

"Murdered."

"War."

Over a short period, only three days, assassins shot Jules's Socialist friends in their beds. Or worse. The radicals were stabbed on the street or in crowded bakeries or outdoor cafés. For all to see.

Paris was mobilizing for war.

Jules stumbled through panicked pedestrians, crossed the place de la Concorde, and a poster caught his eye: *Mobilisation Générale*.

In a restaurant, he sipped on his glass of wine by an open window, and the foot traffic paraded by—the War Office had confiscated all the motorized vehicles and carriages; they were transporting thousands of troops. The band in the restaurant broke into multiple choruses of the "Marseillaise," and with each new rendition, every patron stood and raised a glass.

Paris walked. The poor in their tatters, the ladies with parasols, and the dandies with their winkling gold pocket watches and fobs.

#

When news reached Paris that the Germans were in

France, Jules enlisted. He attempted a conversation with now-distant Delphine, but she did not answer his knocks. She clicked the lock.

He slipped a note to her maid:

My dearest D,

I've joined the infantry. It is not my country or war—not yet. But I feel as if I am doing something important. I hope you understand. Please come to me so we may make peace. Before I make war.

J

\#

He watched Paris empty all day, then ate supper alone in the kitchen with the cook. They listened as an unnerving silence fell over the city. The glasses in the storage pantry tinkled from the buzzing of *les vindangeurs*, the nocturnal garbage collectors, as the workers' vacuums sucked bilge from septic tanks. He had never noticed the noise before. Now the metropolis was a ghostly place.

He mounted the steps to retire. At the end of the corridor, he saw Delphine had left her door wide open, so he stole into her sweet-smelling chambers where he heard the tap running in her bath.

"Delphine?" No answer.

"Delphine?" No reply. He waited for minutes, then water trickled under the door—it was a decided claret tint.

"Delphine!" He tried the handle. Locked. He first pushed with his shoulder, then ran and rammed into the solid barrier. It finally gave. There, in the sunken tub, marble glinting burgundy and slick with blood, Delphine's body floated. Her eyes were open, but unseeing; her wrists split like sliced fruit; her veins drained. What had she done! In his full suit with shoes on, he tumbled into the red water and tried to revive her, commanding, "Don't!"

But it was too late.

He held her one last time, sat in the full tub cradling her for a long time, clasping his arms around her chest to maintain her buoyancy, her body floating limply, legs bobbing like two dead branches in a river, her burnished hair, now stained pink, flashing in the dark and cold water. His gorgeous Ophelia.

✳

JULES TRAINS FOR BATTLE

He'd already enlisted, so he decided to relinquish the lease, bury Delphine. It wasn't difficult. With money, anyone could do anything expeditiously.

He felt nothing. The days were full of marching, smoke, and guns; ruffians spitting and shitting and pissing and talking stupidity and eating horrendous food. There was no poetry there.

But he did not question. Killing a stranger would surely be more natural than killing someone he knew.

He walked through the days with ease; they were days other men might find painful or repressive. The tediousness was a relief. Monotony a salve.

Jules only felt shattered by the world after the sun went down.

He dreamed of dreaming, of lying in a strange bed in a strange land, of a gold-painted woman calling to him for help, a woman Jules was not sure he loved or even liked, and no matter how many monsters he fought, he could not save her.

＊

JULES LALANDE AT THE FRONT

They took fire from the Germans. Jules sat entrenched with his battalion, buried in the front-line foxholes they continued to dig for fear their furrows weren't deep enough. It proved futile, preventing the enemy from crossing the Meuse River, whose waters encircled and traveled through the region much as the Germans had. Now the French waited, hunkered down in miles of devastated farmlands.

In the late winter morning, an inky fog blew in soft sheets off the water to blanket Verdun. Soon, the sun would try to push the mist away, and the curtain of haze would filter off, revealing an epic battle stage behind. Most days were the same: performances with Jules cast as an actor in the best theater in the world. War.

Like any other day on the Front, there was no sleep, and all one could hear were the echoes of death. Yelps of untended men with bits blown off. Chattering teeth in the dampness. Slow clanks of turning machinery. Slops of mud splattering under ambulance wheels.

Half in, half out of his trench, Jules sat and cleaned his gun with methodical strokes, pushing dirt out of mechanisms and contributing his own grit to the already weighty air. As he bent to fetch a fresh rag, something caught the edge of his sight. He looked east. A spot of black sifted through the sky as if heaven was shaking a speck of pepper from the firmament.

The blotch gained speed. As it neared the earth, it grew larger, clearer—it was a red-tipped blackbird plunging to Earth. The creature had trussed its wings as it dropped, and it came down like a bullet.

Jules wondered at a bird's power to fall—an animal winging first into an ascent, and at the high point, twisting around and facing gravity with abandon, diving with no fear, just play. In childhood, Jules had often spied mischievous birds who, after last heaves up through the air, shifted direction, pointing away from the cumulonimbus, and they would spiral earthward, only unfurling their wings at the last moment of their death-defying plummets. They'd then kite over the grass, gliding, ruffling in the breeze as they came to a casual stop. They made it look so effortless.

This kind of avian show was what Jules expected on the day he watched the blackbird tumble. The bird surely would open its wings to fly. But it never did. It never fanned its feathers as others had, never glided anywhere. After the bird's long coil from the shuttered clouds, it did not recover. It *kerplunked* onto the frozen field, twitched, then lay immobile. Without hesitation, Jules dropped his gun and scrambled from the protective berm, and, in the middle of the bleached clearing, he knelt and cradled the fragile bird in his hands.

The animal's weathered feet pointed to the heavens from which it came, its head flopped about on an elastic neck, and its yellow lids, tiny and creased, were as motionless as the frigid air. Jules crouched and breathed on the tender bird, rumpling its downy breast with his exhalations; he could not accept it would never recover its mildness, it would never again pull worms or peck at winterberries.

Didier, his comrade, pleaded with Jules and hunkered deeper inside their trench.

"Take cover! *Mon dieu,* you'll get shot through the head!" But Jules ignored his friend's entreaties and remained with the bird, holding it, and murmuring and intoning prayerful words he'd learned in childhood, words he thought he had forgotten long ago. A warm tingling rose up in his hands then; a gush of power raced through his appendages—a sort of prickly heaviness as if he had posed with his arms in one place too long, and they had fallen asleep. Soon, an electrical pulse heaved from the top of his head and flowed straight out the soles of his worn boots, as if lightning had plugged down his spine. Despite intense discomfort, Jules knelt steady, held the bird, and muttered, and the air vibrated with wonder.

For minutes, he rocked and divined over the fragile creature. He did not know why he did it, but he did it nonetheless. He could not calculate how long he sat and prayed, but after a long time, the corpse jerked; its feet twittered; its eyes fluttered. It was alive!

And as it righted itself on Jules's hand, it shuddered, preening behind its left wing, and then it springboarded, lofting into the celestial sphere. Jules straightened, tucked in his shirt, righted his helmet, and marveled. He watched the bird hop onto a lonely, dead poplar, the scarlet of its wings curving into a smile as it perched there. The bird chirruped his thanks at Jules, and off he flew. And, as it rose in a light-hearted, swooping dance over Didier in the trench, the bird let go of its load and shat on Jules's clean gun.

✳

JULES IN BATTLE

The Battle of Verdun. This is most definitely his trench. And though his fellow soldiers don gas masks, he recognizes them.

Everyone's in uniform, buttoned, tidy.

Terror.

Mud. Men in the muck.

Skewed leg of a soldier. It points to Hell; it points in a most unnatural angle. Not alive. Probably not dead.

Medic!

German artillery rounds. Surrounded.

Shells whistling like train cars screeching out of the station. Booms like two heavy iron plates dropping onto each other. Nearby impacts. Concussions. Every minute of every day.

French 75s barking in fast reports, cracking in long, massive jags, then smashing, short and snappy with a punch to them. Soldiers opening and closing their mouths like baby birds in a nest—anything to keep their eardrums from shattering in the deafening racket.

On a bloodstained brancard, a soldier. Right cheek shot away. Right cheek jelly. No jaw, teeth, or lips. His nose plastered in. Or is it his eyelid?

Blood streaming. Boots and boots of it.

The Battle of Verdun.

The roads. Troops on the march. Long lines of multi-axle camions, enormous 280 cannons, ammunition trains, *ravitaillement* wagons, kitchen carts. Miles and miles of vehicles and TRPs and howitzers. Countless columns stretching out of sight beyond the horizon.

Aviation hangars, fields of motor parks, artillery barracks, dug-outs, every conceivable lean-to. All camouflaged. All brown and olive. Low-ranking officers' tiny cars skedaddling at high speeds.

Grating and slow caterpillar-wheeled motor-tractors. Mud-stuck, house-sized mounted guns. Sludge-spattered dispatch riders. Ripping staff cars. Rattling artillery trains rushing along.

Mayhem, mayhem, mayhem. Verdun.

This ravine. Twenty kilometers wide and ten k. deep.

300,000 lost. Traveling stench. Every inch pockmarked. Shell craters and bullet holes.

Salvos for forty days. Sky the color of lead. Mire oozing in the heat last hour. Mire freezing the next.

Shells blasting, spraying debris geysers. Feces-riddled mist. Dead horses rotting. Overturned wagons, spoiled cabbage, moldy bread.

Jules Lalande's battalion. Medic!

But Lalande is Swiss.

He should not be here.

Medic!

Verdun.

✳

JULES LEAVES

By June, the second line trenches outside Verdun fell to the Germans, but neither Didier nor Jules would see the defeat. Shrapnel whizzed into their ditch and smacked Didier in the arm and separated his torso from his spine. Jules folded him back together and tourniqueted his arm. And though his friend was now only mush and shattered bone, he spoke, and his words made sense.

"You're Swiss. Go home," Didier said, and his eyes did not close, they just looked beyond Jules's shoulder and lost all color. Oh, how Jules tried to resurrect him, how he attempted his tricks as he had done with all the battle-injured animals! But, alas, Didier lay in a lake of blood. He was gone. The shells kept firing, landing close or even inside nearby trenches. The sound was beyond all sounds, the sound of death flying by.

And though he was in peril, Jules held his friend for minutes, hoping for the familiar, prickly feeling to invade his arms and hands and body, the sensation he experienced whenever someone presented him with an animal's corpse. He waited and prayed and cried, but the healing never came. He was cold, though it was June and the mud steamed. And then he realized maybe Didier was right.

Jules stood upright under heavy fire, climbed the edge of the battle line, and walked away.

"I am Swiss, I am Swiss, I am Swiss." Hands in the air, he scurried through bullets and missiles.

It was the last thing he remembered.

The medics found him forty-five miles from the Front without any weapons, with no gun or bayonet or dagger or razor, wandering the road, face black, body skeletal, a hole in his helmet. Who knows how Jules got there?

✳

AT THE CABARET VOLTAIRE, JULES FINDS PARADISE

Out of the hospital, Jules hopped an army train. And the soldiers, mostly Brits or Americans, happily let him ride along. He did not know where he was going. He just knew he had to get as far away from the trenches of France as he could. In a one-horse town, close to the border, the local officials arrested Jules as a spy. They tried to send him back to the middle of France. He did not cry. But he gave the lugging officers his saddest, emptiest look—he was not talking.

And lucky for Jules, he had his Swiss papers. The interrogation officers were soon brushing off his jacket and sending him on his way.

Continuing his journey, he found farmers traveling the backroads willing to give him a ride. For long stretches of his journey, he rode in rickety buckboards. And he slept best in hayfields and dirt. Those rustic conditions were optimal compared to muddy trenches taking fire from all directions. He was at peace. Except when he dreamed of the Front.

When he made an entrance into Zurich, it was a momentous occasion. No one lay palm branches at his feet. No, he was more a prodigal son returning home for a feast. Though he had not a penny for a crumb of bread.

It was a gloomy day, but he felt cheerful as if the sun

were high. There was no bustle there as he'd encountered in Paris, no foot traffic, just quiet streets where the *Föhn*, a peculiar dry Alpine wind, aggravated the stones. His head filled with the scent of the mountains, and he made it to the lakeshore, where he sat on a bench and willed away his hunger. The town's pet swans gorged down their feed, bickering and fighting, gliding, nipping at one another. The cygnets trailed behind their mothers in broken lines.

Well, he owned a black suit and a white shirt, something he could use. He fancied waiting tables, but knew nothing of working in restaurants. Except he liked to eat.

He unwrapped his suit from its brown paper wrapping which he'd tucked under his arm the entire journey. Behind the bushes, he dressed, then left his peasant's attire buried under pine straw.

He walked in his oxblood shoes, cast-offs from the hospital. Perhaps no one would notice they did not match his attire. Jules spotted an old cathedral, a pious and upright structure, made his way through the winding streets of Niederdorf, where he inquired at every café for a position.

"Perhaps you had better get yourself to Spiegelgasse," a few proprietors condescended, glancing disapprovingly over their spectacles at his scruffy dress. And when Jules could take the rejections no longer (though, he retained an airiness in his step), he asked for directions to the red-light district. The man he stopped raised an eyebrow, then glanced at Jules's dirty shoes. He pointed the way and shook his head as Jules walked away at a fast clip.

Jules pushed open the door of the Cabaret Voltaire, and a cloud of smoke greeted him as if he were entering a hazy fairy kingdom—it was as if everything a person might see or do there was not real. There were students, deserters, spies, bourgeois, everyone crammed into the pub/gallery/cabaret. It was an extravaganza. Someone on stage recited nonsense: "Gadji beri bin blassa glassala laula lonni cadorsu sassala bim." Everyone talked at once, but no one said anything. The candles sputtered; there were ugly people, ugly sounds, nasty smells, thrown glasses and food, sloshed drinks, burning long pipes, and rude, rude, crude people who kicked and elbowed and screamed and nudged and scratched for a better view of the beloved, defiled, tiny, monumental stage and its garish, delicate, crazy performers. Indeed, Jules was genuinely pleased. He had come to paradise.

#

They never spoke about where they were. They never talked about where they were going. They lived and recited together in a kind of momentary ecstasy. They slept with each other's girlfriends or boyfriends. They did not discuss their latest trysts over tables in the cabaret. No, they talked about their visions for their new nothingness. They even named it: Dada.

#

It was over in a matter of months. Jules had a few more coins in his pocket and a few well-publicized antics under his belt, but Zurich was too provincial now. He'd heard of Francis Picabia and Marcel Duchamp; their antics were legendary. Now it was time to meet them. He'd see if he could get to his banks. Damn war. He couldn't touch his inheritance now. No matter. Off on an adventure!

※

JULES EXPLAINS HAYING

It was late in the summer before Jules embarked for America, and André Breton accompanied him on the train to Lyon. They found their way to Grand-Maman's farm. They set to haying. Well, only Jules. Breton was a lazy man. Jules warned him harvesting hay was a dirty business, like no other. "This is not a meadow. Meadows are for fools and poets."

There were two ways to mow. Back and forth in straight lines, turning at the end of each row in sharp, right angles. It was genuinely meditative work. Jules fell into a trance when he hayed in lines.

Then there was a second way: the continuous method. One started on the outside of the yard with the trimmings flying outward.

Breton watched from the hot shade, and Jules chose to mow in circles. After all, it was the neatest method and prevented debris from messing the long drive and lane. And so, the grass sprayed out of his path. He traveled around and around, cut the meadow in circles toward the center destination into smaller and smaller orbits of field. It was dizzying.

Of course, the most appealing aspect of mowing in circles was its rapidity. Jules could move the scythe until his arm tired, steering on a curve until there was just a high patch left to the middle of the growth, untouched and scraggly like a Mohawk Indian. There was no stopping or turning with the circular method, no making sure his rows were straight. It was one continuous jag.

But those loopy shortcuts didn't look as clean to the eye as the more exacting and time-consuming rows. No, not at all. Like life. And he knew in his heart he had taken the easy route.

When they completed the afternoon work, with Breton mainly watching with the rest of the workers, Jules found himself wanting to rid the trees of their loneliness, and he left for the woods, still haunted, and faced the crossroads.

※

JULES MEETS TOMMY FLOYD

After the first-round bell, Jules didn't remember anything, but he knew to take his blows. And when Tommy delivered the last counter jab, followed by a quick, deadly uppercut, when the big boxer sliced open Jules's chin like a filet, he, the self-made poet and painter, fell, then sputtered a molar onto the mat. The outmatched Swiss man was smart, though; he stayed down until he heard the last word of the count. Ten.

When the referee announced the bout had ended by knockout, Tommy Floyd, the man who'd been the fierce boxer just moments before, came from his corner to offer Jules assistance and shake hands. He bent down, lifted Jules to his feet as the hoots grew menacing. The mob's jeers went to both corners:

"Go back to your Alps, fucking fruit!"

"Twiddle diddler!"

Tommy smiled.

"Whaddaya say? Get a drink?" he whispered in Jules's ear, spitting from the sides of his mouth. The two men ducked epithets and debris the audience threw into the ring. The mass of unwashed people grew wilder, menaced closer, and Tommy grabbed Jules's shoulder and pushed him to safety. "Move!"

Jules had a new friend.

In the bar, the air was rancid. Cheap women wearing cheap perfume, toothless drunks occupying every other stool. It was Jules's kind of place! He could rub a palm up a whore's warm thigh as he twiddled under her skirt. He and Tommy drank and laughed until late. And with no prompting, at the end of the night, Tommy, the immense boxer, ran an unexpected, tender finger down Jules's cheek, then sniffed and leaned over to breathe in the Swiss man's scent. They both shivered. And Jules forgot all about the prostitute on his knee.

#

BOXER STATUE: A POEM

Beneath my puffing lids, I trance and toss
Titleholder eyeballs
From ear to ear only after
I inspect a crowd
Collected almost by happenstance.
Dockworkers and doorkeepers and magistrates
And a few starlings, too.

Oh, but in the motley place,
There is the man there on the mat
Who, at first limpid word,
At first laughter of his flesh,
Is foolishness. Ha!
I have torn asunder, bruised.
He exposes himself
And I recall the time I bent up
For the evening beside my medicine ball.
A child-man in love with rubber.
An omnivore.
In the company of this blanched statue whom
I savor and purr with my ocean eyes,
I venerate his palm like a sacred bowl.
But his abdominal mile is my
Favourite attraction.
~JL, 1919

#

Tommy and Jules attended every operetta on "The Great White Way," drank bootleg liquor at every reception, called on every arts patron in town. They were quite the sensation. Especially after Jules's well-publicized stunt.

In a Midtown gymnasium, retrofitted for a theatrical revue, Jules stood on the stage and pissed into the hoity-toity crowd—as he had in Zurich. In New York, though, the police arrested him, then released him the next day. Oh, how the audience members (especially those soiled by the performer's urine) spoke in detail about their ordeal to the newspapers, to all their moneyed friends!

"That Lalande fellow is a base individual, not suitable

for our society." Yet, Jules continued receiving invitations to their gatherings.

Jules added to his dramatic repertoire, including literary "readings" and on-the-spot paintings—many of the works he produced were copies of well-known pieces. He could scrape together a landscape in ten minutes, a portrait in twelve.

Wealthy fans sent their chauffeurs around to his dumpy apartment; they showered him with expensive clothes. And they offered him envelopes of bills and more chances to perform. He was a sensation, the talk of uptown and downtown.

No one ever saw Jules and Tommy apart.

#

A POESIE—FOR FLOYD

And while meliphagous
In the glow of your loving,
Our tangled
Waistcoats entwine,
My darling bee
I follow your vast range
And your colors
And in an amalgam
Of Floyd, elephant-seal
And wardrobe
Our arms glisten like watered silk.
Fuck—fuck! The beat
Of the breeches
In the final

Jolting
Spasm!
~JL, 1919

✳

JULES GETS INTO MORE TROUBLE

It was not a bustling party. The bootleggers had shorted the host, and a dearth of alcohol equaled a not-so-jolly soiree. Anyway, Jules felt positively out of place with American society sorts. He stood behind a melodeon in the corner, while gregarious Tommy chatted up the ladies. Lower Fifth Avenue, Gramercy Park. He peered out the window at dusk; the streetlamps flickered, and cars, silver and shined, lined up outside the curb with their foreign chauffeurs waiting. Taking one last drag on his butt, he flicked his burning cigarette into the top of a preposterous hat worn by a giggling-drunk woman.

Jules made his way outside, and the air smelled dank. Heavy rain was on its way. The wind rushed down the side alley, whistling as if gusting through a mountain pass. He gazed down the row of chauffeurs standing at attention, their jodhpurs pressed and flapping like big elephant ears, then tipped his out-of-season hat, and they bowed. Jules spotted a British-looking chauffeur with a wispy mustache.

"Is that motor car French?" Jules affected a flawless, noble English accent.

"Sir, it is an American automobile," the man smiled and then added with a shrug, "but I have no idea how to drive it!"

"If you'll let me? Get in!" Jules laughed, and the man shrugged again, then slid into the passenger seat.

"It's the damnable choke. You almost break your hand to pull it. I'll try to hold it," the chauffeur said. Jules went to the front and cranked, and, in two turns, the auto spat to a start. He then sat behind the steering wheel and pushed the throttle.

"Well, come on then, let's give it a whirl!"

As they laughed and rocketed toward the Lower East Side, he reached out to shake his passenger's hand.

"The name's Andy Cabe," Jules said.

"I'm Forrester Richmond. Good to meet a countryman."

#

It wasn't tricky to procure base employment in New York, and it was necessary—he had to find something with a salary. Oh, the thrill of the hunt; oh, the thrill of stealing something from a stupid, fat, wealthy American!

His day began as it should; he spent his time grooming: scoured nails, combed hair, pressed pants, shined shoes. His new English accent was a boon.

The servant's entrance off the square was the hardest bit to swallow. Side doors? He preferred grand entries. He sat at the table with the other morning employees and waited for the bells. The summons rang at half-past ten. It was the master of the house, Major Cotton. Jules stepped outside to the carriage house in the courtyard. It was a hot day, and he pulled the roof off the limousine, popped on his hat, then steered the motor car to the front, parked on the street, and waited.

#

The salon to the house was as bright as a surgery theater, and he tiptoed through with a certain reverence on his way to the servants' kitchen. There, over a divan. Jules did a double take. Oh! It was beyond coincidence. He'd intended to nick something, anything, but that particular item's existence was a sign. Yes, he had to take it.

The lamplight illuminated Master Cézanne's painting, the one he'd admired in his youth, the one he brought back to the artist so long ago in Paris. Jules looked around, made sure the drawing room was empty; he only heard the shuffle of maids on the back staircase a few floors up. He lifted the picture off the wall, walked out the front door, down the steps.

In a faraway alley where bums sat around a flame, Jules pondered his next move. The unexpected discovery of his old friend, the painting, had thrown him off-guard. He usually had a plan for his heists. But this situation was different. It was a travesty for someone so greedy—his boss, no less—to possess a painting such as Cézanne's.

Oh, Major Cotton! He did not deserve any painting worth anything. Though wealthy and with the means for benevolence, the major had not even pretended kindness. Every day, Jules witnessed Cotton brutally whipping the family dogs, yet the man also slurped his soup like a cur might lick run-off in the gutter. Such a crude excuse for a human. Major Cotton's bulbous belly was so distended he required bespoke suspenders to buttress his trousers. Those straps were architectural wonders.

But the painting. Such a tender, sad piece. The trees

softly scraped across the canvas in spring colors, the clouds shadowy, lonely, looming. Jules thought about burning it right there, but the world would be empty without it. In the alley where Jules hid, he looked at the poor men warming themselves at the burn barrel. He handed over the painting, the frame and all, to the chap with the saddest face.

"Thank you, sir, it reminds me of my childhood home." The smile Jules received was worth every bit of the trouble he knew was coming. He opened his hands over the fire.

#

They called the jail "The Tombs." And he understood why. It was dark and damp. Something out of Dickens. Death settled into the crooks. And in another dark room beside the sad cell where they had pitched him, the police questioned him for hours about the painting, sure he had sold it to a secret buyer. He would not answer their questions. They threatened him with deportation, a long sentence. But Jules just smiled, made himself into a simpleton, a petty malefactor. Art thief? Why he wasn't smart! They couldn't believe such a mute and dumb man could steal something of such importance.

"Sir, we think you're using an alias. If you don't identify your true self, we'll have no choice but to convict you. Or commit you." The threats were useless. True self? What man knew his true self? They led him away. Justice system? Hah, what a joke. His arraignment would convene in the morning.

He smiled as he went back to his cell. So many men incarcerated in those tombs, those catacombs. A few smelled like they'd bathed in sewers. Others wore elegant overcoats they draped over themselves like blankets. But they all looked dismayed. Jules smiled, yes. He had saved Cézanne's painting from a terrible fate. Nothing was as wrong as a beautiful work of art owned by a brutish man. Dumb men had no business possessing beauty.

Jules slept on the hard ledge. The prisoners came and went. There was the clang of the cell doors, the snores of drunks sleeping it off, the sighs of forgotten men.

In the morning, Jules awoke to a new sound: the jiggling of keys. The cell door squeaked open; the detective stood over him.

"No substantial evidence. Gotta let you go." The scrappy detective wore a garish herringbone suit. With a couple uniformed officers, they pushed him down the stairs, and Jules ran out the double doors into the sunlight.

✳

JULES, WELCOME TO THIS NEW WORLD, THIS AMERICA

In this dream, it all surrounds you! Take a deep breath and smell this outlandish, foreign land, this New York. Take a whiff of baking apple pies in brick ovens; frankfurters steaming in black cauldrons; lime dusting street gutters; stale beer on saloon steps. Sniff at the fresh stack of newspapers, the print's ink still wet; inhale the stink of horseshit, piles steaming in the road; snort the sweetness of rotting fruit sagging forgotten on windowsills.

Look at New York! At the old negro fish monger

squatting to feed raw halibut to a tomcat; at the tinker struggling with his cacophonous handcart of candlesticks, pie pans, doorknobs, trowels, cookie tins, copper kettles, forks, horseshoes, clasp knives, and screws; at the bakers' wives tied up in yellow headkerchiefs and stained aprons; at butchers who cleaver sides of beef, tossing offal into bloody pans; at the hotel bellboys donning black tails; at the Navy shipmen in white linen soiled on shore leave; at the vegetable lady, hands knobbed as roots, hawking her bushels of collards and beets; at the stickly shoe-shine man veiled in a nimbus of pipe smoke, thin rivulets of saddle soap dribbling down his pants.

Prick up your ears to the old Jews, hats pulled low over their sidelocks, their payots bobbing as they peddle trousers and diamonds to passers-by; ignore the calls of paperboys yelling to read all about this morning's news, their black fingers smudged with headlines. Pin your ears back to plump whores arguing, young businessmen tabulating, to new-fangled Model T's toot-toot-tooting, to infants yowling, traffic cops whistling, and silver bracelets jangling on wrists of immigrant women—gypsies, no doubt. This melting pot, this stew, this New York! This place where everything is possible! At least this is what you imagine.

You make your way inside the exhibition tent where the stench is sickening: mildewed canvas, unwashed men who've labored long through the day, liquor, old beer, and piss.

"I'd like to introduce myself as the undisputed heavyweight champion of Switzerland. *Je suis un peindre*, Jules Lalande, *le suisse.*" They do not know there has never been a heavyweight champion of Switzerland. How could they? You appointed yourself to the position. Your voice booms out over the bleachers; your Swiss accent coughs out like phlegm. The throng hurls whatever they can: cigarette butts, bottles, and tobacco spit with high accuracy. Someone even tosses a boot, hitting you on the forehead. But you don't mind. You prance your finely-honed body around the ring as attendants sweep the rubbish away. You taunt.

For hours, for days, you've practiced certain moves, weaving, dodging, watching yourself in the mirror. Your fighter's body is the epitome of art, after all. Or the absence of it. And nothingness is art, too, after all. For you are a genuine artist. At least you think you are.

You know your opponent will beat you bloody, but *mérde*, you've conned your way this far, you will follow through. When else would you ever get the chance to spar with the former Heavyweight Champion of the World, Tommy Floyd, the Georgian Prince, with his purple-black bruises and creamy skin glossy in the opposite corner?

❋

JULES SENDS A LETTER TO THE PARISIAN PUBLICATION, *STOP!* 26 NOVEMBRE 1920

Dearest Friends,

C'est vrai—the postmark—New York! What a glorious, uncivilized place. It suits me to no end! I've compiled this primer for all of you if you ever follow me to the New World. Please, do come!

You will hardly recognize me—I have transformed into

an American. Only English, write and speak only in English. It's the only way. Love to all the ladies.
Sincerely your former fellow European,
Jules Lalande

P.S. The following list is for you, my future émigrés!

Tips for How to Become the Perfect American Gentleman:

— Be a splash or two taller than the cop on the corner.
— Scruff will not do! Shave yourself to a soft boy's fleece. Do it to a fault, morning and evening.
— Part your hair. Middle, side, it doesn't matter, just make sure you grease it with some perfumed nonsense. Make the line across your crown crooked.
— Chew on something all the time—tobacco, gum, or even remnants from last night's supper.
— Like chewing, spit all the time, and at the most inappropriate moments—on your hosts' carpets, in the massive halls, at the "theaters" (note my American spelling) with their slick lobby floors.
— Pick your nose, dig deep with your fingers. Remember, skill at flicking is essential.
— –Dance the waltz or reel or even a jig with knees high and your fly open.
— –Let your money jingle loose in your pockets as you walk down the street, preferably striding with a wide gait.
— –Carouse in bars drinking nothing but cheap beer piled to the rim with a foaming head. Let the froth ferment on your upper lip the rest of the day.
— –Loathe women, even your mother.

- –Concerning your wardrobe, button boots and detachable collars are requisite with all ill-fitting clothes.
- –Haberdashery and suits must be two sizes too big or small. –No bespoke anything, understood?
- Outdated styles are most apt if you are twenty years old or fifty.
- Try to look like your grandfather.
- Wear wool in summer, linen in winter. Kick conventions. Or better yet, kill them completely.
- Spats are keen, especially if you want to look like a boxer and everyone does.
- Bowlers and felt hats are becoming, even for non-bankers.
- Straw boaters are excellent in blizzards.
- And always, always, keep your hat on your head, even in a church.
- Respect and generosity are not as important here as cheek. Remember rudeness reigns.
- Never hold the door for a lady or proffer a light.
- And never, ever thank anyone. Especially if a person has given you something—a cigarette, a steady elbow on muddy terrain. Appreciation is extraneous. After all, you are an American; you have more important things to do.

※

JULES'S LIFE CHANGES (AGAIN)

Soon, Marcel Duchamp wanted to meet Jules. He'd

heard all about the antics, the outrageous performances, the stint in jail. And they became fast friends. Duchamp was without peer.

And then one night, they attended a poetry reading. It changed everything. At least for a night or year or decade.

A nude, freckled creature recited her poetry with postage stamps affixed to her nipples and a newspaper undergarment barely crumpled between her legs, her unruly mound of hair poking out on all sides. The woman turned her sapphire eyes (or were they black?) on Jules, and his legs almost buckled. Oh, he recognized the sweet hardened star of pain: Isobel.

#

Isobel was England. Isobel arrived. Isobel would become America.

Isobel, she walked in, and Jules forgot his infatuation with the boxer champion. Isobel, across the salon, the big hat a black swan upon her head. Isobel, with a sparkly ouche attached to her shoulder strap, the emeralds and diamonds shimmering on her creamy skin. Isobel, she fluttered at Tommy with his arm latched to Jules's elbow. Isobel, a saunter forward and a suck at the tip of her forefinger like a sullen child.

Isobel, her penthouse. The expensive paintings, the heavy sofas, Buhl cabinets, inlaid dressers, bewitched ottomans, the satins overlaying velvets. Isobel, the softly knitted braid of hair untwined onto the floor: the pearls, a lasso, the brooch, a buckle. Isobel, the harmony of voice and movement, the pointy bone of her clavicle, the blue freckle on her left buttock. Isobel, her sheer silver dress, the sweet, fragrant nosegay.

Isobel, the signature, the calligraphic painter's hand, the register: *New York State, December 7, 1919, Isobel Lalande, wife. Jules Lalande, husband.*

✳

JULES LALANDE RETURNS TO THE SEA

He advertised in flyers; he posted bills in all the galleries. An event at the shore. "Saturday, May 3, Noon. Come. Prepare yourself for an amazing sight. Be sure to bring opera glasses!" He also ordered formal-style invitations. The borders around the edges of the stationery were colorful—red, blue, green. Child's colors, a thematic touch, bright like party balloons.

Filling the inflatables was an arduous task. Jules had bought the balloons in a corner toy shop and stolen the helium tank from the shop's storeroom. One by one, Jules blew them up. After inflating over two hundred balloons in the warehouse of a close friend of a close friend, he stowed them in a net pen, tethering them with fishing line. He then fashioned a crude seat out of a caned chair (sturdy enough to hold the weight of a 200-pound man) and affixed it with rope to the flock of balloons. He anchored the contraption to a truck bed, and Jules and Isobel rode with their delivery all the way to the seashore cliffs.

The crowd waited below, pinned beneath a glary noon light, diamond flecks for faces, tiny baskets splayed across the sand and grass. Women stood in the tall sea oats in their long sherbet-colored dresses; the men held their straw boaters with both hands against the gusts of early May.

Scores of birds dipped and raided the sand. A solitary sandpiper hopped near Jules after he pulled the truck into the clearing on the cliff. The blanched bird cried out; its rapacious, sideways eyes filled with suspicion.

Oh, the porous and greenly translucent ocean as delicate as a butterfly's wing! The clover on the bank was rampant, too; the swollen heads slewed like waves. And the beach glittered in front of the long shoulder of rocks; it was a black collar tatted out of stone and shade running as far as the eye could see.

Jules smiled; it couldn't be a better day for the performance he had planned. He spoke into his giant megaphone, aimed it toward the crowd on the beach, bowed and made sure everyone saw him point to his wife standing next to him.

"Madame, I am ready." He handed her the megaphone, and she responded in her dark, concerned tone—a real stage voice was never more resonant.

"Please, if you climb too high, use this to deflate a few, and you shall return to us in safety." She knitted her brows in mock fear and pulled a long, sharp comb from her locks, handed it over to him with a flourish and a whoosh of obsidian hair. The scent of jasmine lifted in the breeze. She stood aside.

Jules climbed into his seat on the truck bed, then toed and poked with his foot until he slid off the weights anchoring the balloons. The floating invention hesitated in the stiff wind for a moment. And then it soared. Oh, how his father's friend Santos Dumont would have loved the sight! A grown man riding children's balloons. Pink, orange, green, blue, red. The clouds were so easy to reach, and the onlookers clapped, and before he had lifted more than forty feet, he took his wife's comb and poked at the balloons as quickly as he could.

Pow. Pow. Pow.

He descended smoothly, landed on the beach below, and the crowd rushed down the path to meet him.

He stood with his back to the sea, his arms outspread, the sky a massive block of gray-purple with a storm looming. His snowy shirt shone. He announced his purpose for the anticlimactic scene.

"As you can see, man is not meant to fly in the air. All those silly aeroplanes are a waste of our time. We came from the sea. And we shall return to the sea." Then, Jules flung off his shirt and pants, tossed his white bucks at a stout man who did not look amused. But what did Jules care? Naked and unabashed, he grabbed a woman who was not his wife, and they went into the water together—she was fully clothed. As they bobbed and embraced in the waves, the avant-garde gaped, confused. They did not join him and the woman. *Is the water too cold,* Jules wondered? His plan had fallen through.

The murmurs were of discomfort.

"Do we watch this, too?"

"Is this part of what he wanted us to see?"

The answer was yes: they'd heard of his capers, so, of course, they were confident they were witnessing a show.

The audience dissipated then, stepped over the rubber balloon debris fluttering across the beach sand; the cheerful colors mixed with sea froth. The ladies stepped as fast as they could to exit the strange showing, puffing open their parasols to avert attention from the inappropriate behavior in the water.

"Such nonsense."

The spectators departed for the comfort of their expensive hotels down the road. They attended the usual afternoon tea and contraband cocktails. But it did give society something to talk about for the long, sweltering summer season. And Jules's legend was secure.

❉

JULES DREAMS HIS LIFE

He walked out. The door clicked with finality behind him. But not before he left his key alongside a note on the table in the foyer:

> *Isobel,*
> *We are done. I can no longer tolerate you. My*
> *departure is not negotiable. Stay away!*
> *J.*

He made his way to Florida on the train, stayed only a few months, was happy to leave the alligator-infested state behind.

And then to Texas. How did he go? There were so many roads! And he spotted automobiles even in the most rural places. Few, but he rode in a handful of the motor cars. And old-fashioned wagons, too. One was a pig cart. The smell!

As the land expanded, he left the forests and rolling hills behind, found himself in the middle of vast distances.

The farmstead work was difficult.

Everything took extra effort in the scorching heat—cutting the balls off bulls, reinforcing fence lines with barbed wire unspooled from wheels as big as buildings.

The drudgery could not dull Jules's anger about Isobel and her malevolence. And then he quit the ranch. He wasn't sure if it was pure instinct. Or maybe it was self-preservation compelling him to leave. He wouldn't forgive himself for any form of weakness, but he pushed through his disgust and ran away anyway. Or maybe he was running *toward something*—Jules was not sure.

The coast.

After a hurricane, he found a small, abandoned sloop, something perfect for one man to sail. And as he navigated the Gulf's waters, with measureless emptiness around him, he felt all his needs, even his wants, dissipate. The sea would take him to undiscovered places. There was no need for Isobel out there on the waves. Life was all about the cutting of the bow, the brisk water and stiff breezes and briny air and the battle against moisture. The wetness would inevitably rust and rot everything. And it would steal everything, too. Maybe he would forget Isobel. Maybe.

#

Breakfast, and the Cuban Señora was busy. Jules sat at the crumb-covered table and ate a heaping plate of eggs, not tasting, not chewing even. He was dreaming about a different life. A newfound existence, one without certainty, without words, without acclaim, with no wives or friends or progeny, with aging señoras and fertile hens and hungry dogs, with nothingness and heat all around him.

At her butcher block, the woman stood quartering birds for lunch, tossing innards to roving dogs in the courtyard. She pitched plucked skin through the door to waiting mutts and then shuffled over to the table, propping one hand on her shelf of a hip.

"*¡Aquí tienes!*" She slid a glass of mountain coffee and two shots of cane liquor in front of him, then took his empty plate. The cavernous kitchen, its whispers of fire, its fecund chickens sleeping on their perches—poised to lay more eggs, he was sure—breathed in calculated, living rhythms. He drank the rest of his liquor and coffee in slow sips. He was thinking just as slowly and did not take his eyes off the woman eviscerating birds at the block. Despite her age, she wasn't in bad shape. Long legs. Like Isobel. Only, the lady was no bedswerver. She was kind, yes, but had a recessed chin, and it marred any real chance she'd had at beauty.

Jules closed his eyes and remembered the letter Isobel had sent him by way of Duchamp. It had reached him while he worked long hours at the ranch. During those tired days, he read Isobel's letter hundreds of times, knew it by heart. With no need for the physical reminder, he burned the note before he packed and moved.

The missive was telling—Isobel's handwriting had lacked her usual *facetiae*. And Jules wasn't sure if the words he could recite from memory tortured him or gave him solace.

#

30 août 1920

J,

If you're reading this, I have found you finally. All I know is you may still be in Texas or the South, as word got out you were in that godforsaken place. I miss you. How I wish we might have spoken before you left. Forgive me, dear cousin.

CATE MCGOWAN

Please. I cannot bear your absence.

Know I love you, *mon chou*. Your child misses you.
With all my heart,
I.

P.S. If you doubt my feelings, here is a poesy I composed
for you.

BUILDING

Your thighs are my vestibule
Where space is unmoving,
Where i will unhook my stiff
Bodice in a swoop, let it drop,
Where i yank off your shoes
And throw my necklace
In haste, and other men
Are shadows, blurred
Cheval glass reflections,
People who've moved away.
Our time is so full of
Scratch and rut and freesia
And clutch, i am not me.
Yes, your limbs are my flights
Of stairs. Your shins the steps
I mount and banister until i reach
The top, duck the ceiling,
Press into your big room,
Whiff cedar, vanilla, cinnamon.

Yes, yes, your jaws are taffeta-lined
Drapes drawing open, then closing.
You nibble, scrape the hearth,
Stoke combustion in the grate.
I press the bell, knock. You dwell
Here, are not home, but soon.

He slid down her handwriting, followed the slopes words into their last night together. They had danced in a bistro, their child asleep in a pram. So slow, her hip bones pushed into his leg, so quiet, her scent redolent of lilies. As they swayed together, she had whispered the truth in his ear. It was something he had never wanted to believe, but knew nonetheless. "I shoved Governess Boyle on the stairs. There were others, too. And a fire. Someday I will tell you everything."

He danced with her a moment longer, but his legs locked up, so he pushed into her for balance. He could not breathe. He had to escape. He stopped and pushed Isobel away.

\#

Following breakfast at the Señora's, Jules purchased two mangoes and chorizo in town for his dinner and packed them inside his creel. Amid the commotion of the market, his feet stung. He glanced down and wished he'd worn his shoes; the grime had combined with his sweat, and it now oozed as mud between his toes. Earlier in the morning on the boat, he thought it a good idea to go shoeless—he'd look more authentic, more like a peasant. Now his feet throbbed from so many nicks.

The bells rang for morning Mass, and women shrouded in black lace shawls shambled their way up the steep church steps. On the dusty road, boys kicked a ball through each other's legs.

Past the melon sellers, Jules slipped down the long alley, and no one noticed him standing outside the bakery window; the lane bustled with foot traffic as the shop filled. Maids jostled each other, hurrying to purchase the day's bread. He was invisible with his concealing costume of a fellow peasant. No one could spot the refined weave of Jules's linen shirt. He congratulated himself for fitting in with the masses.

There, by the open window, he eavesdropped on the baker's widow, Valentina, gossiping about visitors to the town. Lovely Valentina, whom he had charmed during his brief stay, was a woman he knew talked to anyone and everyone. As usual, she was effusive, exclaiming the exciting news.

He understood almost everything the baker's widow said: "A couple, señora, I met them yesterday. *Hombre* . . . and a lovely English lady . . . Isobel . . . *hacienda*." Did Jules just hear his wife's name? Only a trick of the mind. It was most certainly the day's heat affecting him. No, not her name.

He made his way through the pedestrians and market-goers, focused his tired eyes in the glaring sunlight as best he could, and saw colorful posters ruffling up and down the lane. Handbills fluttered affixed to buildings and poles; they imparted a festive air. On the notices, scarlet and orange like holiday flags, there was a rendering of a shadowboxing man with a flat nose and the name, "Tommy Floyd." Yes, there was Tommy drawn in caricature, his pose formidable and exaggerated, his massive head, and there was his body's bulk of muscles, but on the poster, it was all out of proportion.

An advertisement for a fight.

Tommy Floyd was going to box there in Cuba. But why?

And Jules was now sure the heat had gotten to him. Jules had not heard her name. Isobel.

#

There! Riding in a carriage down the street. The big man rode past in one of the town's hired coaches. He was a man from Jules's world. Yes, yes, it was none other than the American boxer, Tommy Floyd, sparring partner, opponent, good friend. Champion.

Panic. If Tommy spotted him, what would Jules say? Jules was a thief and beggar now; he was no one. He was nothing.

Jules slumped behind a yucca garden and checked his disguise, and as Tommy drove the horses by the town's shops, dogs and children scattered out of the road to let the fancy carriage pass. Jules moved under an awning and watched Tommy snap the reins as he made his way up the steep hill road.

Above the town, in plain view, the carriage moved at a fast clip along the switchbacks toward a stucco hacienda. On the hillside crest, at the house, the carriage pulled to a stop, and the tiny figure of Tommy Floyd stepped down.

Yes, Jules could make out the boxer's muscular shape, miniature like a toy soldier. Tommy stood less than a mile from Jules.

Tommy breathing Cuba's bright, cloudless air.

Jules walked along, following the carriage's trail of dust. A subtle, smoky powder clung to the air. He picked up his pace, sprinted the lonely route, hacked in dirty air, but he pushed on.

Faster, he had to get to the big house, had to make sure he was not dreaming. He had to know for sure. Faster.

His heart hooked to his ribs, and as his body ached up the rise, parrots in the sparse jungle screeched and squawked on either side of him—*eeeh-ak, eeeh-eeeh, eeeh-eeeh!* In moments, he mounted the stickled grade and moved past the flat sugarcane steppes; he slipped through a tract of waist-high vegetation, spikes dancing in gusts from the ocean. And when he arrived at the residence, he was breathless with exhaustion and exhilaration, but he kept going, dodging past the parked coach on the gravel drive. The horses remained in their harnesses; they jittered and sweated, heads glistening and bobbling in the afternoon heat. Like the equines, Jules dripped in a bare liquid way.

He crept to the side of the house. His breathing slowed. Calmed. He crouched, skirted low, then crawled on his haunches along the edge of a ravine, concealed himself in undergrowth at the back of the property. He was yards below a balcony. He had to see his old friend, somehow square Tommy's presence. Jules needed to understand. If Tommy spied him, Jules would concoct a good story, and his old boxer acquaintance would welcome a reconciliation.

So, as Jules lay close to the earth, concealed inside the encroaching jungle, in the lush plants, his heart gave way to the quiet. He burrowed his face close to the moist soil, caught the scent of his own fluorescence. He imagined the beetles and bugs below him digging and crunching, going about their business of living. His eyes flittered, almost closed.

But then a thunderclap. Jules jolted upright: a voice shattered his feeling of safety. Isobel's voice. Through the large house's lifted windows, its gaping doors, her speech stung like an open-handed slap. She was calming a baby.

Though he could not make out the words of his wife's distant, precious-sounding talk to the child, there was no mistaking her raspy, dark tones, even out there in the overgrowth and circling bugs. He brushed his face as if to swat at flies, but it was Isobel, her sing-song, he wanted to push away.

It was time to leave. If Jules stayed moored on this island, surely, Isobel and Tommy would see him somewhere in town. But only if he remained. No disguise of his could fool Isobel. She knew them all. And she had mastered what he could not. She had killed what good was inside her years ago. Now, she was a terrifying container of everything. Isobel moved through every moment.

Escape was his only option. Now. But somehow, he could not budge. The truth of it all did not matter as he hid under the house in the swelter of day. He felt an unwelcome rush of unearthed tenderness, an excavated aching traveling the distance, as he peered through the orange orchids and choking vines. If only he could see her face one last time.

He'd had a moment of recognition, a moment of quietness, a revisitation. It all came back. He had loved them. Isobel. And the baby.

"*¿Señor? ¿Señor? ¿SEÑOR?*" a child screamed at Jules. No more than five, the dirty urchin, a dark and shirtless boy, had stolen through the tangled woods and now tugged at Jules's sleeve.

"*¿Señor? ¿Señor? ¿SEÑOR?*" The caretaker's or housekeeper's son, no doubt. And the little monster had found him, was dangerously close to revealing Jules's hiding place. Isobel and Tommy would hear, peer out the window, and see Jules if he could not silence the boy.

"*Shhhh.*" Jules implored and smiled, then motioned for the boy to sit and quiet down. He then held up his hands in surrender, adopted a modest expression, one of defeat. Of course, a grown man could lie anywhere he pleased, in the brush, on the road, in a tree, but the child was suspicious and would not have it. There was no mollifying the boy.

"*¿Señor? ¿Por qué aquí? Yo sé por qué.*" His register reached a high pitch. Louder with each word. Jules held his finger to his lips again to shush the kid. There was a pause, as the boy pondered, then frowned and pointed. And he returned to yelling. "*¡Aquí, aquí, aquí!*"

The boy would surely ruin everything with a scene. Silly, dumb child. Jules's rage was quick, complete. He acted; he didn't think.

He pounced on the brat, his heft knocking the wind out of the boy, then clamped a hard hand over the little one's filthy mouth, and Jules whiffed sour breath and the scent of play. The boy struggled; he scratched and kicked. The smell of crushed leaves was all around them—the sharp odor of ruin, and the child whelped and bit at his fingers; Jules's own blood mingled with the boy's, trickled down his wrists, but he did not relent, no, he seized even tighter as the urchin fought.

Jules's grip tightened on the boy's neck and mouth; Isobel must not discover him. She would not find him hiding, ruined, penniless. The shame. The child kept fighting, and so did Jules. It was a hushed battle of wills and scrap.

It only took moments, a minute, maybe two, of pinching the boy's mouth and nose, of squeezing his neck, of listening to him kick at the fat, creeping plants. There was the crackle of stems under the boy's feet no louder than the sound of raindrops in a deep forest, and then with one last jolt, the child's neck popped. He wilted into Jules's arms. No more heartbeat.

The horror. The child's eyes remained open and questioning, but they clouded over. His last breath bored into Jules's ears, and there was an echo of his struggling whine, of his fast, labored panting. Jules rolled on his back and lay there until his heart slowed, but his senses heightened. He watched sweet-smelling pipe smoke billow from the house toward the understory of trees. And he listened to the plaintive yelps of puppies crying far away in a barn, a high sound like many bells ringing.

Isobel stepped onto the balcony then. So close. But he didn't think she could see him. She stood leaning like a corbel and gazed directly at the spot in the brush where he secreted. He reached up to his scalp. He'd lost his hairpiece. As he'd struggled, he also swallowed the cotton batting disguise tucked inside his cheeks. He was exposed—but she would have seen through his trickery anyway.

Nothing mattered now that he had seen Isobel's face.

Jules covered the dead child with his shirt, the linen dark with stains, and he lay there and wished he were dead, too. Oh, what had he done?

#

He was sure Isobel had spotted him in the brush. And they were not so different, after all. She had killed, and he had murdered, too. He was a hypocrite.

He walked to the water. To the boat. No more lies, no more inconsequential scribbles. He had felt real life in his hands and instead of resurrecting or fostering it, he doomed it to inconsequence.

The waves crashed on the beach ahead. The only right and good sound, and so he followed it.

#

He waded to the sandbar, and as he slogged, he lathered his hands in seawater, rinsing off the dirt and blood. The crimson trickled away into spume; it was the last he'd see of the slain boy. With his back to the sea, with outstretched arms, he opened his bloodstained hands. An offering of contrition.

It was too late when he spied Isobel running across the beach after him, yelling his name. She staggered through the sugary sand and called out to him. But the name she shouted, "Jules! Jules!" meant nothing to him. He would no longer accept himself by his given name. He would never be a monster. He would escape the words and personas and dreams.

Oh, what kind of cavalier was he? The undertow lugged him and gently beckoned him to the boat, to the dock. He swam around the point and reached his sloop, untied it from its anchor and drifted, sails down, furled, then aimed away from shore and out to sea. He gazed back at the island one last time.

His boat wrapped around the surf, and, in response, the

tide spun the hull with a mighty force. The waves embraced him, pulling him toward the center of the world. Sweeping, yes, gradually sweeping him deep and far.

#

The fishing trawler had been out for several days when they found him; his boat long smashed in the currents. The men joked to each other that he was the biggest catch of their season. Some believed the waterlogged stranger's survival was miraculous. It meant hope for their vessel. Others thought he was responsible for the hundreds of fish they'd found already dead and floating. And for the red tide. They were convinced there was a curse upon those who found him.

He was dreaming when they discovered him there, swimming among the fish. The warm sea had washed away his memories. He'd sunk far beneath the surface, surrounded by a school of black grouper, his clean hair a glistening halo, specks of gold flickering in the sunlight like soaked mica stones. It was almost funny how he never sensed the fish, his companions, were all dead. Not even as their slithering corpses brushed his arms and legs.

Swimming in seawater was simple, it slid across his skin. He was weightless, aloft; he'd taken flight. He was a dolphin. Or a ruby-winged bird. He ignored the growing heaviness stitching his lungs, filling them. He opened his eyes. There was a shadow on the water's surface; he spotted the prow of a trawler. The grey hull augered a crease through the blue sunlight above. And he never saw the nets.

Within seconds, the men pulled him aboard the vessel.

They were celebrating Christmas. An old fisherman dressed as Saint Nick, drunk and dirty, was the first to see him. All those aboard the fishing boat had thought the drunk was sea-mad as he muttered, "*Una sirena, aquí . . . Mira mes amigos, una sirena.*" The tipsy Saint Nick, alone, reached with scarred hands and pulled an exotic creature aboard, and then set about separating the sea from the swimmer's lungs, slapping his chest the way he'd seen women beat the dirt from rugs.

The sea left Jules's near-drowned form as quickly as it had entered him. The water sputtered out. And then, his gaze fixed upon the drunk's flushed nose, which, with years of drink, had exploded into the shape of a wild mushroom. The man's Santa costume stunk of sweat and chum; the once-white cuffs were black from handling nets. As the old man worked to revive Jules, the grimy ball of his Santa hat bobbed and bounced. And though Jules gave no sign of fear, the man whispered kind, calming Spanish, as if comforting a fretful baby. Jules slept then. The dreams called to him like sirens from the shore.

#

Jules became fluent in Spanish. Quickly. And, as he learned, his visions changed. Often in his dreams, a boxer visited, his voice sharp, accusing. But it was Isobel who was there every night. She spoke English in flat American tones; other times, she spoke French in halting patterns. The sharp rise and fall of her voice would move closer, then away again, until months passed and her words held no meaning other than the click and murmur of cyclic sounds. Her cadences dredged up the day he'd heard her calling to him from shore. And then, he'd wake from his dream with a start, screaming in horror, as his child, whom he had heard fussing in the house while he murdered another, toddled toward him, dirty, shirtless, no more than five, asking, "*¿Señor, Por qué aquí? Yo sé por qué.* Sir? Why are you here? I know why . . ."

#

Not long after Jules's rescue, the cook, the drunk, Juan Piñon, a ragged man in his sixties, took Jules in as an apprentice. The old man was suspicious, but generous. The first day, Juan watched Jules cut vegetables, and he was sure he had witnessed a miracle. *Este nunca ha estado en una cocina. Pero este aprende. Y rápido. ¿Cómo preparó esta comida en solo diez minutos? Sí, salvé a este dios dorado del mar.* [*This one has never been in a kitchen. But this one learns. And fast. How did he prepare this meal in only ten minutes? Yes, I saved this golden god from the sea.*]

Juan didn't know Jules had come to understand Spanish so quickly; Jules comprehended all the words the man whispered.

Cooking was like writing, a process, one element or stanza after another, a careful melding of components like creating villanelles or sonnets. It was finding all the right adjectives and verbs, the perfect seasoning, faster and quicker, the rhythm crucial. Jules stewed the day's catch with potatoes or rice from the stores, lowered the filleted fish into steaming kelp and boiling ocean water, stirred in dried herbs from old cans forgotten in the galley.

Jules kept to himself, indeed, kept the mediocre cook believing he and his shipmates had rescued a fair person who'd been adrift for a long, long time. *Ah*, the chef would say, clucking his tongue as he prepared meals slowly, *este es demasiado inteligente Ah, el mar le ha arrebatado el mundo. Una cáscara y un cerebro, eso es todo lo que es. Este no tiene más preocupaciones que vivir y morir. Él no tiene nada, ni bocas que alimentar.* [*Ah, this one's too smart. Ah, the sea has taken the world from him. A husk and a brain, that's all he is. This one has no worries but living and dying. He has nothing, no mouths to feed.*] As Jules listened and watched, he mastered every kitchen skill, learned how to spice, how to combine ingredients.

All the while, Juan sipped his cheap sherry, shook his head, watched as the fantastical man moved like a speeding steamboat. Jules took over the galley without wanting it.

#

In the Santiago port, when the long winter catch was over, and they'd brought in their last haul, Jules gave every man, all well-fed by his apprenticeship, a hardy clap on the back and a farewell in his now-fluent Spanish, *"Adios, mis compañeros."*

After anchoring, he made his way back up the coast to visit Valentina and his favorite Cuban haunts. He stayed for a month or so, remained in hiding. And then, when domesticity and boredom were too much to take, he traveled to Havana and found a Moroccan vessel headed to Southampton. He signed on as a cook. His guilt was all but forgotten.

#

THESE LOWLY OBJECTS

TELL ME OF OCEANS, OR, AS A LOCK OF HAIR FELL FROM THE DUNE AND A MILLION SENTINEL CRABS SCUTTLED ACROSS THE COASTLINE

[A poem attributed to Jules Lalande, found in an abandoned journal, written in English, 17 janvier 1925]

While decks pause in the rhythm,
Back and forth, back and forth
And the clouds swirl like twirling ropes,
I throw into
The Ocean,
An offering to nobody—
A precious little letter.
The letter lost, a precious little body,
The waves drink it up,
And I see its profound figures leap
In the bitter air,
They penetrate
The drowning of water.
And this bold boat,
This beautiful turbine-driven vessel,
Whistles. It goes, it goes!
It pushes thunder
Trailing its long white puff,
After a golden vapor.
It dreams, as I do, of oases,
Of ports in the heaven of glass.
And the trouble of my heart calms,
The purity of equality.

The sea.

#

When not in the galley on the Moroccan ship, Jules would sit on the upper deck, perched on a pile of coiled ropes. From where he was, he could hear the crew below playing cards, drinking, arguing. He could not understand how the men so easily could ignore the sea and sky. They did not care for the depths or for the ocean's petticoat waves surprised in spray.

Their indifference baffled him. How could anyone float in the slow, undeniable traffic of tide and not taste its cathedral limits, the rush running inside every soul? The water's lushness drugged him with its downcast lullaby to the deep. Every evening, he watched the shimmer of parchment sunsets until they faded into almonds of moon, the gulls gathering and shrieking in shadow.

Those same waves would soon bathe a distant island where washerwomen scrubbed laundry on the shore. Oh, the universal oceans! Maybe, if he gazed at the emptiness long enough, at the fluency of whitecaps on the rough surface, he would find a hidden geometry, a map of meaning for his own destiny.

Soon he'd return to civilization, though he was not sure how. The dreams, they haunted him, the arcades of stars and sleeping fish. He did know, for sure, he'd come back, somehow reunite with the museum of sea and sky for all time. Odd as it was to contemplate oblivion, he found comfort in accepting its inevitability. It was enough, after all, to believe all of him, all the personae, all the horrors, even the ocean itself, would someday disappear into nothingness. It could only be true happiness to dissolve into something so immense and complete.

#

PARTRIDGE

In winds of current, the death ship, a rusty wreck, lay perched on the reef. The waves swayed its bulky shell. To and fro, to and fro. Back and forth, back and forth. If it had only been an empty vessel. However, its various instruments, its bilge room, its hammocks, and its clocks were annoyed with creakings of the tide. A regular drift had long ago lulled the ship into a game called "Waiting for Rescue."

The ship's sole responsibility and inhabitant, Titian Partridge, was much more patient than the craft. He did not care about the changing sea world swimming by the reinforced hull. Soon after going down, Partridge's breath had left him; his corpse had rotted. Yet he survived. As the ship settled on its side at the bottom of a chasm, the gashes in the ship's aft rushed, then lulled into a seeping of water.

Partridge came to terms with the idea he might live forever in the cramped space. Those first years were not so intolerable in the bottle-green depths. Yes, it was true Partridge's skin was gone, and his joints leaked. But there were stacks of books, somehow impervious to the ruin of water, and whooshing gold sunfish inhabited them. Numerous schools swam through his library, as Partridge commenced his education. Shakespeare, Chaucer, Hemingway, and a woman writer, too—Austen. He liked Austen best, her stories promised fulfillment in romance, in completing oneself with another.

Partridge read on and ignored the fish weaving through his ribs in chasing games. And he began to wait, too. Yes, his hip bones, shoulder blades, and skull were like irregular lustrous pearls anticipating discovery. Soon, someone would recover this ruin of a craft, they would hoist it up from the depths, and he would become whole; he would be flesh once more. Partridge's partner, the ship, Ariel, would live again, too. Maybe.

#

Jules walked into the gym in South End, and the boxers in the place hushed, then drew their breath as if someone had thrown a torch through the window. Tommy Floyd did not spot his old friend as Jules came up from behind, shadowboxing, mimicking. Jules then grabbed hold of the bag and peeked around at the exact moment Tommy threw a tight one, clocking him. He fell to the floor.

"I know you hate the French, Tommy. But I'm Swiss," Jules moaned, rubbing his cheek as he remained sprawled.

"Jules, is that really you?" Tommy, stunned, grasped the bag, tried to balance himself. "They said you were dead. Everybody said it."

"Well, I'm a ghost, then." The American hugged the wind out of Jules.

"Where you staying?" Tommy asked.

"With you."

#

The real Jules Lalande, if ever glimpsed, was handsome, some would say dashing. But reality did not matter to a man of Jules's ilk. The dreams condensed and grew queer inside him.

At various times, as a master of masquerade, he had passed himself off as a pugilist, poet, professor, and prospector; made himself into a sailor, critic, editor, and chauffeur; and gained the reputation of a dandy, forger, cardsharper, and thief. To all, he was the toast of three continents, a lady-lover. A man-lover, too. A bounder, a roué, a lothario, a cad. Jules Lalande was everything and nothing. Dada.

Certain circles, yes, still relayed his story: one day, Jules Lalande, *poof*, like a rabbit down a hole, vanished from Cuba. No corpse, no note. They all said, *Maybe he's drowned on the high seas or reinvented himself in a faraway land*. Parisian and New York denizens were confident he would undoubtedly return. *Perhaps he's taken up the language of a new lover*, they whispered and laughed, as they fucked in their bright-shuttered boarding houses and sipped bootleg absinthe in out-of-the-way cafés, drinks glowing and verdant as fireflies.

The pectorals of the lost Jules, the boxer who'd departed, had measured more than forty-two inches around. The ghost of Jules, the absurd, outrageous poet and painter, haunted all of Dada. One day he'd been *un fripon*, the next, a chic host wearing a velvet smoking jacket and evening fez, the dangling, silky tassel swishing across his forehead.

Isobel, with the long nose, tall legs, and rope pearls, whose eight-foot-long necklace trailed her like a wedding train, the woman he married on a whim so she'd wrap those legs and beads around him, well now, she, too, assented to public opinion. He was lost.

The vulturous crowd all concurred; of course, he'd return; Jules would surely glide back into view. Yes, yes, of course, he would, he had to come back to them. Didn't he?

ISOBEL WRIGHT LALANDE

Leave everything. Leave Dada. Leave your wife. Leave your mistress. Leave your hopes and fears. Leave your children in the woods. Leave the substance for the shadow. Leave your easy life, leave what you are given for the future. Set off on the roads.
—André Breton

ISOBEL WRIGHT CONSIDERS OCEANS, LAKES, AND A CANAL

They found Jules's boat in an open tropical bay. A freighter had carried it back to Havana, stowing the yacht in its hold. And, after everyone else gave it a once over, it was Isobel's turn to peek at the craft.

By circumstance, Isobel was already at the dock, enjoying the cooling fan in the heat, waiting in the cruise line's lounge, waiting to depart to New York, then England. She was on her way home, already packed, her passage not leaving for hours. A man arrived with the news of Jules's yacht's presence. In his clipped English, the Spanish concierge relayed the vessel's whereabouts.

"A ship has docked on the other side of the yard. It carries Señor Lalande's boat. Police are there. I have seen it. I do not recommend the sight. You want to see, too?"

"No, I can't bear to look," Isobel said. But she had to. She left the baby with his nanny, slid out of the room and into a taxi before the attendant could say another word. What would it hurt to see Jules's torn-up boat? She was sure it was a splintered mess.

The big ship, creaking with rodents, filled with stench and dark sounds. Isobel was grateful for the perfumed kerchief she clutched to her nostrils. She gaped at the shell of Jules's destroyed boat. The shipping company refused to unload it from its large carrier, and thus, the investigators did not know what to do with it.

There, silhouetted in the lantern glow, the broken shape hardly resembled any seafaring craft she'd ever seen, the bow fractured and jutting its broken bones. She gazed at the sun-cracked deck, so odd in this dark cavern of a ship. It was if the light-damage was a joke, for surely this vessel would never see the sun again. Nothing else remained. No mast, no personal belongings. Just the crudely lettered name on the side: "Isobel." This was the last place Jules had stood before he disappeared into the depths.

#

Isobel still heard from Valentina, the poor widow, Jules's Cuban mistress, a woman thick with child (most certainly not Jules's child), after Jules went missing, after Isobel had returned home to Britain, after the two women's long, aimless search for the man. Valentina telegrammed for weeks from Cuba, Florida, or New York, where she had settled temporarily. Every few days, there was a knock on the door. The same delivery boy every time. He looked at Isobel's maid with increasing pity. There was never any news, just the slight words of an abandoned mistress who was frightened, a woman six-months pregnant with a child who most certainly was not Jules's.

"No word yet." Always the same three words. No.

Word. Yet. Three desperate words. Especially the word "yet."

Valentina did not just send telegrams; she wrote letters, too. Long ones, with implicit pauses. "I can't mourn, not yet, I still have hope . . . I won't do anything until there's proof." And she also sent Isobel a single photographic portrait—Jules and Valentina looking so wide-eyed, scared, titillated. He cut quite a figure, a dashing man in pinstripes and linen waistcoat. The woman was elegant and proud with freesia blooms clutched to her heart. Dark everything. They were in a market somewhere, all was a blur, but they stood still, pristine, a halo around them. Now the unfortunate woman even shipped Isobel two of Jules's paintings—old works she'd found behind the wall of his abandoned workshop.

Jules's past now hung on Isobel's walls.

There were other letters about Jules, too, but they were always from some friend or solicitor, asking for money or word about the elusive poet and painter. The 9th Duke of Burlington. Yes, her second cousin, who was as infamous in his death as his life, he was a popular man, and she was merely his wealthy relation and estranged wife, mother to his child, someday the 10th Duke. To the world, her closeness to the man did not matter. She was not sure if she liked her degraded status.

Lately, she received letters from Tommy Floyd. Short, to the point. The same words as Valentina's: "No news yet." Yet.

Oh, how Isobel dreaded each trip downstairs in her home! On the long marble table in the vestibule, the letters would sit, waiting. But Valentina's notes were easy to pick out. Shell-pink envelopes, fine linen stuffed full of sadness.

The hallway's polished veneer walls, shagreened with a tint of sickness, would close in on Isobel whenever she tromped from her suite and saw a pink missive lying unopened there in the entry.

But the last few evenings, she had surrendered to ennui, sitting in the library, watching the flames jig over the logs, subsisting on a steady diet of fish soup and dry toast. The maid would *harumph* when she brought in a tray. But tonight, Isobel stood, left the child in his nanny's care, and cloaked herself in lavish fur, pulled on a muffler and rubbers and set out, sludging along the street to a café, and the bleakness of it all clobbered her—people tucked deep into their coats, feet slopping through dull, slushy snow. No faces. People all going to meet someone, all trying to accomplish something.

Isobel fingered the slim letter nestled far down in her coat pocket, as a cut of wind pushed against her; the icy blast drafted up. The city was bleak this time of year. She shivered, wound her big scarf tight about her neck. If only there were something, anything about him. How could she love him so, especially now, especially when she was sure he was gone?

Over the pedestrians, the gaslights perched like thin-necked beasts. Every so often one would slowly glow in the dusk, then flicker and flush bright, illuminating people's shoulders and the crystalline snow. She made her way inside, found a window table in the teeming place. Beyond the glass, outside on the sidewalk, the world continued to stream by in currents. People clutched cases and packages. A few adolescents leaned against the window for a moment, rolled and lit cigarettes, then folded back into a snake of pedestrian traffic. Wriggling smoke lingered in their absence. Across the boulevard, snow-glazed on a slate roof. A motor car stopped under the blue streetlight.

Her stew was too hot. She blew steam off the spoon, gingerly tongued it, then pulled the unopened letter from her coat pocket and set it on the table. Picking at the edge with her fingernail, she knew she'd have to open it. Valentina would expect a response. After all, months ago, the woman's telegram alerted Isobel of Jules's disappearance, the words creakling with panic: sailors had found Jules's boat wrecked off the coast of Cuba; Jules was nowhere. It was not unusual for him to drop out of sight. But this time felt different.

Isobel dipped into her cooling stew. She slurped a spoonful as she inspected her name: "Isobel Wright." Valentina had lovely handwriting. Isobel glanced again outside the window hoping she could find something to press away all of this; but no, it was just Parisians, workers' pants and coats, the glacial pace of shoes, a flood of feet.

Where was Jules?

It was past dark now. All the gaslights flickered like stars. Another automobile stopped. Isobel's own reflection appeared in the window glass, a specter sitting alone in a half-empty café, a lonely woman with a hollow, troubled expression gazing out at a boulevard.

\#

Isobel had once been another person. Though now, that Isobel was dead inside her.

It was a happy childhood, even without parents.

They built sheet forts on chairs in the nursery; they stood on the top floors of the manor and gazed at the distant countryside; they crawled into high hay in the barns and hid, watching the grooms argue and fight; they ran under the moonlight to watch meteors rip seams through the heavens.

They only had each other. And it was enough. Jules and Isobel's governess and the housekeeper had told them they were lucky; after all, they had no scars. Isobel knew better. And Jules made up for it as best he could. Her big cousin. Laughing, thinking up games and fun things for both to do. Particularly in the lake.

Yes, it was at the lake where they would fish and swim. And Jules had fashioned a rope swing for her, suspending it out over deep water. They took turns swaying higher and higher, finally letting go, dropping into the cold abyss. Jules, his gold-flecked hair dripping, would yell, "Jump! Isobel, you can do it!" And Isobel would hesitate, a skinny girl clinging to a sharp thread of rope, clutching to that primitively-made swing as it built up momentum like a pendulum. She doubted the water below, its slinky movements; she suspected something lurked in its depths or something had changed since her last jump.

Every time, as she swung high above, she'd wait until the surface settled, after the rings dissipated from Jules's last drop, until it was a mirror of aquamarine. But then, she'd force the fear away with Jules screaming, "Jump!" and down she'd go, flying with glee.

#

Months ago, Isobel watched Jules escape to the ocean. She had seen him go. Many weeks later, his lover, Valentina, sent Isobel a panicked telegram, which finally found Isobel newly-arrived in New York. The woman requested Isobel's return to Cuba. For a reason Isobel could not explain, she felt obliged to assist in the search. She booked passage again, brought her toddler along.

The day he disappeared, she had watched Jules swim into the deep, was sure he'd circled around the island. He always had some strategy. She knew his tricks. Surely, he could not be lost at sea. And Valentina, so oblivious, had no idea Isobel had been there when he'd gone.

It was all Isobel's fault. He'd left because of her.

None of this made sense.

With puffy eyes, Valentina met Isobel and her young child at the port. The grieving mistress tried a smile. Her face was full, her belly bloated from pregnancy. Yes, she was expecting. A gaunt woman, pregnancy had filled out the Cuban's beauty, made her new plumpness appear as if her body had been waiting for years to lug a baby.

Together, for a week, Isobel turned her family's sugar plantation into the two women's headquarters, organizing local volunteers for a futile on-foot search, making coffee, and serving trays of food. They met with the useless *los policías*, whose officers were convinced Jules had returned to the mainland and gave up any water recovery. Many of the men required bitter quinine after beating down stalks through the hilly jungle terrain.

Valentina baked pastries and bread for the search parties. It was her gift. After all, she was a baker's widow.

The men grew exhausted from days and days of looking. Before Isobel had even arrived, another search had been underway: the caretaker's child who was also missing. They finally found the boy's decomposing corpse hidden in dense underbrush close to the hacienda. The flies led them there. The men turned all their attention to finding Jules now. They were convinced he had not been in his boat or had even left the island.

"Did . . . he, *aye cómo,* drink?" asked the short, big-chested Cuban *la policía* in broken English. He tipped his finger to his mouth, mimicking a drinking motion.

"No!" Valentina and Isobel responded in unison. The three stood in the large kitchen, a group lit by a single candle on a long plank table, coffee urns turned over after a long afternoon. Valentina's buttery *los pastelitos* still piled high on platters.

The policeman then pointed to Valentina's bulging belly. "Did he know about that?"

"No . . . *tal vez.*"

"Ah-hah."

The man turned to Isobel, "*¿Quién es usted?* Who . . . you?"

"His wife . . . *su esposa . . . esposa separada.*"

"And?"

"We were also close when we were children. Second cousins." She looked to Valentina, smiled, apologetic. "We haven't spoken for a while." Of course, it was a bit of a lie.

"*Si,*" the policeman jotted notes on a notepad.

They spent days looking for Jules, days filled with conjecture. Pointless days. It was only after the sugar fields were raked, after the sheds bared, *las posadas* visited and upturned, beds and all, after every dark corner was bothered; it was only after the police finally decided it was prudent to search the water, after fishermen brought out the nets, dragging the bay, flatboats humming over the water's curling surface; it was only after Isobel heard the men tell a sobbing Valentina, " . . . *muerto,* Señora . . . *No hay rastro por ahí*"; it was only after they found nothing and gave up; it was then they called off the search.

#

Months later, the uncertainty still haunted her. Isobel looked around the café at the merrymakers. A large woman sat on a man's knee, who loudly slapped her muscular thigh, and everyone drank their wine with zeal.

If only Isobel could have seen Jules one last time. There was the other photo Valentina sent her last week. Over the years, Jules's face had changed into a sharper version of itself. He had sharp cheekbones. She couldn't tell if he looked happy in the picture, wearing a blue detachable collar and a newsboy cap, playing chess with Marcel Duchamp. They sat in a park on a bench, and Jules held a white pawn between his thumb and forefinger. She hardly recognized him. So different from the robust child she'd known in their early years.

There would never be reunion news from Valentina, just mementos. Isobel knew now. And, anyway, Valentina's letters had winnowed to once a week. Still, Isobel dreaded every postal delivery. She wondered if she might someday receive messages from the missing man himself. Perhaps one day she'd discover a postcard on the table from Bali or Singapore written in his scratching hand.

Now, she once again fingered the unopened envelope of Valentina's letter and smiled. She pulled her spoon from her stew. She traced the wet utensil over the envelope and doodled a drawing, and the paper crinkled as she moved it to the blank side, near the flap. She fashioned the face of a boy. Round mug, freckles dotting the nose. She wrote

"Jules" below the caricature. She wrote the name again above it and beside it. Jules. Jules. Jules. She scribbled a border, doodled in sunken cheeks. The details faded before she finished, and the pink envelope curled toward her.

She looked up, and outside, an old woman stepped in front of the window, shielded her eyes, peered in and past Isobel; the lady frowned, then turned away. An auto stopped, discharged a single passenger. The man looked right, then left, and disappeared. The street was empty, the wind off the nearby Seine gusted through the leaves on the promenade.

Isobel wondered if, all those months ago, Jules had stood on the deck of his boat, unsure and heartbroken while drifting in the middle of an angry, storm-swollen Gulf. She still could not make sense of the timing. But that was the way of Jules—she'd never understood how he made things happen. She'd watched him swim half-naked through the cresting waves, then vanish.

Was he a strong man, possessing the same trace of authority he'd exhibited when they were young? Or did he look down into the whirling currents and give up, not wanting Valentina or another child, not sure if he was even the child's father? Did he let the fast water churn him under and away from everything he'd ever cared for? Or did he dive in after a long sail, abandoning his boat? Maybe he lost his footing in the rain and plunged into the dark, cracking his skull on the edge of the bow, breaking open his head like an egg? Did he float, or did the spinning water swallow him up?

Well, he was gone, it was all Isobel knew for sure.

Across the way, a couple strode with locked arms. The wind burst, and they separated, pulling their hats low. The man then walked a distance up the road, but the woman hesitated, froze, arms crossed, and, when he came back for her, she waved him away and leaned against the brick wall, looking down the boulevard away from him.

Isobel stood and folded into her coat.

She left Valentina's unopened letter on the table under the bowl, then turned, no trepidation, until she hurried, rushing to get back to her nannied child, who was always running a fever or coughing or crying. She crunched fast on the cold roadways, went toward the river, to the water's edge. Winter barges broke the icy currents, and the soft, sloshing sound of water offered no solace, none at all.

※

ISOBEL WRIGHT CANNOT REMEMBER

She cannot remember summer. She cannot remember what makes her name sound active, why her bell rings.

She cannot remember the weeks of summer flame stitching themselves together into a patchwork of heat, the sky the color of boiling oil in a bucket, and the grass soutaching the welt of the lake, coloring her reminiscences.

She cannot remember twinging for living tints the way she does this November, wanting flowers, cutting naked branches with a blade, and in the mudroom, dipping the brown limbs in a crock's murky water, positioning the stems in a maid's bay window. She cannot remember hoping for red flowers from the out-of-season quince, buds bursting into her home the way soft nipples harden after tweaking.

She cannot stomach summoning from the past, cannot bear to remember. But she must.

She cannot recall how, long ago, her uncle was kind and accepting, showing her his study, with its scents of cedar and a smoldering pipe in the dish, sweet smoke lavishing the air. The duke writing his manuscripts, painting landscapes. She cannot remember his encouragement, "You are bright as a penny, young Isobel."

She cannot remember the lifting and falling tones of Jules's voice, the way he looked driving his pony down unmarked dirt roads for the aim of escapade, or when he smirked, showing her the proper way to look over the precipice of a gulch: on her belly.

"Come on, Isobel, it's not scary. Be brave."

She cannot remember his arms, his shoulders, his knees, his close-cropped hair, all his beauty taking her over. She cannot.

She cannot remember the sea spray spattering his blue coat as he jogged ahead of her, jumping from rock to rock, looking for tide pools at the beach. Her hands no longer remember the weight of his. Or what it felt like pushing him as she had heaved others, shoving him hard and watching him fall.

She cannot remember lighting the match, only the fire and the screams reaching her before the heat. She cannot remember the schools, the looks, the fear alighting faces of everyone she met.

She cannot remember the verdant trees in Cuba, how she was always hot in the home despite her nakedness, or how the breezes in the window choked in the hallway before reaching her. She cannot remember air folding both the stench and flowers together, all redolence of the fields and lilac and cattle manure. Or the speckled jungle resonating with the high-pitched tunes of parakeets, trogons, and todies. Or the sugarcane fields, the perfect lines dissecting the distance, bent workers and their music, laborers singing as they tossed cuts into baskets. Or the cats snarling; the children with sticks chasing hoops; old men sitting on porches snapping peas into bowls, their throaty gospel crooning, Spanish and lilting, reaching her on the veranda. Or the sky turning aurulent, then lavender at the end of day.

She cannot remember craggy undergrowth obscuring the stars. Or her hands cupping icy well water, the cold so welcome; or her lover, standing at the fire in the late gloaming, smelling of dirt and salt; pressing her ear against his chest, his breath catching, only his breath, no other clamoring, no symphony of night; no crickets, no cicada or nightingale trills, only sinking into his quiet rasps, his breathing shallower; reaching between his legs, around his thighs, the rough fabric too coarse for her chapped skin; leaning in to study him, his angling head, his parting lips; and then the returning din of the rainforest, the insects and loud tree frogs.

She cannot remember watching as Jules disappeared into the edge of woods, the shadows swallowing him as he crossed through penumbras, tumbling into summer night; his hands running through her hair, under her blouse. Plummeting into jungle grass, blades swallowing her up. And she cannot remember winter.

She cannot remember feeling Jules's heaviness on top of her, feeling her heart contracting at the heft of him. She cannot call up the memory of standing at the washbasin, watching Jules scrub his nails after a hunt, the shape of his hands resembling her own.

She cannot remember if she lay awake when she lost him or slept deeply in her Cuban bed, the summer's heat scorching the hills, the hay in the barn sticking to the soles of her shoes; cannot remember waiting, watching the sunlight move across the walls and face of her young son.

She cannot remember nuzzling that son on her stomach for the first time, his umbilical cord still pulsing, and his wet head smelling like something belonging only to her, pressing her nose into his hot hair, her child's aroma too overwhelming, too like his father's.

And she cannot remember what it was like to nurse the baby's fevers, the heat turning his skin a scalded color, making him whimper in his sleep. And she does not want to remember, cannot, cannot remember finding her four-year-old cold, burying him, the ground swallowing his too-small coffin, the house so quiet without his play.

She cannot remember feeling a failure at life, no family, no.

She cannot ever recall wandering alone through the now-gone, monstrously large house, dodging the holes in the floor, navigating the roofless sections.

She cannot remember the sensation of standing at her mirror, running her fingers over the pentimento stretch marks on her deflating torso, the vanishing fragments of all that she bore, the memories no longer searing and jagged, now fading like the pale pinkness of an old scar.

She cannot remember; she cannot remember.

She cannot forget.

She cannot forget watching the sky at sunset with Jules, the lilac turning wild in stratified layers of cirrus, each line tracing identically, all fading copies of the others below, stacking, then dissipating into the ether, climbing higher and higher, augmenting, duplicating, copying it all down so someone else can live the same lies, smoothing the visible, leveling the invisible, leveling it all.

She cannot forget his final inhalations and exhalations, serrated and irregular: inhaling, pause; exhaling, pause; she cannot forget imagining him standing below her window, peering, imploring.

She cannot remember anyone or anything alive; she cannot remember the dead. She only forgets. Now it is winter, so she will not, cannot remember.

TITUS PIDGEON

Our brains are dulled by the incurable mania of wanting
to make the unknown known, classifiable.
  —André Breton

TITUS PIDGEON MEETS TRISTAN TZARA

Titus Pidgeon, reporter extraordinaire (at least he liked
to think of himself as exceptional) was in Paris once again—
always a pleasant consequence, and Tristan Tzara, the self-
proclaimed master of Surrealism and Dada, would greet
him at the station. As Pidgeon stepped off the train and
onto the jammed platform, he was surrounded: lovers
kissing with mouths open, tongues searching, and hands in
each other's hair; families hugging, reuniting, or saying
tearful goodbyes; giggling girls swinging bags of candy;
linen-suited men commuting home after office jobs,
tugging at waistcoats and securing straw hats in sudden
summer gusts. Pidgeon wondered how he'd find a stranger
in such a bustling place.

"Pidgeon?" The query came from behind. He turned,
and the speaker was not who Pidgeon had expected. A
slight man, not over five-and-a-half-feet, Tristan Tzara
hunched his shoulders as they shook hands. He squinted
his monocled eye in a rapid flashing succession like a
flickering candle. His skin, waxy and wrinkled with a
jaundiced cast, hung a bit from his jaw. And, as he refused
to meet Pidgeon's gaze, he glanced over Pidgeon's shoulder,
a greasy swath of hair flapped over his forehead.

"You'll be staying over, I expect?" The voice was bullet-
fast; the Romanian accent muddied his perfect English.

Charming somehow, despite his questionable appearance.

A long car waited at the curb; the driver stood by the open door. In the backseat, Tzara, *tisked* and looked out his window as Paris streamed past.

"Paris. It changes so." They made their way past the Arc down the Champs.

"It's not far now."

Inside Tzara's large townhouse, the winding, carpeted stairs led up to an office loft. Tzara ascended halfway and turned abruptly, then smiled, genuinely. A surprise. He pointed to the door below the stairs.

"Your quarters are on the other side. I believe you'll find what you need for a comfortable stay. We shall talk after you've rested. I have not much to say."

Pidgeon changed his shirt and socks, set his case on the bed, and went to the drawing room, where the butler poured him a brandy.

"Sir?" The servant proffered the glass with just a bit of derision. The bare room was dim, unkempt. On its high ceilings, he spied a couple cobwebs swaying in a draft.

"Monsieur Tzara requests your presence."

The elegantly appointed office was too warm, its walls tufted with mohair velvet the color of sand. A sculpture of shapes forming nothing found in nature sat on a columned stand by the window, where the open curtains pooled onto the floor. Light streamed into the stuffy room, added to the heat. Tzara sat at his desk, a long cigarette holder balanced between his plump fingers.

"I know you're here about Lalande, of course. It's not such a long story—I did not know him really. He was after-the-fact. Lalande often joked he had bad timing. I think he was right."

Tzara sighed, gestured with his cigarette holder in a broad, effeminate sweep.

"Please, do sit, so I can tell you what I know. I was hoping we could go about a pleasant evening. I've made reservations with the cook." Tzara's dramatic movements and his affectations bordered on buffoonery. The man was so sure of himself, and it made him interesting. Pidgeon would abide dramatics. Anything so he could discover more about the fugitive Lalande during this short trip to the Continent.

"So, to begin." Tzara blew a curlicued trail of smoke, then his cadenced accent filled the room.

✳

TRISTAN TZARA'S FIRESIDE CONVERSATION WITH TITUS PIDGEON

Had you been there, dear Monsieur Pidgeon, you would have seen something of beauty. And hilarity. Those nights in Zurich were a chaotic cacophony of all the arts—and they were about nothing in particular.

Let's say you could go back and see it for yourself. After you turned into a narrow alleyway in the Spiegelgasse, perhaps you might have bumped shoulders with Lenin (yes, Lenin!) as he scuddled on his way, shunning the crazy artists of Zurich. You would've seen old Nikolai growl in your direction as he crossed to his temporary home at No. 12. Of course, there at his own haunt, he held court and sipped coffee and planned his own personal revolution. Not like ours, of course.

So, if you brushed off your jacket after a chance encounter with Lenin and went on down the alley, you would have seen, at No. 1 on the corner, a skinny, five-story brick building: The Cabaret Voltaire. Our home.

The door would swing open, and the sweet stench of pipe smoke would wrap you in a dense blanket. Your eyes would sting, and inside, once you wiped away the tears, you'd spy a wobbly stage, tables, and chairs for fifty people. But with most performances in the space, you'd see more than a hundred pushed together, all odors and moisture. And some nights, you might not have entered because the crowd was so large, so you'd stand outside on the cold walk. You might have milled about with the unfortunates for a time until you crammed your way in to observe paintings and posters tacked to the wall (my friend Hugo Ball put these up always at the last minute). Those canvases and such were the work of great ones: Arp, Kandinsky, Klee, Leger, Picasso. Not much care in the handling of those masterpieces, I tell you!

You'd take your place among the loud, lazy students who propped their feet on tables, huffing from their long Alpine pipes, exhaling rings of smog. And the noise! You'd cover your ears to the talk! All sorts of crude conversations! Painters, dancers, sculptors, infiltrators, and draft dodgers from other countries. Crooks and tourists.

On the stage, like a giant, lurking tarantula, an out-of-tune piano waiting for its first song. To the left, from where we made our entrances when cued, silhouettes dressing behind yards of scrap linen draped over a trestle.

#

During our first soiree, Hugo Ball sat down to the piano and played something formal like Debussy. The throng hardly noticed; they chattered and ignored the dull melody as the piano tune plunked like heavy feet echoing down a hallway. And then the beautiful Emmy came on stage to sing. Her guttural German songs could awaken love in even the hardest heart. And that night, she never looked lovelier than when she crooned, her cropped hair burnished under the soft spot, her buck teeth horsey and white as if she were some cartoonish beauty out of a Wagnerian opera. I was transfixed, as were all the men and boys. And then Hugo, still on the piano, broke out into a dance tune, and the audience members turned over the tables, flapping their arms, kicking their feet high. Wild. Not many women were attending, either. I think the place was too mad for a sensible female. It was males dancing with males. The scandal!

As the crowd swirled and bounced in a frenzied type of cavorting, Emmy recited a gory poem against war, dramatic and damning, while Hugo went ahead and played another jaunty jingle. The discord! The song was angry, rightly so, as many of the men in the room had been at Verdun! Tiny Emmy pounded her chest, her ripe nipples hard under her diaphanous shift (oh, and you could see their outlines in the rust-red lambency). She snarled out her words (written by Hugo, of course) feeding the frenzy. Everyone gavotted and joined in the vitriol. As a pack, they began to growl, too, just like Emmy.

It was our group's first real collaboration. It was magnificent, though not what I had envisioned. Only later, when I was at the helm running the place, did things turn into what they should have been all along. Confrontational.

I remember, too, the moment the mantle passed to me. Hugo and Emmy would leave soon after. That night, we carried Hugo on stage with his legs in a blue cylinder he had dug into all the way to his hips. Hugo costumed as a big cigar! Over the long tube, he wore a cardboard coat, painted in gold scrolls on the outside, crimson inside. On his head, Hugo sported an enormous blue-striped miter like a bishop might wear. As he arrived at the front of the stage, Hugo stood solemnly, entirely still, and recited a poem, all cockamamie brilliance. I have memorized it from many years of repeating it to myself. Here are the first few lines:

gadji beri bimba glandridi laula lonni cadori
gadjama gramma berida bimbala glandri galassassa
laulitalomini
gadji beri bin blassa glassala laula lonni cadorsu sassala
bim

As you may surmise, the poem was nonsense, as were our endeavors at the cabaret. But Ball enunciated, inflected using Italian, French, Russian phrasing, so everyone thought the verse meant something. And he whispered with the voice of a priest intoning the most holy. The crowd hushed, and Hugo's face ignited from within. It was a moment, a real spectacle! What I aim for always!

Though we did not understand what he was saying, the words were beside the point. The underlying feeling, the wave of sound hit us all like a hammer. I was supposed to follow Hugo with something more spectacular. Though it was wholly appropriate to start off the night with liturgy, I think, because we all believed we were starting a new religion. But we believed in nothing.

At the time, I remember thinking Hugo was mad and hurting our fun with such gravitas. Now, as I look back, I think of my own youthful hubris. I wanted nothing more than fame and attention. Hugo wanted to change minds. And that was what mattered. Yes, we were radicals. Believing in nothing was what fueled our performances.

As you probably know, I have my own milieu now, my own personal mission. Our group's ideas are so much more radical than anything Dada could devise. After all, as you know, I coined the word for our Zurich nothingness. Dada, indeed.

After witnessing all the Cabaret Voltaire madness, Monsieur Pidgeon, you would probably have walked back down the hill and headed into Lenin's more tame entertainments. Ah, I see your disapproval. I sense it. You English!

But you don't care about this? You are here because you want to know how Lalande fit in? He was in the audience the night of Hugo's poem. I imagine him, his hair a dirty grey-black from his travels, his sad eyes transfixed. It would not be long before he learned all our tricks—and more. But I did not know him for long. He performed, yes; he even threatened a public suicide. It was scandalous—and beautifully magnificent.

You should talk to Marcel Duchamp. Hah! And André Breton, the idiot. Breton knows all about Lalande. Took photographs. It was one of his pedestrian passions. Personally, I find the pictures more impressive than his poetry. I know you came to me, the expert, about this, but Breton is the one you really want.

Of course, you can stay here for as long as you desire.

How about dinner? I'm hungry. All this talk of nothingness makes my stomach realize it's empty, dear sir.

Mind you, Lalande understood our nihilism. More than anyone. And how perfect—now, he is nothing, too. And nowhere. You wonder if I have seen him in recent years? No, I have not. He left us to go to New York or back to England or somewhere, I think. I never saw him again.

But one night he did have the world at his feet. And that gun was not loaded.

✳

MARCEL DUCHAMP PLAYS A LOSING GAME, AND TITUS PIDGEON WATCHES

Pidgeon gave up talking to Tzara. The man's ego made him impossible. But the reporter did settle into Tzara's home as his base in the lovely city. Pidgeon would first speak with Marcel Duchamp, and he would have to muster courage, for Duchamp was a man he greatly admired—he'd written about the chess master's performance in the last Olympiad (for his newspaper, he'd decorously penned an accolade of the man, a feature about the artist's famed congeniality and artistic pursuits, unusual for a master. Alas, Pidgeon's editor at *The Times* had omitted all the color and anecdotes in the short, Section C, two-paragraph article. "Journalism is not poetry, Pidgeon. Nor is it adoration.").

Duchamp was a technical genius. He had just recently published his solution to a particularly rare endgame position; it was, Pidgeon imagined, inspired by something genuinely divine—Pidgeon translated it and pored over it many evenings as was his habit with every new piece of chess literature. Of course, when the chess world read about the Lasker-Reichelm position, the strategy solidified Duchamp's reputation for brilliant endgames. It was something like this: Black could only linger, anticipating defeat by White, who waited out the delay to win.

Patience paid off for only one foe. Endgames were such an essential element of chess. And so much more satisfying than a stalemate.

#

And so, Pidgeon went to call at Duchamp's gentlemen's club, aimed for reserve, hoped he would keep his admiration of the chess master in check.

Pidgeon sat in the back of the leather-upholstered, sound-proofed room and watched Duchamp, who was stationed front and center at the primary table. Chess aficionados pushed forward from behind a silk dividing partition. The large room was silent—except for the sound of ticking clocks. And then Pidgeon's thoughts turned to Lalande. Was he Black or White?

During a long span, at least thirty minutes, observers cocked their heads, motionless, and Duchamp did nothing but twine his fingers through his long forelock, staring at the pieces before him, avoiding the anxious glance of his young opponent. He wore a starched ivory shirt, the collar turned up around a rumpled silk foulard ascot. He'd pushed the tweed jacket's sleeves up to his elbows. Casual, insouciant style.

And then he jerked upright. Everyone roused, gasped.

Duchamp then made a goofy expression, stuck out his tongue. He knocked over his queen, smiled, stood, and stretched. Whispers filled the room. He'd lost.

Pidgeon followed the artist as he lit a cigarette and stepped onto the sidewalk.

"Sir . . ." Pidgeon began to explain his presence, though his mission was distant from his thoughts.

"I know who you are, Pidgeon. I've been warned, and I will not speak ill of the dead." Duchamp sputtered English with the affectations of a Frenchman who had lived in New York. He inched down the sidewalk away from Pidgeon, then leaned in against the stone building to face the reporter. "Perhaps if you were writing an homage, I might consider letting you borrow our correspondence, but only if you do not speak another word to anyone in this town. You are dredging up hurt feelings, and I, for one, do not desire to open a wound that pierced my heart."

Duchamp looked deep into Pidgeon's eyes, assessing the reporter's potential for betrayal. Pidgeon nodded his head, understanding. They shook hands. Pidgeon smiled then, but Duchamp continued, hitched his thumb toward the club's entrance.

"No one told you? Dear Pidgeon, only members are allowed inside. Well, you should be on your way. You'll get what you're after. Good day." Duchamp threw his cigarette to the walk and ground it out with the toe of his shiny shoe, walked inside without giving Pidgeon another glance.

#

Pidgeon was already on his way to bed at Tzara's in the guest quarters when the outside bell rang. A messenger had arrived with a delivery, a portmanteau stuffed with years-old correspondence between Duchamp and Lalande—right up to the time of Lalande's disappearance. The young messenger tipped his hat and spoke in perfect English.

"Sir, I was told the contents of the case should not leave my sight. I must return these by noon tomorrow. I shall wait on the premises until you are done."

Pidgeon sighed. His eyes were almost done-in from fatigue. He reached into his pocket for his magnifier and commenced reading. He only found four letters with salient information. The rest were full of romantic nonsense.

※

TITUS PIDGEON READS JULES LALANDE'S LETTERS TO MARCEL DUCHAMP

To: Marcel Duchamp
2 février 1920

Cher Marcel,

I am, as you know, still in New York. Though my circumstances have changed. I am in what they call the Tombs. It is not a fancy catacomb, but the jail. I have been accused of stealing something important. Though, in truth, you must know that your art is sacred, not just important (if you understand me). And all art is such. It should be appreciated.

I cannot sleep in my cell. I continue to have the most terrible nightmare. Perhaps you can explain what it means. I see this all as if it happened in history, to someone other than me. Was there ever anyone in England who died this way? Answer me this and let me know when and if I return.

My dream goes something like this:

A ship makes it to port in record time, and my main character (me?) hops the first slithering train from Liverpool. It is a short trip to the big town—sheep pastures and girls wearing silly felt hats. People bumble large valises down the aisles. He (me?) pulls his cap brim down low.

The wait in Waterloo station, it lasts forever! The glass, the bustle! The people, all speaking English, all hurrying somewhere. Galvanized announcements for destinations, the mixture of voices like off-key orchestras! London! The man (is it me?) tugs up his collar, adjusts the waist of his old sweater, and sits on a bench. He has nowhere to go. Not yet. A bobby comes by a few times, looks the man up and down. The man's beard is scraggly; to the policeman, he appears a drifter or vagrant. Only after the policeman spots his stuffed burlap bag, does he understand.

"Move along!"

Our protagonist wanders the streets, finds himself drawn to a large church. It is evening. He presses the door. It creaks open. Inside, the candles burn low, the gold altar shimmers, and he lays in the back pew in a King's Cross cathedral. And then high-pitched whistles rouse him; he's been daydreaming about a fair woman; she is whispering in a language he cannot understand. As he reaches for her, she screams, high-pitched, lips stretched, her open mouth revealing a scored tongue, mangled. He runs out the church doors, the shrill sound of police whistles louder outside in the evening. Dogs bark. People shout.

"There he is!"

"Get him!"

They tackle him on the steps, take him in a wagon to Scotland Yard.

The case is strong: some bum stabbed by a stranger. Our dream protagonist fits the description of the suspect. His barrister even believes he is guilty. Especially when he will not give his real name or address. That is a crime, too. No identity in the empire is unthinkable.

"Do you have anything to say for yourself?" the judge sneers, and the protagonist shakes his head. The jury frowns.

"Due to the nature of your heinous crime, Mr. Smith, or whatever your name is, you are at this moment sentenced to death by hanging. May God have mercy on your soul." Our condemned man gazes out the window and watches the grey filtering through the day, no colors. He lies in his cell, day after day and scratches poems into the stone floor. And when it is not optimal, he utilizes his shit and blood for ink.

Outside the tiny barred window, high in the stone wall, he catches glimpses of birds, clouds. It is morning.

Perhaps they've forgotten him, maybe they will.

And then there is the knock.

"Mr. Smith?"

Three jailers enter with shackles and chains. The walk down the stairs is challenging; the chains are heavy; he shuffles.

In the yard, the scaffolding's wood smells fresh. His shackles are replaced with rope. His hands are tied loosely behind his back. The trees are budding. It's spring. The guards, with their backs stiff and their faces blank, stare unfeelingly as they throw a hood over his head; he feels a noose positioned around his neck. He listens for the thump of the handle, and then he swallows. He waits. *THUMP*. The trap opens, and down he goes, down. And then he feels a snap, and his neck burns, but his feet keep plummeting. His feet push down, down, slow, but now onto solid ground. There is a gasp. And he wriggles from the noose; the hood comes off as he ducks through, and then he is in the courtyard; he is running; he is opening the gate, running along the street; the whistles grow faint. He walks with purpose. And there in the morning rush, he is lost once again. Never to return.

Oh, Marcel! This is my dream! It haunts me. What can I do but keep dreaming about it?

On another subject, I will be leaving here soon. When I return, I hope we can have one of our long talks about art and poetry. Can we discuss our usual topics well into the night? Perhaps a game of chess? You know I am your only worthy opponent. Tell that to Apollinaire! And no duels for anyone until I return. Then you will see I have become a great shot. I need a theatre.

Yours,

Jules

———————

Rrose Sélavy, a.k.a. Marcel Duchamp
Care of Suzanne Crotti
Paris, France
14 avril 1921

Dearest "Rrose" (Marcel)!

I write from Texas by way of the state of oranges. Yes, Florida was baffling. You will have a laugh that I, with my ugly, flat nose, disguised myself as a woman. And as a dancer no less!

The Seaboard Atlantic Railway. A wobbly system of passenger trains and cargo holds. It took me two days to reach the isthmus (isn't Florida shaped like a phallus?). It was hot, something to which I was not accustomed. I accept high temperatures now, especially here in Texas, where it's a dry heat, not like the kind we had in France. And Florida was all humidity, miserable to be honest.

So much for the weather. I know this sounds positively boring.

In the horrible sunshine, I took the train to a river, where I found work picking oranges in a grove lost to the horizon—citrus as far as the eye could see. Days steamed on and on, the fog boiled off the river in the mornings and at night. The air was dull with moisture, beads so thick, every moment of every morning, noon, midnight. At sunrise, the encampment rolled out, and we each had eighty baskets to fill. We worked every day until sunset. I found the work rhythmic, hard, but in some strange way, cathartic. My hands stiffened, froze into claws still caressing the round fruits long after I'd settled down to sleep in my cot. It took days to train those many finger muscles!

Ah, friend, but you would be proud of my attempts at manual labor! I put out sixty to seventy baskets in half a day. The foreman was impressed. Would you expect anything less from me? My fellow pickers were not so happy with my speed, though. Would you expect anything less from base humans? All day, every day, as I worked, all I could do was see Isobel, hear her laughter. And the baby. Oh, the baby. How I missed my child! How I wish I could forget him! It made me work faster. I did not hear my fellow workers' comments, the growing grudges from the men around me.

"Who does this foreigner think he is?"

"Make us look bad? Not for long." And then one day, my ladder mysteriously went out from under me, and I thudded to the ground. The foreman threw a spit bucket over me. I was dizzy with the sweet scent of oranges rotting in the hot grass, the trees in rows all around me. I'd sprained an ankle and a wrist, and my head felt like the split oranges in my basket.

The landowners, the people who owned all the groves in the area, the Thursbys, were kind enough to take me, an injured worker, into their big house. The place, built on a midden, was lopsided. The hill felt as if it was always shifting, the shells refusing to crackle under the house's foundation—but perhaps it was my injured head. Those must have been some hungry ancient Indians because it was a tall hill of refuse. Crushed crab, oyster, clam, and mussel shells.

The Thursbys put me in their parlor on a cot. And it was pleasant enough with the air from the river and from the nearby spring breezing through the open windows. I did not sweat for the first time in weeks. Within a short day, I came into the family's good graces. And—*a-ha*! The daughter was the one who cared for me. Minerva. Before you start smiling, I have to tell you about Minerva. A perfect name. Her hair, however, did not slither off her head, nor did it charm me—she did not have much hair, to be honest. Dear puffy Minerva. She liked me.

A week into my recuperation (yes, I milked it!), Mr. Thursby had hatched a plan. He was a tough-skinned man, face wrinkled as boot leather from years in the elements.

And his wrinkles often showed how he felt. I would have to marry his daughter.

"Son, you're good and all, even with the funny accent. You seem a gentleman. It's a good deal. You'll have the spring here and the oranges when I'm gone."

Well, this Minerva was a rather large woman, which is not necessarily a bad thing, in itself. Softness can be right. But Minerva was not someone I could share a life with: she had a tonsure, was missing three front teeth, and walked with a leaning squeak.

"No sir, I will not marry her."

And before old Thursby could fetch his gun, I scrambled out the door. I still had an injured ankle, so I hobbled, but I picked up steam, Minerva screaming for her father to shoot. I limp-ran down the shale road. And so I was sad to say goodbye to the comfortable house and its refreshing spring, sad to bid *adieu* to the aqua creek and its coolness, sad to bid *au revoir* to the alligators lurking in the shallow waters and to the Seminole trees leaning close as if they were sipping from the stream.

Minerva's wails traveled down the road with me for a good mile or two. I felt no pain but that of haste. Please know, dear friend, it was no good to stay. I couldn't do it! A four-hundred-pound woman would have crushed me in the marriage bed.

I moved to the next town down the line where the freight steamboats docked. The hamlet had its share of speakeasies and brothels and burlesques for the sailors, and I devised a perfect disguise so Thursby couldn't find me. It was a real costume of majesty—I'd taken some of Minerva's clothes. On washing day, I had watched her hang her wet laundry out on the line. It wasn't hard to stow a few garments in my croker sack.

Well, I made a beautiful dancing girl, after a few alterations to Minerva's dresses—the extra fabric helped, too, as I just moved it around a bit, added some ribbons. I didn't need to compensate too much with a needle for my broad shoulders. My face—all it took was a close shave three times a day. I didn't bother with my legs, as I wore stockings and did not take customers. Well, you can imagine how lovely I was with hairy gams below my garters! I named myself Bessie the Swiss, and the wig I stole from a shop, all blonde curls, I must say, really complemented my coloring. The men loved me. I made more money working there than anywhere else. It certainly was preferable to picking oranges!

But then, as with all deceits, it did not last. Remember, alcohol is prohibited in this strange country, and the bathtub gin my employer served was potent. Men could easily go blind on the stuff. When a drunkard decided he liked me a tad too much, he found more under my skirt than he'd anticipated. He pulled out his pistol (everyone, it seems, has a gun in Florida, and everyone who has a gun in Florida wants to shoot me!), but I made a quick exit (the man was so inebriated he could not run without stumbling), and I went farther up the road, to a luxurious enclave, Winter Hall.

I found work at the college there.

At Rolley, a pretentious art school for scions, I pretended to be a French dancer who'd studied with Nijinsky. The poor students did not know what to make of me. I wore a scarf tied pirate-style on my head and stole bright women's attire from clotheslines in the area. I was a sight! The dances I choreographed, many taken from my recent dancehall gimmicks, were all hips and legs. A kick here, a *battement* there. I remembered my days in Zurich and all of Sophie Taeuber's steps. The boys tried to follow along.

Marcel, I must be wholly honest here. I found the designing of dances something euphoric. As if moving around the living pieces of a puzzle. Mornings we would hold our class in a neglected house off-campus. And Marcel, they had no idea I was a fraud! And, because of that, I wasn't!

All went well until one of my affluent students, Alfred, befriended me. He was a kind boy, a dancer as you've never seen! Well, his parents invited me to their home, a mansion set on a lake.

The dinner party boasted at least thirty guests—the town's society, the *nouveau riche*. They sat on either side of a long table. During the meal, we discussed the aggressive alligators I'd heard about. Apparently, hundreds of them lurked in many of the area's lakes. I did not believe the big reptiles could thrive so far inland.

"Ah, but just last year, one of the town's children was dragged off her swing and into the water. They found her torso a week later."

I had to see the reptiles or at least the lake for myself. After the long, hot candlelit dinner, Alfred offered to show me.

"Any other brave souls want to join us?" The young students, all Alfred's college classmates, giggled and followed. The adults sat with their brandies and cigars and pooh-poohed me.

"A risk. No, I'm comfortable here," Alfred's father said without moving his lips.

We excused ourselves and made our way to the lagoon. Our little college group threw off our shoes and carried bottles of champagne onto the dock. On close inspection, the lake was cloudy, eerie in a deafened sort of way. The crickets and frogs creaked so loudly we could barely hear one another. A girl with red hair yelled above the din to no one in particular.

"Would you like to play a game?" Well, I smiled. You know me, Marcel, I am always up for a game. And I had to maintain the devil-may-care Frenchman's ruse. I thought this would be some sex play. But I was wrong. Hah! Unfortunately, my delicate Alfred was the butt of a joke.

"Let's play 'Where's Alfred?'" All the girls squealed with delight. And then the game began. Alfred sat on the dock, his head in his hands.

"Where's Alfred? Did he fall into the lake and SINK?" someone shouted. They all laughed. It was malevolent laughter.

"I'm here," Alfred screamed. They ignored him.

"Is he some alligator's meal?"

"I'm right HERE!" They looked right through him.

"Is Alfred a *drowned* rat?"

"Here, here, HERE." No, they still pretended the boy was nowhere, no one. The questions continued in the twilight. "I'm here. I'm HERE. Stop this! Stop this!" But his cries and pleas made no impression on them. They walked to the end of the dock, where he sat and pretended to step *through* him.

"Where's Alfred? Where?" Having had enough of their silly game, still in his tuxedo, Alfred dove off the dock. No one cared. They poured more champagne and gossiped as if the boy hadn't been there at all. Perhaps I should have done something, but it was now dark as ink, and the mosquitoes were nicking every bare spot on my face and arms. And then someone noticed Alfred had not resurfaced from the water.

"I'll look over here!" The boys stripped down to their shorts and dove in, dunking and resurfacing many times to no avail. Two girls huddled together, whimpering about snakes and alligators, and I stood on the dock, surveying the scene. Far off, on the other shore of the lake, in the moonlight, I spied the clothed figure of a man as he crawled onto the bank. He shook and shimmied like a wet dog. I smiled. And so, it was how Alfred and I became friends.

Subterfuge is such an effective way to solidify bonds, am I right, Marcel?

Many nights with my new, young acquaintances, I played games such as the one I just described. For our finale, the last game before our fall dance recital, the students kidnapped me from the studio early in the day, then bound and blindfolded me, shoved me in a footlocker (for some reason Alfred was not in on this gag—he later explained he would have no part of it).

After carrying me a long distance, they extracted me from my coffin, tied my arms behind my back, giggled, and pushed me into the swamp. Birds called to each other above, and Blindman's Bluffing through the forest, I knocked into something hard, hit my head, and fell to the ground. There was moisture on my brow, and the laughing stopped, and footsteps petered out. No sound, save the beating of bird wings.

Only when I snagged my blindfold on a branch could I see where I was! I promptly walked out of the woods and onto the road, where I followed the lake two blocks over to

Alfred's house. I flung my body against the back door. And the maid recognized me.

"Lordy, mister, who did this?"

She cut my restraints with a cleaver, then bandaged my head.

I returned to the college the next day and tendered my resignation. I never saw those miscreants again—except Alfred; every one of them failed to show themselves for dance practice, and funny, I cannot remember their names, so you'll have to excuse all my general descriptions of these events.

You know me, I leave those who would hurt me behind.

For a week, Alfred and I practiced his dance, and Alfred absorbed it all—he was compact, but his physical gifts took on a spiritual dimension. The boy could do things no ordinary human would find possible, and with this tangible magic (*I* made it happen!) and in his dance, he transcended the corporeal.

The auditorium was full and hot on the night of the performance. When the locals heard only one dancer would perform, many came to see the spectacle, expecting a laughable show.

The ballet started naturally enough, with Alfred cutting horizontally across the stage in darkness, pirouetting in beige wrappings we had nearly grafted onto him like a second skin, arms hanging at 90-degree angles from the elbows; then he repeated his gestures farther and farther upstage. He was operating on several levels at once, tilting his head with an ardent, glistening face, flowing in and out of the musical phrases lovingly. (Yes, I sat at the edge of the stage and played a tribal rhythm on a big water drum. The beat grew and grew and grew, resonating through the hall until it was deafening.).

Each repetition built upon itself, spinning a strange, fresh pattern, and Alfred would add adjustments and slowly metamorphose. Out of nowhere, a whipped leg, a swift *battement*, a measured *rond de jambe*. He'd stretch, then fold his limber torso, all while circling the center in a feverish, crazed whirl. And then, just as quickly as he sped up, he would stop, dragging his leg, trailing an arm in long beats. The lights crescendoed, slowly rose as the music quickened. It was like a birth or an awakening. Terpsichorean ecstasy.

And when it seemed Alfred was too spellbound to continue, he eased center stage, cambered his legs, bent his knees and arched his torso, jutting his head back, back, back. Then he stomped his heels, syncopating with my growing beat on the drum. Alfred danced removed from his body, maintaining the same serene expression no matter how he twisted and thrashed. He burrowed into my music. Like Sufi dancers I once saw on the Dark Continent, he transported himself (and me and the audience). I was witnessing the materialization of wonder.

Marcel, this performance came alive, and it will live with me forever—even its simple gestures. The dance was not perfect. Probably another reason it was impressive; oh, how Alfred lovingly regarded the currents of my music and the shape of my choreography! I'd infused my simple beats with warmth, and he made them complicated music. It was downright elegiac. Oh, how Alfred made us all fall in love with him as he fell in love with the music.

Physical emotion, a manifestation of beauty.

I left Winter Hall the following night, after my ballet's great success, even discarded all my belongings and made my way to Texas. How could you do this, you ask? I do not know, but shedding my outer membrane is so easy. Like a snake or a lizard.

In fondness for beauty and nothingness,

JL

———————

Rrose Sélavy, a.k.a. Marcel Duchamp
Care of Suzanne Crotti, spouse
Paris, France
13 juillet 1921 (Almost Bastille Day!)

Dearest "Rrose"/Marcel!

There are so many roads to Texas you would not believe it! And you will be happy to know I've seen some North American desert—untainted emptiness different from the Sahara! (Don't let Isobel discover where I am, please.)

I've been in this state for weeks; I'm now finishing working the lines on the Square D Ranch. My goal is the Gulf, where I hear the turquoise water is something to behold. The idea is what keeps me going here.

The ranch work is hard, twisting wire every day around posts, making it taut so the cattle cannot push through. Invariably, the dumb bovines escape, though. So, every week, we walk acres to patch the holes. They say this ranch is bigger than the state of Rhode Island. Though I've never been to Rhode Island, I believe they're telling the truth.

I will soon quit and aim for the coast.

I had so much to write this time; my hand is tired, though, and so are my eyes. Especially the troublesome one. My regards to Picabia. Please let him know I am not

shunning him. Wish me luck, dear friend.
In fondness for beauty and nothingness,
JL

Marcel Duchamp
Care of Suzanne Crotti
Paris, France
9 septembre 1922

Dearest Marcel,

In my last letter, I mentioned the Gulf. I made it! I finally quit the awful ranch. The hot work became unbearable. I made it a few more months, wore through five pairs of leather gloves, and was nicked all over my arms from the barbed wire. Anyway, I was lonely, needed to see the water.

I chose a place on my map called Corpus Christi because I loved the name: "The Body of Christ." I only carried that map, a blanket, hat, rope, my last pair of gloves, a pencil, and bound journal for its paper. I haven't written a single verse since I got here, but I was sure I'd find a good poem or story if I moved closer to the water. I was right.

I walked along the dusty road into town, finally close to my destination. The flowers were blooming like mad, and the atmosphere was an unyielding yellow. Then *cra-aack—* a spike of lightning, dry and bright. The cottonwoods and mesquites clustered closer together. The sky blanched— another flash—*cra-aack*! Like a seam ripping. The hair on my arms stood on end, electrified. Hail pelted down as if heaven aimed to stone me.

I ducked under a mesquite tree, waited out the storm. I couldn't see well, even across the road. As the wind manhandled the tree around me, I thought I spotted a sign through the blurriness. The trunk swayed as I leaned into it. The storm finally eased, and in the aftermath, I found all the flowers had shed their petals, which were purple, wet, and stuck amongst the melting eyeball hail.

I could now read a posted sign across the road. It was hand-painted in red—"Get Right with God." Under the words, a crude arrow pointed toward a path. Curious. I'd experienced a certain religious mindset since I'd come from New York, something I did not yet understand about America. And so, I turned down the wide drive with patches of wet weeds alongside, and soon, I spotted a single-story warehouse in the middle of nowhere, in the middle of a field. A twenty-foot-high white wooden cross rose from a broader area beyond.

Dirty tents surrounded the cross. They spanned the landscape as far as I could see. It reminded me of Verdun. And there were people, hundreds of them milling around. More arrived in wagons. Children chased each other in quiet play. Women rocked babies. Men stood together sipping from water cups, looking at their feet. Unbridled horses moseyed in a large pen by the woods. The place was eerily silent.

I had a feeling this encampment was something I'd often heard about from my fellow ranch workers: a revival. I wasn't really sure what needed reviving. As I stood in wonder observing the strange crowd, a man in an expensive suit sauntered through the outer ring of tents and passed me, then entered the large, squat building. I moved forward, too, and the throng joined me. They started singing as they marched. And then at the building's entrance, we all stood together, waiting for admission. The day's rain, which had just passed, now rose as steam through the air.

Inside, the sweltering place was outfitted like an auditorium. My feet sank deep into fresh hay on the floor, and I found a seat on a wooden bench. On my right, an old woman slumped. She cradled a piglet on her lap. A family with at least ten dirty, mewling children sat in front of me, and there were men to my left who appeared to be bachelors or many brothers. The makeshift theatre was the size of a modest opera house, and believe it or not, Marcel, the interior had a stark beauty to it. Someone had hung large cone-shaped crystal chandeliers from the rafters, and candles lit up the hollow shell. Painted bed sheets, intricate murals with images of the Bible, enveloped the walls.

But what really drew me in was the portrait of Christ at the front. This strange version of Jesus on the cross looked distinctly like a real person. He sported square teeth and a more squared jaw. But unlike other Christ on the Cross paintings, there was no grimace of pain or suffering. He looked euphoric.

The chandeliers swayed, and the crowd muted as if they knew something was about to begin. A lone figure moved down the aisle, a small-framed woman pricking her way to the center on the hay covering. At the front, she balanced on a ropy man's elbow for a moment, then teetered up makeshift steps onto the stage. The stage creaked as she stumbled just slightly, and, as she grabbed the sheet with Christ on the cross to catch her balance, she giggled. It was roasting hot; I wiped my forehead on my sleeve.

The woman spoke into a megaphone in a breathy, schoolgirl voice, "I'm Velvelee Wainwright. The Lord loves you, and so do I!" The audience jumped to their feet and clapped wildly. She smiled, a little slip of a thing, so tiny up there; she'd piled her red hair high on her head in multiple buns, wore a full-sleeved dress sewn from cheap satin. It was a style from the 1880s, not the 1920s.

"Isn't she just beautiful?" asked the old woman to my right as she caught my wrist with her bony fingers. I nodded, not sure if she meant the swine she was holding or the lady on stage. Velvelee, in her weird clothes and slathered stage makeup (she could hardly keep her voluptuous eyelids propped open under the weight of the puce greasepaint she had painted onto them), was a convincing actress.

"Let's tell the Lord how much we love him and how much we need him. He forgives us every fault, loves us for who we really are. Halleluiah! ♪ *'Amazing Grace, how sweet thou art, to save a wretch like me . . . I once was lost, but now am found♫ . . .*" Folks poured into the aisle to dance a jig or something. Strangely, like the other people around me, my heart lifted with the song.

Everyone held their hands aloft, including the feeble old woman next to me (she'd dropped her piglet to the ground at some point, and the miserable creature squealed and hid under the seats). They all proclaimed, "Thankew Jeesus!" I shocked myself by raising my own hands.

As we all stood there with our arms upstretched to heaven, a drum roll pounded from outside, and a strange man bounded down the same aisle Velvelee had so tenuously traveled. He leaped over the steps and dove onto the stage, landing and sliding on his round stomach like a big, rolling ball. Somewhere from the side of the stage, a fiddle warbled, and a guitar twanged, and a harmonica wailed. The audience roared. The man jumped up and grabbed the megaphone from Velvelee.

"You people know what you want. You want JEE-sus, SWEET JEE-SUS, to come into your lives, into your hearts and souls. Sing Alleluia. I say, Allelu-YAH!" Velvelee shook a tambourine, moving in jerky fits and starts as if she were a marionette. The man continued. "There's evil in the world, I tell y'all! But Jesus will save you."

The crowd exhaled "Amen" as if it were as natural as breathing.

I must tell you, Marcel, this pageant was a work of stagecraft. The people worked up to a riot as only I had seen in Zurich. And it all centered upon the ringmaster who worked the indigent crowd into a frenzy.

"Our legacy is God's promised land; our money goes to get you there. Can you sing Hallelujah?" He looked at the worshippers and smiled, eyebrows raised in question. "HALLELUJAH!" The resounding response drew a chuckle from the minister. And then the buckets came around, the sound of coins falling into tin receptacles jingling louder and louder as more and more money was added at the pass. I avoided the offertory by keeping my head down. When I looked up again, Christ on the cross in the painting stared back at me, and well, I realized it was a ringer for the man on stage—pinkly sunburned skin, those square teeth, big and flat, and wide, square jaw.

Velvelee spoke up again. She had her a smaller megaphone now, a scarlet cross crudely painted on its side.

"If you can just open your hearts, folks, you'll know that sweet Jesus loves you no matter what. Give up your sins.

Turn away from Satan. Fight him. And remember to give more than you receive. Am I right, Asa?" The man smiled, teeth as big as grave markers. Velvelee listed decidedly to the left and moved her shoulders up and down in silent sobs. A twangy guitar started up again. And her tambourine ting-tinged. "Go to your purses and pockets. I love you. God loves you. He died so we can live."

I found myself a bit teary. The old lady next to me offered her tattered handkerchief as she made her way down the row, pushing her weight on a cane, her tie-up shoes scuffling, and she scooped down once every row to peer under the seats for her escaped pet. She wore a worried expression, her face tight.

I left to strains of "Onward Christian Soldiers," and the song followed me back to a spot I found in the empty fields. I fell asleep and dreamed I felt the hands of God push me out of heaven after I'd floated up too fast into the clouds. The flying pigs laughed at me as I fell back, and I woke with a start to the sound of a dry cough in a tent a few yards away. The field was awash in moonlight, all the tents, glowed with burning lanterns inside, a galaxy on the flat meadow. It was so beautiful, Marcel.

I shook off my dream and the heat, then went to a close-by pond for relief. As I stood there, waiting to dive into the cold, a few adolescents laughed on the opposite shore with a lantern illuminating their play. I smiled and jumped in, and sure enough, the water jolted me awake, and I swam and swam under the surface until my lungs tightened. When I emerged on the other shore, a frog chorus greeted me, a high-pitched wailing and grunting. And those children I thought I saw, well, they weren't children at all.

Yes, I had swum into some sort of strange midnight

baptism. Asa, the minister I'd seen on stage, was there. All the men who'd sat together next to me in the audience during the revival were there, too. Indeed, there wasn't a single woman in the water. I tried to dive back and return to the other shore. But Asa grabbed and submerged me before I knew it. I kept my eyes open. There, in lantern light spangling through water, all dreamy and otherworldly, I saw those men's lower halves. They were naked and engorged.

I freed myself and swam back the way I came. At least now I can say I'm officially "saved"—the term I kept hearing folks say. Obviously, these people are not as pious as they would have us think, Marcel.

The next morning, I woke early (by my standards at least) and visited the worship building. A dawn service was underway. I came in late and slipped into the back row. Asa stood on stage, waving his arms, screaming, "Let 'em in! Let 'em in!" It was so strange! Fire and brimstone first thing in the morning is a difficult thing to stomach.

And, honestly, Marcel, I couldn't get the sight of all those men's erections in the pond out of my mind. Sanctimonious buffoons.

I quickly grew bored with the spectacle—it was the same kind of performance I'd witnessed the day before. Then things shifted. The people started speaking in what they call "tongues." It was Dada with a religious bent, Marcel! It was! About this speaking in tongues business. Apparently, angels speak in a language quite strikingly like our own Dada choruses. It was all a great ruse, but everybody else was doing it, so I just "blah, blam, ahh-edddd, aaaaahhhhh-ed" right along, rolling my eyes around and frothing at the mouth.

I got tired of trying to keep up with all the gibberish. It went on and on. Then I turned and saw my own salvation. Yes, there in the back of the building, by the door, was the Big Bin. No, it wasn't a replica of the clock in London. Yes, I was relieved to realize at least someone there was smart enough to devise a pun. The Big Bin was a receptacle where people contributed all their donations, wrote out prayer requests, and slipped them into the big wooden container's slot. If you want to know what it looked like, it resembled an old election box

So, I got religion! So to speak. Everyone was preoccupied talking to angels, so it was easy. With no detection, I stood out in the open and pried open the box. The hinges and lock were flimsy, and my nerves were steel, maybe because of all the speaking in tongues. No one heard the crack of the latch. No one saw or heard the lid squeak open. The religious hullabaloo up front was an excellent distraction. The simpletons kept yammering and faith-yelling.

And I hit the jackpot, Marcel. There was a pile of bills and coins in the Big Bin. I pocketed what I could and ran. Praise God, indeed!

I headed to the coast half-expecting some kind of Christian cavalry would come after me. But no one followed.

I finally made it to Corpus Christi. It was a bustling town with streetcars and cobblestone lanes and jetties and piers and smiling fishmongers. Note I said, *it was a place*. After I explored for more than an hour, I passed a kindly woman who was sweeping her stoop with a crude broom. She looked me up and down, saw my mean predicament, and took pity on me. She didn't know the wealth I held in my pockets!

"Hold on there," she said as she disappeared into her humble home. She came back with a cloth handkerchief wrapped around a slab of cheese and wedge of bread. I nodded and gave her a crisp bill. She curtsied; her expression was one of amazement. A dollar is a lot of money for Texas! And then she kept on sweeping. I found a park bench and ate my lunch, not sure what I would do later for sleeping arrangements. I fell asleep as drizzle fell.

And then I awoke when the tempest arrived. Oh, it was a sight! The heavens turned inside out, and the clouds turned a forest green shade and lowered their lids, and a deep, haunted kind of darkness descended in a line across the horizon. The rain came. And the winds swooped in. People in the houses around the square had yanked their shutters over their windows, only minutes later to watch latches unhinge and jettison into the sky, planks flying into oblivion as if they were bits of paper lifting on a zephyr.

I found myself one moment lounging in a park under a pleasant shower and the next bracing myself against an iron fence. I watched roofs fly off the buildings all around me, and the plants and shrubs uprooted in the city square. I held on, I held on, and then I could not grasp any longer, as the wind bombarded me in blasts and threw me off my feet. The storm was speaking in its own tongue. Perhaps it was punishment for stealing from the faithful, but I didn't repent. I needed cover. I staggered, pushed into the wind, made my way to a big oak on a corner; I climbed it, slipping, sliding, barely making it to the first level of limbs.

And then the water rushed from the sea. The water came, the water came, and my feet were dangling in the roiling soup, so I scrambled up the moss-covered trunk higher, higher, as murky waves overtook the town. I held onto my branch for dear life even as the winds tore the pants from my legs. All my ill-gotten money! Gone!

I watched as the water surged higher and higher. Boats and bodies floated past, but I couldn't see much, really, because I was blinded by sand and rain and salt (with the sight I have—you know it's already somewhat impaired), and the wind pressed against my lids and cheeks, pulled at my skin as if it were smoothing out a wrinkled sheet. The force of those winds, and, oh, my fear! I yanked off my wet, torn shirt, twisted it around my left wrist, then looped it around the shaft of the sturdy tree, turned it back around my right wrist.

I anchored there, holding on for dear life in the crook of a branch. The wind! *AWHOOOOL! AWHOOOOL!* The smell of sickly brine. The sound, my ears, the smell, my nose. The storm flew past for hours, and the aggravated clouds drummed with thunder, and the tree swayed, and it swirled me, and I was sure my perch would be swallowed into the heaving sea below. Lightning lit up the darkness like a struck match, and the raindrops formed in spears.

Perhaps my accidental baptism at the camp had been a good thing. Because I survived the devastation. I thought the hurricane had receded, and a two-man sailing yacht drifted right up to my safe bough as if the craft had been guided by a hand from heaven. The boat thumped into my tree, and it stayed moored under me for minutes. I took it as a sign and jumped onto its deck, lying there in the still-furious waves until they calmed. And then the sun shone, and the clouds disappeared into cerulean, the softest blue you've ever seen.

Nothing of the town was left; it was all under water,

save a church steeple in the distance only a few feet above the surface of the murk. A dog house floated by, a shoe, a head of purple cabbage, and a bright yellow pillow. I wondered about the kind woman who'd given me cheese and bread. Perhaps she'd been baptized, too.

The sudden temperate weather only lasted for minutes—I had no idea I was in for a second round of pain. The storm picked up again, and my yacht and I made it out to sea. I slid on the deck as I lay on my belly, too exhausted to move, held onto the lashing ropes flinging around like tentacles. I did not go below, because I didn't want to sink if the vessel broke in half. And I only had my shirt, which I'd had the wisdom to put back on. I know that's a cliché, but it is true. I only had the shirt on my back.

I don't know how, but I endured. And the boat saved me. When the worst of the storm was over, I found some clothes and food below deck—when I had the energy to stand and wobble down there. The rain smelled like petrol, like the death on the Front, but fishier. Precipitation kept falling, and I saw the strangest things floating with me, like a railroad crossing signal, and the arm raised and lowered in the waves.

I am now mailing this missive to you from somewhere in Cuba, though I do not know precisely where I docked. No one I have met seems to have a map. I am close to Santiago or Havana, though. More stories later, I promise.

Perhaps you need some real old-time religion, too, my friend! Rest assured, my redemption is guaranteed—at least today, that is!
JL

P.S. I am penniless right now, so apologies for the reverse

postal charges. I do hope you understand. Know I shall reimburse you when I see you. With drink or song. Or maybe a dance!

P.P.S. If you see Isobel, please do not tell her where I am or where I've been.

#

Pidgeon read the last of Lalande's missives, found no other useful information in Duchamp's messengered suitcase. He wondered about the dates on the letters—there were such extended periods with no correspondence in between, but the events seemed to occur chronologically one after the other. At least these disparities were something interesting he could investigate. Some of the gaps in information did not make sense, not really. Bugger. He was tired with yet another long day of travel ahead. At 4:37 in the morning, he closed up the valise and shuffled down the back hall to the servant's kitchen. The messenger, sleeping at the table with his head on his arm, roused effortlessly and was pleasant as he plopped on his cap.

"*Au revoir.*" The young man smiled drowsily and waved as he left, wending down the middle of the deserted boulevard, swinging Duchamp's precious case.

Pidgeon returned to his room to find his bed turned down.

✳

NOW PIDGEON VISITS ANDRÉ BRETON

"Ah, so that obese rat, Tzara, sent you here! Tzara was once a good friend . . ." André Breton stood in his entryway, surrounded by masterpieces, an enormous wealth of art—Picassos, Mirós, Giacomettis. At the sight of so many works of high standing, the investigator's chest tightened; his breath would not leave him.

Breton cleared his throat, and Pidgeon refocused on the man he had come to see. When Breton spoke again, he was all mulligrubs, defensive.

"Yes, yes, I know you visited that little Tzara. Nothing's a secret for long in Paris. You work for *The London Times*. You're looking for Lalande? Why, indeed, we all are. You know he's gone, perhaps even dead? No one can hide in this city." Pidgeon noted Breton's impeccable English.

On a marble side table, the reporter spied a stack of proletariat posters and a Russian newspaper. He had read many of Breton's fascinating exegeses on art and literature. And the reporter's attention slid again to the paintings on the walls, crookedly hung, skewed strangely from floor to ceiling. Breton followed Pidgeon's loving gaze.

"Yes, those are my true friends. Though I forget they're there most days. Here, let me take your coat—you won't hear anything from me in a rush."

They sat by the fire. Pidgeon was thankful—the weather had turned uncommonly cold. A dog lay at the great auburn-haired poet's feet, whining in his sleep.

"You must be interviewing many who knew the great poet."

"Is that what you call Lalande? A great poet? Many think he was a great painter."

"*Ah*, so you have spoken to *many*. Well, if you had come to me first, I might have cleared up a few things. Lalande was before his time. Sadly, though, no one has seen or heard from him in years. No one. Not even that demonic wife of his. Tragic. You would not know about my strange friendship with Jules Lalande, would you? Well, we knew each other before the war, but really, there was a defining moment when Lalande was my patient. I have never told anyone else. I guess there's no harm telling you if the man's deceased."

※

BRETON SHARES PHOTOGRAPHS WITH PIDGEON AND TELLS SOME STORIES

Sit back, Pidgeon. Here, let me fetch this old box off the shelf there. Can you help? There, there. See, this box. Someone must have spent weeks carving this arabesque pattern. Feel that relief! Such deep cuts. I keep this locked. Only I have the key, which I wear right around my neck.

Here. See, here are some photographs of a time that is gone. People who are gone. Perhaps their stories will avail your research.

As if evening's a bed sheet tucked under the sun's chin, look, look out my window, you see? The night is so beautiful, creeping along, catching the day with its shade, covering the light to save some bit of warmth.

That box holds my dearest memories. Of course, I am the famous man so many describe; I am an enigma, true. André Breton. But I suspect you know that, dear sir. So, what? Some say I have a hollow heart. No, it is a resonant heart.

I often view the photos this box contains; I fan them out, shuffle and deal them as if they are playing cards, and then I pick one with my eyes closed. I hold it close to my face, open my eyes, and I'm transported. You will see I was a photographer and took these with my own camera. Or I paid a handsome lot to acquire them from some crook. I used whatever I had so I could find these. Blood or kindness. Whatever it takes.

Yes, when I show these scenes to a few of the many who lived through those times (and there aren't many remaining), they ask me why photographs are so precious. These images evoke moments lost. Each is a *memento mori*. Each captures a perished person or someone who doesn't matter anymore. Each reveals relationships or feelings no one can replicate.

Tell me, does every gentleman of means want to be a writer in this new age, this modern century? I think so. When Lalande intimated this specific desire, I felt a tug of jealousy, for he had a way of seeing the world, you see. A capacity for solitude I can only imagine. He possessed a singular vision with a comprehensive understanding of all God's creation, too, yet still, he brought intimacy or delicacy or whatever to his poems. His manner inspired even the hardest heart to warm to him.

Oh, Lalande gave me many things. But this box is the most prized—other than his friendship, of course. You will see it has the Burlington family coat of arms carved into its side. I took his gift as a promise of friendship. But amity was useless in the end. Jules Lalande needed no one.

THESE LOWLY OBJECTS

BRETON SNAPSHOT #1: THE CAFÉ, OUR CHURCH

Ah, yes, this photograph is from before I knew Lalande, though I'm sure he was a patron here, too. Before the war, everyone who was anyone went to le Café de Flore. Here everyone congregates at the tables outside under the jade awning. The boulevardiers in their frock coats and monocles, *chapeaux hauts de forme* and *chapeaux melon*. Ladies in their eclipsing hats, high collars, gloveless, sipping on a cup of tea or even absinthe radiant in the daylight. A street cleaner in blue denim sweeps the walk; a gendarme in his short cape rests against the pole. Plumes braids boots—officers. So many duels in those days. I was privy to a few. They were expected, too, you know.

Everyone in theatrical costumes for our secular church. For we were all worshipping—art, music, literature, life. Anyone could enter, buy a drink. See that *garçon*? Really an adolescent, as all waiters were at one time. He holds the tray so expertly. I remember him, zigzagging his way through the crowds like ivy. His deep-set eyes peering out as if he is lost in a forest, the awning casting a shadow like a tree canopy. I wonder if he is still there or if he died in the war.

I wonder if I ever saw Lalande there and did not register his presence. Not likely, for he was memorable.

BRETON SNAPSHOT #2: SAINT-DIZIER HÔPITAL, TERMINUS, 1916

Ah, the big war, the place and time, where and when. Every day, honor and horror shook hands. I met Lalande there, as you know.

That is me there in this photograph; I'm second from the left, standing in the ward of the psychiatric center of the Second Army. What a sharp mustache I had!

And what a dismal place. Quiet, except for the screams. I was transferred there. Five months in Hell. The men were mere lumps in their beds. French, British, and American flags flew from the beams. The walls were whitewashed. The smells! Most patients had only scratches, but some wounds had a decided stink. Always there was a bustle from the capped attendants and nurses who wore long headscarves. Doctors in aprons lined up for new patients at the entrance every day.

And see, we all look weary. Observe everyone here lined up for the portrait, no smiles. No one smiled. Why should anyone feel happiness in times like those? But the ideas I came upon! The dreams those soldiers suffered! I still feed upon them!

At that time, I was so unsure about what I wanted out of my life. I was writing poetry in the style of Mallarmé, doubting my future in medicine. Then came along this elegant talent. Jules Lalande. The war was outside. We heard it. We saw it. And felt the effects. And the doctors inside would shout doltish prescriptions and diagnoses: "Hysteria? There is no such thing! You have an upset stomach. That is it. Or cancer, perhaps."

Ah, yes, the ward of the psychiatric center of the Second Army at Nantes. Let me tell you about it.

During the Great Conflict, as always, I began a dawning day with so much to do, but it could be so tedious, this important work, yet I knew it carried weight. As a medical novice, I first sat in on all the sessions of the great alienist,

Raoul-Achille Leroy. I soon graduated to my own patients.

Neurological issues are always so subjective! But I believed I was freeing minds and consciences. And what I was doing was as important as the surgeries I saw other doctors perform when the thousands of wounded arrived.

It was already mid-1916, and the Western Front still held fast against the Germans, though the Anglo-French forces were hobbling, barely maintaining their lines. Men died, men lost limbs; there was so much—so much death, so much poisonous gas, so much noise, so much ugliness! And it was almost too much for me. I resided in a field hospital close enough to Verdun the battles were less than a day away. I had five injured soldiers a day, only five, and my patients took it out of me.

In my first session of the day, Chasseurs à Pied Francoeur cried over rumors of his cheating wife back in Paris, and then he fainted off his chair. But this was normal, as the man fainted often. I revived Francoeur, as always, by holding the man's hand and easing him back to comfort.

"I can help you sort out your feelings. Perhaps you might not focus on the details of your wife's supposed infidelity? Focus on your reactions to these fears?"

I then prescribed a tonic for relaxation, and my parting words to the poor soldier were encouraging: "Be kind to others."

Francoeur was still sniffling as the nurse walked with him back to his bed.

Next, I listened to a nervous *dragon* at noon, and then, at one, I saw a young *caporal* suffering from an imagined sexual disorder. My time with these men was dreary, as always. But it was necessary. At two o'clock, my favorite patient arrived with an orderly who wheeled him about in a chair. Sous-lieutenant Guy Aglionby was a man who had lost both legs but whose charming smile belied his phantom pains. Today, the lieutenant was having a crisis of the ardent sort.

"*Docteur*, I haven't heard from my wife in Liverpool. Should I write her a letter? I'm trying to compose a poem in English, but I can't find a word that rhymes with orange."

"Well, of course, you can't! It is the only word in English that does not rhyme! No matches for that one. Many a revered poet has tried. Wordsworth, Byron, Blake—I am confident they all attempted it. But really, do you feel less than satisfactory because of this inability?" And right there, after some prying from me, Aglionby forgot his afflictions and began to brainstorm anew, settling for words sounding slightly like orange, terms and names such as "torrents" and "Lawrence." He was undoubtedly fluent in English— and cheerful after such a productive time with me.

"*Alors, Docteur*, you are truly a miracle worker." And as the hour closed with a handshake, the officer passed me a fat cigar from the slim case he hid in his robe's pocket, and then flashed a smile and motioned his waiting attendant. Aglionby turned in his seat and waved to me, as the orderly pushed him down the hospital corridor. I watched the legless man stiffen his back before they departed, and the door closed behind them.

Through my window, I kept them in my sights as the two individuals slogged in the mud, the chair wheels gunking and spraying. They then picked up the pace down the lane on the grassy hill, and dodging ambulances zoomed past at breakneck speeds, scooting around other bandaged and scarred men, sad soldiers sitting in chairs or tottering on crutches, and finally, as they went out of sight, the orderly and wheelchaired man's combined silhouette grew dark against the violent, war-time sky.

I sat and continued to peer out at the camp and all the patients dressed in hospital pajamas, all of them aimlessly pacing about in the muck. And then there was a whistle in the low clouds and a scary delay. *BOOM!* A cloud of smoke puffed above the scrappy forest—the shell originated from the Front many miles away. Funny, no one in the yard even flinched. I frowned, licked my cigar, patted a flask in my breast pocket. I peered farther out to the west, to where the horizon folded over the earth, cinching the afternoon like a worn-out belt. Somehow in this craziness, I was satisfied with what I could do for these men.

Yes, I remember the day so well.

After lunch at the officers' table, I sat in my quarters and waited. Just the day before, another Freudian had visited with me. He was a well-respected man who'd given me oblique descriptions about a problematic case he was passing my way.

"I just can't work with him. You'll see . . ."

For me, a first face-to-face meeting with a particularly unusual patient was always riveting. Indeed, at the end of the day, what a troubled man wants is solace or meaning. I tried to give them a sense of purpose—I knew so many soldiers who could not find comfort in comrades, chaplains, or even wives safely tucked in at home. And anyway, a medical aficionado like me hated easy cases, the lackluster men—the barely disordered were usually so drab. Oh yes, I hoped this new case would arrive with serious issues. I needed a challenge. I was done with nervous boredom.

I went outside to meet the new soldier under my care.

This man had a head wound. Yes, some shrapnel pierced clear through his helmet, grazed his temple. His best friend perished in the same mortar attack. He spoke of trying to resurrect his friend. Such fodder for my research! What injured people try to make real! Or not! What you can interpret in those dreams and wishes if you try!

He was one of those courageous types who wouldn't cry out in pain even if I took a straight pin to his heel. Not foolhardy or stoic, mind you, just brave. The man sat in a chair outdoors with a blanket over his knees, crows shrieking in the split-leafed trees. These days, we call what he experienced "shell shock." His face was so familiar—I thought I recognized him from somewhere before the war. Paris, perhaps? But I was so unsure. I just could not place him.

He did not speak, and I assumed he would never talk again. I tried for twenty minutes to elicit some reaction. None. I gave up and went back inside. I would try again in a few weeks.

And then he initiated treatment. A week after our initial meeting, there was a knock on my jamb. Outside the plank door, the tall man loomed in the warm lamplight. Beefier than most of the scrawny, starved patients I usually saw, the haggard man had a long scar along the top of his shaved scalp, and his pate was shiny with sweat. Again, he seemed so familiar; he scratched at his sharp-featured face with a delicate pink hand. He introduced himself properly.

"Are you Dr. Breton? How do you do? I am Dorian Libellule. *Désolé*, I was not able to speak to you last week. I am improving now." His elocution was better than an Englishman's I had treated. I smiled. Something nagged at me. I just could not place it. Maybe his familiarity was a trick of sinister light. The man-who-called-himself-Dorian-Libellule followed me to the small desk. I motioned to the camp chair alongside.

"I suppose this chair will suffice." Dorian winced as he folded into the seat, and there was a spark in his eyes. His accent was British. Or was it French? Uncanny. He propped on the edge of the rickety seat as if it might crumble under his weight. And I considered it just might.

I smiled to myself and began.

"And why are you here, Monsieur?"

Dorian did not answer, but shifted his focus, pointed to a disfigured artilleryman down the hall sitting on a cot.

"See the craters on that man's face?" Outside the open window, an attendant pushed a legless boy toward the common area. Dorian pointed at the boy's dressings. "And look at that soldier. How pure white are those bandages. Imagine how they are healing, how those scars are such a monument to survival from infection, from death. Death is not such a bad thing, but if you can avoid it, why not?"

"What do you mean?" He had piqued my curiosity.

"I can raise the dead," he said.

I was not sure how to react to this disclosure. Surely, he was speaking metaphorically. So, I raised my eyebrows, waited for him to elaborate.

He did not. He left and returned the next day when I had an open moment to see him. And then he spoke right out the gate.

"I'm unsure of my faith. But that's not it. The miracles keep occurring. Perhaps the seven-headed beast with ten horns has arrived on these battlefields." And as the strange fellow talked about the Book of Revelation, he stroked a large crucifix hanging from his belt. What a unique location for a cross, where a watch fob would usually hang! It gave Dorian the countenance of an out-of-place monk. "I was raised Catholic. My parents are buried, so you needn't ask about them—I know how this all works. What's worrying me? Lately, I've been raising the dead." He repeated his outrageous confession from the day before. I had not misheard him the first time. There was a long pause as I fully comprehended the statement. Dorian certainly noticed my expression. He continued.

"Yes, it's true. I raise the dead. And it's so simple. I first feel the heat in my hands and spine, then I place my fingers on a corpse, and I say a few words, and the dead being's spirit, whether human or otherwise, comes back from wherever it went." Dorian leaned back in the rickety chair, crossed his legs. It creaked angrily. I jotted quick notes in my journal, barely looking up. I was so excited by this delusional man's admissions, by his familiar timbre I wanted to transcribe everything verbatim. He continued.

"Often these days, I read Bible passages and try to make sense of my gift. Genesis is especially informative. Beginnings. Did you know there were two trees in Eden?" the man asked, and the doctor nodded. "Well, Adam and Eve chose the wrong tree. And I think perhaps I'm the first human of all time to pick the right fruit. Yes, I'm certain I'm fulfilling some destiny God has aimed for all along." Dorian looked away then, scanning my makeshift bookshelves. I watched him as he mouthed the titles, his eyes finally stopping and alighting on a manual of illustrated war maladies. I pushed for more.

"Go on—I'm listening. I understand what you're saying."

"So, I tried to give up all the sins." Dorian looked down at his hands, turned them over and over. "And, of course, I want to avoid death—I'd rather stay here and resurrect the lost souls that find me." And then there was another long pause, and while I tried to compose myself (I was not usually at a loss for words), Dorian broke the uncomfortable lull by singing in a soft, querulous croon. He held his hands aloft as if he was a priest blessing the Eucharist: *"Tantum ergo Sacramentum / Veneremur cernui, / Et antiquum documentum / Novo cedat ritui; / Praestet fides supplementum, / Sensuum defectui."* And as Dorian crooned the sad chant louder and with more confidence, tears marched down his sharp cheeks. His Church Latin was perfect, and the benediction (a song I had heard many times) asked God to look with mercy on lowly humans.

I listened and watched Dorian and was reminded of my own adolescent Sundays, when the country priest gave boring sermons to the rigid congregation, and, after a long proselytization, organ music would break the stale air, lifting to the rafters, and the staid Catholic women flushed and prayed passionately, whispering, *"Mon Dieu!"* after the rousing offertory song. Dorian continued, and each refrain grew louder: *"Genitori Genitoque / Laus et jubilatio, / Salus, honor, virtus quoque / Sit et benedictio: / Procedenti ab utroque / Compar sit laudatio."*

The song skidded to a stop with Dorian's "amen," and the big man's eyes widened into blank reverie. Silence filled the room. I had to say something.

"Oh," I tossed out, referring back to Dorian's last speech, "you're almost a martyr who delays entrance into heaven so others can go in your stead. How honorable!"

Maybe compliments would draw him out some more.

"That's it!" Dorian said, slapping his broad knee. "I knew there was a reason I'm here!"

"Well, then, I canonize you a martyr and saint." I chuckled as I made the Sign of the Cross with my fountain pen. But Dorian did not laugh; no, he scowled. I could see the man was troubled as his attention shifted to the window, and his eyes squinched together in thought.

"You know, I'm not so sure you should play at making me a saint." I sighed, peered over my reading glasses. Dorian continued, "Yes, only God can . . ." His voice waned as his stare cleaved onto something outside, and he went quiet. I followed the man's sightline. In the unusually hot evening, up the mucky meadow, a dark-haired boy, no older than seventeen, pushed a wheelchair with a shriveled, palsied soldier hunched over in the seat. The boy winced in the fading, searing sun and was so short he could barely see over the invalid. Heaving in starts and jolts, the wheelchair jammed to a stop in the warm sludge. The boy rammed his head into the back of the chair with extra effort, trying fruitlessly to mount the slight hill. The contraption would not budge, and the passenger jostled in his seat.

"Those are some pitiful souls out there," Dorian said, his voice trailing off again, and before I could say anything in response, he hurried outside and made his way to the clearing. He circled the steadfast teen, gesturing, and when the boy shook his head, dissented, Dorian continued arguing with him, then wrenched the wheelchair handles away, bouncing the vessel free from the mud. Then Dorian took to shaking the boy's shoulders. As the two argued, they forgot about the chair. It descended the hill, skipping slowly, squeaking into a flagpole, and stopping. The crippled man slumped to the ground.

To my relief, I could see the patient was unharmed—he was like a puddle on the ground, still shaking and squinting as if nothing had happened. The boy ran down, hoisted him back in the chair, brushed him off, righted his knees, and the convalescent's head lolled, his expression returning to the same oblivious stare he'd displayed before he made his downhill trip.

The boy turned to continue his Sisyphean task, but only after he shook his fist at Dorian, who stood atop the hill for another moment and then tiptoed backward, re-crossed the yard to the hospital.

Inside again, Dorian had no awareness he'd done anything wrong. He plopped into the seat as if he owned it. "See. I care about people. God knows about my goodness."

I stifled my laughter. This man was undoubtedly delusional.

God. What a silly notion! It had been years since I'd given up my own bearded, fire-and-brimstone deity. Now I reasoned I could use my own spiritual experiences to help this patient. Perhaps I could talk sense into Dorian. And so, I did not hesitate—I stood and opened my traveling trunk on the other side of the desk. From inside, I lifted a gilded urn. The gold container was certainly a macabre object, much like a smaller version of something one might encounter in a mausoleum.

Many years ago, I had bought the jar at les Puces after reading Nietzsche. I was determined to supplant my own disabling faith with a more secular, more beneficial philosophy. I would rid myself of God. And I did!

And so, when I realized theology no longer ruled my

conscience, I made my way to the city's bazaar feeling a weight lifted, and I perused the stalls for hours. When I found the perfect urn, I then purchased a puppet. I returned home to scoop fireplace ashes and the doll into the container, sealed it, and glued a label onto the lid. It read, *"Dieu c'est mort."* ("God is dead.") I performed my own cremation of divinity, laid the beast to bed.

And I kept the relic jar with me as a reminder of how far I had come, of how I had rid myself of a god who had always judged me unfairly. I even carried it with me to the Front, the puppet body parts jiggling around the cinders inside the reliquary.

So, the day when I spoke with Dorian, felt I could trust him to understand my past, I retrieved my no-god and gingerly placed the vessel in his hands.

"You see, this is my memento of how God is dead to me, and well—" I paused, searched for more words. I wanted to share my cure from, my relief, even my contempt for all the pain I associated with religion. But I felt some apprehension, as this was as much as I had ever shared about my personal life with a patient. The jar rested in Dorian's open hands, and when he responded, he voiced concern for my soul.

"You'll be left with this weighing on you." He grabbed hold of the urn then and shook it vigorously, his face crimson as a sphincter. "Isn't this a bit too much responsibility? God is not dead. You have made him so. Perhaps you should make a confession; maybe your soul is lost until you do." Dorian shook the golden urn again, and it rattled and shimmered in the sun's last rays.

I had not calculated this reaction; I had made a mistake; I had divulged too much. And so, I gingerly reached to retrieve the fake ossuary, but Dorian pulled away from me, hunkered down in his chair and clung to the prop, pulled it tight against his torso. The ceramic clanked against Dorian's cross belt, and there was a whiff of dust from under the finialed lid.

Bile rose in my throat. The man's voice was louder now.

"Rid yourself of this, for you will need to resurrect someday." And then Dorian's voice trailed up to a high-pitched register, which made him sound like an injured cat. "And to think I came to you for help!" I looked away, glimpsed out the window, tried to estimate if the man could grow violent. Two moths flew close to the glass, and tap-tap-tapped; they were mating in a fury, no reason to their flight, just a mad flash of silver wings in the dusky lamp-lighted pane.

Dorian stood and hovered over me; his stale, panting breath ruffled my hair. I looked down to the floor, glanced at the man's thin, long feet and beat-up boots. He had inked wispy crosses in different colors on the tongues. Red, blue, green, orange. And, funny, the man wore no socks. I drummed my fingertips on the desk. Dorian repeated himself.

"Are you going to surrender this sinful object?" His fingers whitened as he gripped the container. I shook my head slowly.

"No, I will not. God is truly dead." Nothing else could be said.

"Then, I'll save him for you." Cradling the jar in his arms like a baby, Dorian stomped down the hospital's corridor and hurried past the cots of injured infantrymen. At the front entrance, on the splintered flooring, he turned slowly and looked back at me down the lengthy hallway, pursing his lips together angrily. I matched the man's stare.

We paused there in a gaze for a long moment. Dorian's hands trembled so I was sure I could hear the dead god, the puppet, jangling inside its decanter all the way through the hospital. And then, as if directed by something outside himself, as if seeing something I could not, Dorian's focused gaze moved upward, little by little, to a point somewhere on the ceiling. His fevered manner calmed, and his face brightened as if illuminated by a supernatural spotlight.

After a moment of gawking at some high, fixed point, at something I could not see, Dorian nodded a response, then blurted out a sharp, pained yawp. And, as if prompted by some authority outside himself, he tiptoed all the way back to me, sidestepped in a crouch and lowered the funeral jar to my feet. Dorian then jogged out, dodging patients in the passageway.

After the man's departure, I wrote a lengthy letter to my friend and colleague, Jacques Vaché, incredulous at the exchange I had just experienced. And as I wrote, I realized Dorian, a man I thought I recognized, was indeed someone I knew from my days in Paris. Dorian was Jules Lalande! Transformed, taller, more immense, sharper, and I finally recognized this man was a specimen I would never find in a book, a case no one would believe. He had shifted his shape and voice enough, disguised himself, so I could only place him after-the-fact. We would meet again after the war, but we would never acknowledge our encounter. So utterly strange.

After I wrote my missive, I sent it along by a messenger to the other hospital, the one I hoped I would never see, where sawbones and vile infection bunched into every corner.

The next day when I made my rounds, Dorian was gone from the hospital, and the amputee who lay in the bed adjacent to Dorian's complained his money and pocket watch were missing.

Years later, I heard the story from Tzara, our good friend. Lalande had made his way to Zurich at about that time. I saw Lalande a year or two after in Paris, and we began a short-lived friendship before he disappeared again. Forever that time.

God is dead, surely.

Anyway, back to the photograph. Dorian, also known as Lalande, is far in the back on a cot somewhere. I see him. You do not? He was not one to smile broadly, even for photographs—now I wonder if he had terrible teeth?

BRETON SNAPSHOT #3: THE FRONT

Let me unfold this paper. It is a wrap for the next photograph. Yes, this was Lalande's photo. And yes, it is his writing on the back of the photo. I do not know who took the picture. It looks almost like a postcard, doesn't it? Yes, Jules showed me this gruesome scene only once. And he cried as he described what he saw.

You see, he was there. That is the Battle of Verdun in the scene. Or what is left of it. And that is most definitely a trench. Terror. Look at the dirt, look at the men in gas masks. I am not sure why he kept this. That is his handwriting here on the reverse, recognize it? See, that's his script? I found a package—the photo and a piece of paper folded around it—by accident. I was looking to reacquaint myself with Rimbaud and reached into the bookshelf, and as I thumbed through, it fell out quite by accident. I have no idea which Rimbaud poem Jules was reading at the time. I wish I did!

In any case, look at Verdun in this panoramic view! See, there's a dead man cut in half. I was at the Front, too, but never directly in Verdun. I visited the lines on occasion to understand the gore my patients encountered. And once, German artillery rounds surrounded my corps, even though I was far off from the thick of it, standing with high-ranking officers.

The memories haunted him, I am sure, and he choked them down. He seldom talked about the horrors. So many. One I remember is his description of a soldier lying on a blood-soaked litter, his face obliterated, right cheek entirely shot away. Jules told me he could see the innards of the man's face—sinew and gristle. No jaws or teeth or lips left. Nose half-gone. Blood gushing with the man's last breaths like pumped liquid from a well.

Verdun. Jules called it the most horrific place anyone had ever known. He held out the picture, a gory still of a landscape with a group of scared boys up front in the foreground, their indistinguishable features behind their masks, their legs wrapped from their ankles to their knees, their uniforms still tidy in the middle of Hell.

Hmmm. At one time, I had Lalande's written comments about this photograph. It was in his usually lovely handwriting, but the scrawl was a little more scratchy and uneven. It is missing for some reason. Most unusual.

BRETON SNAPSHOT #4: THEN I LEAVE THE WOODS, STILL HAUNTED, AND I FACE THE CROSSROADS

THESE LOWLY OBJECTS

We took this photograph right after we'd met back in Paris. The war was over, though I am not sure when exactly. Yes, yes, we took the train to Lyon to visit his grandmother's farm. It was late in the summer.

We helped with the haying. I always thought haying was a romantic sort of toil, you know, like the Barbizon painters depict: women in ballooned skirts and clogs, sleeves rolled up, fraying straw hats. Bent over, tossing loads into wagons. But I learned the work is tedious, bloody, and torturous. Not like war, of course, but a quiet kind of torture: brushing scythes, the sound of dry grass, and bleeding gashes.

In this photo, the scent of salad permeates the air; the dust glitters. The men with their bandaged hands' splinterous cuts. I had Jules stand right there in front of the gate with the other workers. Off to the side, someone's parked the hay cart. Pitchforks, see? Jules looks slightly out of place, don't you think, in a brocade waistcoat and linen shirt? He corrected me when I said I was confused, as I had always romanticized the labor and thought haying was a dreamy thing.

"Hay is a dirty business, like no other. Only meadows are for fools and poets."

"Then what is there for fun in this godforsaken place?" I asked. Jules looked at the tree line. And spoke, his tone strange.

"Then I leave the woods, still haunted, face the crossroads."

BRETON SNAPSHOT #5: LE PARC (DU ROTHSCHILDS?)

As you know, Pidgeon, I write a good deal about art, ideas. You are familiar with my work. But with these photos, I possess nothing concrete other than intuitive knowledge, some primal thread to the past. It feels good to *feel something*. I know you will think it is so French of me, but it is who I am, after all.

Take this photograph with the question inscribed on the back: "Le parc (du Rothschilds?)." I am not sure if that is really the place where we stood that spring day, but I wonder. Does it matter? Jules was somehow related to the illustrious de Rothschilds—the British branch, so we were allowed on the grounds often. Look at the old trees; we ambled through tunnels of dark allées. Then I chased a pheasant or one of the harts through the deep forest—those beasts, tame and wild alike, easily survived in the natural zoo of a property.

And then, I found a berry bush. Blackberries. Lalande goaded me. He laughed as I puckered. "Dear André, surely you are aware they won't ripen until summer, silly man." Such a young man, Jules! So full of happiness and rigor. But then his mood darkened as we approached his family's cemetery, sheltered on a hill by a willow. I was hesitant. But he laughed, darkly.

"Why, you shouldn't worry about the dead. The departed can't do anything but haunt you, and even then, often abandon all hope of bother." It was then I laid out a proposition. He would work with me on my magazine and live with my wife and me. And we would visit his home in Switzerland once the railroads ran again on a full schedule. "Oh, but it is bleak there in winter. Do wait until summer. Like with blackberries."

Why couldn't I take a better picture of him than the one you see? This one's darkish, but really, the sun shines, and he is lying on a grave, his arms clamped along his sides and legs straight and rigid, and he's laughing; the willow behind him dances in a breeze. You see the stains on his fingers? They're discolored with the unripe berries he ate with me.

BRETON SNAPSHOT #6: MAX ERNST'S

We all pose outside Max's show. Jules and I are on the ladder as we hold a scale. Tzara hangs upside down from a bicycle from a second-floor window.

"Who knows who weighs justice (or injustice) in this world?" Jules asked as we posed. I threatened to let go of the scales. His monocle dangles from a strap. We were jocular, having fun. Black suits and all. Though we look rather dour here. Soot drifted down from the sky like flakes of snow—it was an omen, I thought.

Passersby crossed the street to avoid our shenanigans. Who is that in the doorway? Isobel. We called her the fair devil. She haunted our photos and thresholds even though I do not think Jules ever saw her. We never told him she was with us. I was sure he would not remember her, anyway. Of course, this was before they met again in New York, I hear. They got married, you know.

BRETON SNAPSHOT #7: LALANDE SHADOW-BOXES ON THE SEINE'S SHORE

I tried my best in this composition to capture Jules's hard muscles, the ligaments of an athletic boxer. His smooth chest, the long curl of hair over his brow, the flattish nose and puffed lips. Here he shadowboxes, while everyone around him lounges on blankets, baskets brimming, and the women laugh, drink from a passed bottle of wine. You cannot see the color, but let me assure you the buff grass is turning emerald; the smoke is the same color in the photo as it is in real life, black-grey industrial filth whiffling out from stacks farther up the river. There was much gaiety. And Lalande's trunks, striped red, white, and blue, were the subject of laughter and a patriotic song or two.

BRETON SNAPSHOT #8: MAN RAY TOOK THIS

Ah, a recent photo, only fifteen or so years ago. Or is it closer to twenty? We all sit around Man Ray's garden. The trees are bare, like naked ladies, such excellent bones. There is Duchamp, see? He is engaged in a game of chess with Lalande. You know Duchamp? The grandmaster, a legend here in France. He gave up all we hold dear, all the canvases and forms and ideas, and now seeks thoughts a little less permanent. The battle on the board. With royalty, heads of state. He is making moves.

Jules, my dear friend, did not like the ideas of inequity, of class in chess. Though he won the game, I recall. Oh, Man Ray laughed. We all had a good laugh. Duchamp is not smiling.

BRETON SNAPSHOT #9: INSIDE THE STUDIO

This. Monsieur Pidgeon, dear man, this photo captures the last time I saw Jules. It was in London. Years later. Attic apartment or studio—no art hanging, though. So stripped and sad. All the canvases face toward the peeling walls like errant children punished for evil deeds. Lots of bits of writing, poetry (which I read—it was delicious). Newspapers stacked on the floor and tables. Rather an empty place, except for solid furniture, with entrails and springs leaking out from the tears in their upholstery. Lustered light from the tipped windowpane creeps along, see? That was the scene. I begged Jules to continue his work with me.

"Stay! Stay! We will create a world here. Or Paris. We can move to Paris," I implored.

"No, I am done creating worlds in this dead place. Paris is just as bad. I need to find young ideas," Jules said. He looked so certain. Yes, I begged my dear friend not to leave again for America or wherever he wanted to hide, for I somehow knew I would never see him again. He was going to book passage soon, and I was right. I never saw him again.

Some say he is still around. But would I not hear from him? I know you want to find him—a story? A mystery? Readers like those kinds of stories; intrigue makes readers feel smart. But there is really no story. He has not sent me a letter since. Not one note. He is gone from this earth. I believe it. Truly. He was too fleet-footed, too busy moving from place to place to answer my fatherly worrying. Eventually, he would have tried to respond to my letters. He would have come back.

See how in this picture, he sits in the chair, a king. He is not smiling; the war is forgotten, his writing, his performances. It is all forgotten. Can't you see? But he did not forget me, did not forget to write to me; no. He is already gone. See here, with that expression? He is already disappearing into places unknown, walking away in his mind. His body is there, but his mind is not. There is nothing more to say about Jules Lalande.

✳

PIDGEON REALIZES NOTHING ABOUT JULES LALANDE

Pidgeon listened to Breton's final anecdote. Breton was exhausted; Pidgeon was exhausted. They were both weary with longing for something impossible.

No one would ever, could ever find Lalande if he did not want to be discovered. Pidgeon was beyond sure of this reality. Yes, Lalande was gone for good.

Those closest to the mysterious man had not seen or heard from him in years, and at every lead, Pidgeon had come up short. Oh, yes, his hunt had been futile; he had found a few traces, indeed. But he could not corroborate most of what he'd heard. It was some ridiculous legend wrapped in a mystery. There was absolutely nothing concrete he could write about for *The Times*.

As he departed Breton's home, Pidgeon mused to the artist, "Isn't disappearance all one can expect as an outcome?" Breton nodded concurrence and said nothing more. As Pidgeon turned the corner on his way to the station, Breton stood on the stoop, hands limp at his sides.

#

On the ferry home, Pidgeon attempted to wrangle understanding out of Lalande's stories. The man was now only a composite of a few people's memories. Soon, those memories would die, too. Without the layered tales, who was Lalande, really? Who was a person if he could bury himself under more than thirty personalities and toss away the people who loved him?

When he returned to London, Pidgeon would have the dreaded, inevitable conversation with Mr. Talbot, his editor. There was no Lalande. No subject to interview, nothing to excite readers. A vague mystery. It wasn't enough.

#

It was a dull, shadowless day. He bought his fish and chips from a vendor on the corner, the meal held together with string and greasy butcher paper, and he sat on a stone wall, feeding birds the bits he could not stomach. Drizzle fell, but he kept his umbrella clasped. The moisture felt right, real. His tired eyes could barely make out Big Ben in the distance, but he could hear the time nonetheless. Back to the newspaper.

Mr. Talbot beckoned him.

"Pidgeon!" Mr. Talbot and the fat cat publisher, Mr. Pryor, sat hunched together at the desk.

"We've reached a conclusion. Not another pound for this Lalande nonsense! We've got another story for you. Talk to the assignment desk. There's a woman in Bristol with an 80-pound potato. Perhaps you can cover that."

Pidgeon shuffled through the bustling newsroom to his desk, dodging reporters running with copy edits or clacking on their typewriters.

There, on his desk. An envelope, blazing white.

He gingerly raised it to his nose and sniffed. A trace of bergamot or cherry. And a Paris postmark. May 6, 1936. An address written with a flowing hand, curlicues around the letters.

No return information.

Sure, the slants and slight grazes indicated a trace of Jules's influence, the chiaroscuro of the man's magical hand, his propensity for long-vined, lowercase y's and g's. However, there was a bit of a faltering difference, a slight wobble to the letters due to a feminine, arthritic hand.

Inside the envelope, he discovered another enclosure. Someone had opened and resealed the smaller envelope, no doubt the sender. On a sheet of nubby cotton paper, someone had scribbled out a note. It was the kind of stationery Jules Lalande had once used. Pidgeon checked the signature. Isobel Wright (she still did not own her married name, Madame Lalande).

> *Dear Mr. Pidgeon:*
>
> *For quite a while now, I know you have been searching for my late husband. I must inform you I received notification from Cuba. Word came by post. Apparently, Jules lived there until recently when he passed away from a high fever. He was buried in a plot by the sea.*
>
> *I've enclosed the last bit of writing his attendants found on his desk. I have read it and have included it here in a small envelope. It appears to be an unfinished letter he addressed to no one in particular. I have no need for it.*

THESE LOWLY OBJECTS

There was a manuscript enclosure, too, a kind
of autobiography, but it is absurd fantasy. I have
chosen not to share it with anyone. We must get on
with living.
Cordially yours,
Isobel Wright

Pidgeon would not read Jules Lalande's re-sealed letter until he was somewhere secluded.

But why had Madame Lalande chosen to share this private correspondence with a lowly reporter? And oh, how he wished he could visit the man's burial site (and who knew if a plot really existed?). It was too far to travel for an investigation only to discover a ruse. And he was confident a woman like Madame Lalande, entitled and deluded and malevolent, would never deign to publish Jules's autobiography or move, then entomb her hated husband's remains. Lalande deserved to be interred in his rightful place with his family in the crypt. But it would not happen. It was apparent the woman was conflicted, ambivalent. One thing Pidgeon had learned. Trepidation bred inaction. So be it. He was done.

Pidgeon would no longer chase ghosts. The time for heroes was ending, another war was in the air, and interesting notions about art were dead.

At mid-afternoon, Pidgeon left the newsroom. He slipped the letter into his breast pocket, hooked his umbrella over his arm, and walked all the way to his real home, determined to rededicate himself to a staid, dark life. Pidgeon would sit in his muffled library, surrounded by servants. He would read Lalande's last correspondence and sit by his fire, wait for the end through the night, through the months and years ahead. Dreaming of the sea and air.

＊

JULES LALANDE'S LAST LETTER

Dear Ones,

Most times, my memory is accurate, ringing high and bright; other times, it misses the mark, the bell swinging slow, its clapper skirting the belt. It is the tenuous nature of memory. Especially mine, with its many lies to remember and propagate. An old proverb says it best for me: the palest ink is better than the best memory. Too bad that I never truly wrote anything about life, feelings, until now. I am not that old, yet I am not well.

Lately, I've been thinking about Yeats's poem—

A COAT

> I made my song a coat
> Covered with embroideries
> Out of old mythologies
> From heel to throat;
> But the fools caught it,
> Wore it in the world's eyes
> As though they'd wrought it.
> Song, let them take it,
> For there's more enterprise
> In walking naked.

Unlike Yeats, I believe there is much in the enterprise of wearing a discrete coat of song. All my life, I tried to fashion my jacket out of stories and myths. I sewed used mismatched linens quilted, my stitching fevered, and everywhere I went, I picked up scraps of cloth and new patches of color. Now, I look in the mirror and admire my collagistic coat's beauty. Mind you, I stole the materials. I am a thief. We are all thieves, aren't we?

During my life, this coat of mine itched. My left sleeve was too long; the right one too short; the throat was tight; the breast was bulky. So, I threw it off, let the fools wear it for a time, and I traveled unburdened. I slid naked over fresh grass green as the first day of spring. I dipped naked into lakes as blue as my wife's eyes. Occasionally, in folly or haste to cover myself, I hooked a branch, tore open flesh, and bled. Then I returned to my coat, licked the thread, and pushed a silken strand through the eye of a needle, sewing a new panel, a new story, and song.

Dear reader, how is your own coat taking shape? Do you wear it too long, too often? So, you're naked from sun to moon? Are you burned from exposure yet? I, myself, took chances—with or without my coat. It was the only way to live. You should, too.

Now I try to patch my memories, adhere odds-and-ends of my story to a larger tapestry. Many have woven monstrous tales about me. I wish I could iron out the folds. It is not knowing something that always leads to madness. And so, my story begins with my pre-eminent alias, and it ends my last and most authentic self. Obscure, but true. And yet I never did discover anything, did I?

Obscurity is nothing to

REPRISE: FOLLOW TITUS PIDGEON

*You don't understand what we are doing, do you? Well,
dear friends, we understand it still less.*
    —Dada Manifesto, 1920

If, on a particular March morning in the late-1930s, you
stood on a corner on the selvedged sidewalks of Paris and
paid attention to certain passersby, a man named Titus
Pidgeon would have walked by as he made his way to police
headquarters. If, in that boundless city, moments before a
second great war, a time well after the first, you were into
spying or snooping or even casual voyeurism, and if you,
an observant person, were to look up after tying your spit-
shined oxfords, you might easily have felt compelled to
follow the interesting Titus Pidgeon, a stooped figure, a
man who just happens to be a sartorial mess: all unpressed
tweed and crumpled linen. Not exactly tall, not exactly
short, certainly trim. And if you were to shadow that
unkempt figure, crossing street after street on a dim
morning, tailing at your own jeopardy and hazard, you
might have shuffled only steps behind your quarry, finding
yourself at the center of the great city designed anew by the
amateur architect, Baron Haussmann. You would have
crisscrossed through a jumble of perfectly formed city
centers, *les quartiers,* not sullied by the stink of the Old
City, where you also walked, where the smell flowed out
from the bowels of decrepit sections of that megalopolis,
where even the most romantic still held their noses. You
would have traveled through over a dozen arrondissements
with no seeming destination, until finally, the frowzy man
crossed le pont Saint-Michel of that fetid river, the Seine,

to the île de la Cité. If you stood at that intersection of old and new, you would have watched your mark duck into the chief law enforcement's immense structure, a building wrapping through the neighborhood, a splendorous edifice, its elegant frontage belying all the calamitous investigations transpiring within the stone walls.

La Sûreté nationale, 36, quai des Orfèvres.

And if you stood close enough to peer into that building's marble lobby, you would learn the slumping man you've followed was much more impressive than he first appeared.

Titus Pidgeon, reporter for *The London Times*.

But.

If you stayed in the shadows just moments longer, hidden, maybe even searching for your eyeglasses in your breast pocket and slyly slipping them on, hooking them over your ears so you could make out more detail, you might have also noticed this Pidgeon chap slumped more when he spoke, his busy hands birdlike and nervous when he gesticulated, squinting in quick-succession blinks as he conversed with the gendarmes.

If you were patient and stood still so as not to be detected, you would then spy Pidgeon's nervous countenance falling away at odd moments; you would discover quite by accident that this Titus Pidgeon possessed a milky, opaque eye only detectable at certain angles in direct sunlight, which he avoided at all costs. You would see Pidgeon's wrinkled cheeks and hooded lids smoothing to a more natural countenance. And if you kept snooping, you would witness Pidgeon's slump disappear by degrees, bit by bit, the non-stooping, now-tall man, now with his guard down, would transform into an individual with a criminal's malevolent bearing.

If you viewed Pidgeon's metamorphosis, you would perceive the charming quirks had all dissipated, that his façade had always been a mere cloak of gussied skin and costume, that he had been concealing some wholly different person below a disguise. If you saw all this, you would be convinced Pidgeon was quite possibly nefarious. If you beheld Pidgeon's shift in appearance, you might have doubted yourself, perhaps it was all a trick, a fata morgana, the result of a long night, mirage by way of fatigue. If you thought about it, maybe this Titus Pidgeon was not Titus Pidgeon at all. No, no, no.

ACKNOWLEDGMENTS

You don't understand what we are doing, do you? Well, dear friends, we understand it still less.
   —Tristan Tzara

Some chapters in this book are adapted from stories appearing in McGowan's story collection, *True Places Never Are*, and used with permission from her publisher, Moon City Press.

Additionally, "Jules Lalande's Power" borrows some aspects from McGowan's story, "Certain Smile," which appeared in *Barren Magazine*.

Any similarity to Henry James's *Turn of the Screw* is not accidental; any resemblance to other texts is not coincidental.

ABOUT GOLD WAKE PRESS

Gold Wake Press, an independent publisher, is curated by Nick Courtright and Kyle McCord. All Gold Wake titles are available at amazon.com, barnesandnoble.com, and via order from your local bookstore. Learn more at goldwake.com. Here are some of our recent titles:

Zach VandeZande's *Liminal Domestic*
Kyle Flak's *Sweatpants Paradise*
Melissa Barrett's *Moon on Roam*
Brandon Amico's *Disappearing, Inc.*
Dana Diehl and Melissa Goodrich's *The Classroom*
Sarah Strickley's *Fall Together*
Andy Briseño's *Down and Out*
Talia Bloch's *Inheritance*
Eileen G'Sell's *Life After Rugby*
Erin Stalcup's *Every Living Species*
Glenn Shaheen's *Carnivalia*
Frances Cannon's *The High and Lows of Shapeshift Ma and Big-Little Frank*
Justin Bigos' *Mad River*
Kelly Magee's *The Neighborhood*
Kyle Flak's *I Am Sorry for Everything in the Whole Entire Universe*
David Wojciechowski's *Dreams I Never Told You & Letters I Never Sent*
Keith Montesano's *Housefire Elegies*
Mary Quade's *Local Extinctions*
Adam Crittenden's *Blood Eagle*

ABOUT THE AUTHOR

Cate McGowan is a fiction writer, essayist, and poet. She won the 2014 Moon City Short Fiction Award for her debut short story collection, *True Places Never Are*, published in 2015. *These Lowly Objects* is her first novel.

CPSIA information can be obtained
at www.ICGtesting.com
Printed in the USA
LVHW011915171219
640814LV00001B/67